NORTH EAST INDIA

A Systematic Geography

NORTH EAST INDIA

A Systematic Geography

N.N. Bhattacharyya

RAJESH PUBLICATIONS
NEW DELHI - 110002

NORTH EAST INDIA

A Systematic Geography

Published by :
Sanjay Gupta
RAJESH PUBLICATIONS
1, Ansari Road, Darya Ganj, New Delhi - 110002
Email: rajeshpublications@gmail.com
rajeshpubdelhi@gmail.com
Website: www.rajeshpublications.com

Ist Published in India : 2005
IInd Revised Edition : 2008
IIIrd Edition : 2011
IVth Revised & Enlarged Edition : 2015
Vth Edition : 2018
VIth Edition : 2019
Reprint : 2024

ISBN (13 Digit) : 978-81-85891-62-0
ISBN (10 Digit) : 81-85891-62-1

Typesetting by :
Ritu Pandey
New Delhi - 110002

Printed at :
R.K. Offset Process
Delhi-95

Preface

North East India is a unit of land that is considered to have a unique character, based on local geology, topography, soil, climate, natural vegetation, regional economy and human way of life. The central concern of this study is areal differenatiation i.e. the examination of the arrangement and association of geographical phenomena that distinguish one area from another.

The book has been designed to provide students, teachers, planners and other readers as much knowledge on all topics as is desirable from the point of view of a region. The work contains two parts: Part I–North East India as a whole and Part II–States of North East India including Sikkim. For presenting a meaningful analysis, the Part I of the book is divided into 14 Chapters which have been weaved into a composite mosaic. The geography of the individual states has been discussed in Part II of this book in a lucid and simple geographical style. So this book will be very useful for the students preparing for graduate and post-graduate courses in regional geography in various Universities of Eastern India.

Every care is taken to incorporate up-to-date data in preparing this book. It is believed that there is still much room for making this work more perfect. Any suggestions for improvement of the book, inclusion of new matter and mistakes in facts etc. will most thankfully be accepted. The data and source materials of this book have been drawn from various books, journals, magazines and Govt. reports which have been referred to in the book at appropriate places with thanks. Special thanks are due to Mr. M.L. Gupta of Rajesh Publications, New Delhi for undertaking early publication of this book.

Guwahati **Narendra Nath Bhattacharyya**
19th June, 2005

Preface to the Second Edition

I am very happy to note that the First Edition of the Book has been well received by the readers. In this edition some additions and corrections have been made in the text. I feel highly grateful in placing the second edition of the book in its present form.

Guwahati
9th November, 2007

Narendra Nath Bhattacharyya

Preface to the Fourth Edition

The Fourth Edition has been further revised and enlarged with recent information. I hope it will also be well received by our readers.

Guwahati
26th January, 2015

Narendra Nath Bhattacharyya

Contents

List of Figures

1

Introduction

Comprising seven states, Assam, Arunachal Pradesh, Meghalaya, Nagaland, Mizoram, Manipur and Tripura, North East India is located between latitudes 22°N and 29°30'N and longitudes 89°46'E and 97°30'E. It covers an area of 2,55,083 square kilometres and supports a population of 38.5 million (2001), i.e. it accounts 7.7 per cent of the land surface of India and contains 3.74 per cent of the total population of the country. The region borders with China, Bangladesh, Myanmar and Bhutan. With its long border extending over 4,800 km, it occupies an extremely strategic position and it is connected with the main land by a narrow corridor of foothill land in North Bengal. The width of the corridor is about 33 km on the eastern side and 21 km on the western side and the link is subjected to occasional disruptions due to heavy rains and floods. Such terrestrial location of North East India makes it into an isolated pocket which is one of the important causes for alienation of its population. Thus the strategic importance of the region highly significant.

North East India is a land-locked region. It is physiographically not a homogenous unit. The region has Tertiary mountains, Archaean plateaus, river valleys, intermontane plain and piedmont plain. The Tertiary hills and mountains cover a major part accounting 60 per cent of the region, spreading over Arunachal Pradesh, Nagaland, North Cachar, Mizoram and Manipur. The senile plateaus are represented by Meghalaya and Karbi Anglong district of Assam which account 12 per cent of the whole area. The major plains are the Brahmaputra valley. The Barak plain, the Manipur basin and Tripura piedmont plain and these constitute 28 per cent of the total area of the region. The

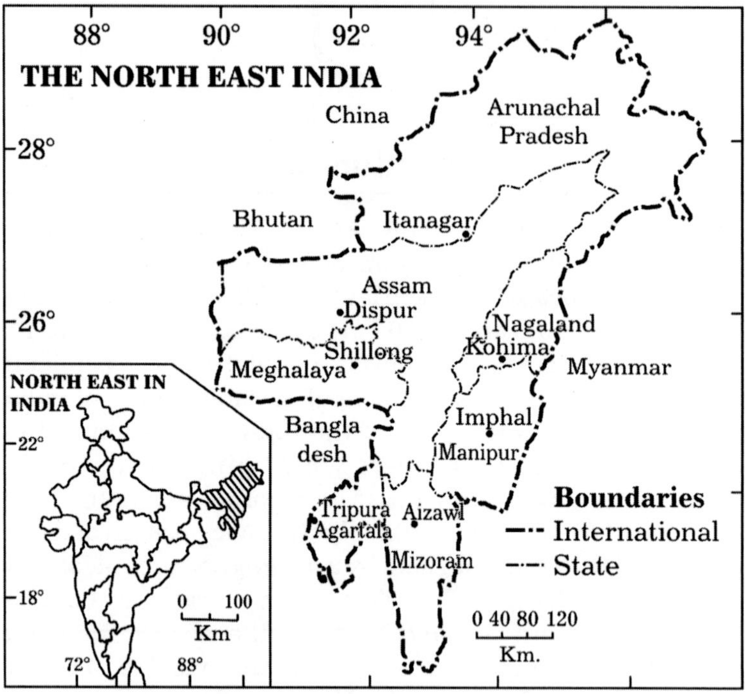

Fig. 1 : The North East India

climate of the region may be identified as tropical monsoon with local variations, the hot season being shorter than usual with low average of about 30°C. The terrain condition, soil types, rainfall, humidity and temperature conditions of the region support an altitudinally distributed vegetations which provide habitats and niches for different types of herbivores and their predators, birds, insects, reptiles and fishes. The region is endowed with a variety of minerals, like petroleum, coal, limestone, sillimanite and a large reservoir of hydel power potential.

The economic structure of the states of North-East India is dominated by agriculture and allied activities. But the land under cultivation in the region is only 16 per cent of its total geographical area. It varies from 2.5 per cent in Arunachal Pradesh to 7.2 per cent in Manipur, 9.4 per cent in Meghalaya, 4 percent in Mizoram, 15 per cent in Nagaland, 36 per cent in Tripura and 45 per cent in Assam. The shifting cultivation is the common mode of agriculture in the hilly areas. Flood, bank erosion and drought conditions in certain areas are the main hurdles to the development of agriculture in the plains. The predominance of primary sector, untapped energy resources, inefficient transport and communication systems, lack of entrepreneurship and marketing facilities etc. are the major factors for the slow growth of industrial activities.

It may be mentioned that barring Assam most of the states of North East India are late comers to the process of development as they were created subsequent to the first decade of planning. The Naga Hills district of Assam and the Tuensang area of NEFA (Arunachal Pradesh) were separated for the formation of Nagaland in 1957 in the wake of insurgency there and it was elevated to a full state in 1963. After conceding Nagaland it was very difficult to keep the other hill areas of Assam from getting their respective state. Meghalaya was formed with two hill districts, namely Garo Hills and United Khasi and Jaintia Hills of Assam on April 2, 1970. Under the North Eastern Reorganisation Act of 1971, Meghalaya was granted full statehood along with Manipur and Tripura, Arunachal Pradesh and Mizoram were made union territories and these two administrative units also gained full state-hood in 1987. This way Assam has been truncated and treated as it were, a guineapig for experimentation of small states with lingering apprehension for further fragmentation.

Three important groups of people inhabit in North East India. They are the hill tribes, the plain tribes and the non-tribal population of the plains. The share of tribal population is over whelmingly high in Mizoram, Nagaland and Meghalaya (85-95 per cent) significantly high in Arunachal Pradesh (64 per cent) nearly one-third of the population in Tripura and Manipur are tribes and over 12 per cent of Assam's population consist of tribes. Thus the region has just 12 per cent of the country's tribal population and they other than those living in Assam, enjoy political power as their states were created mainly on the principle of tribal dominance. Barring the khasis and the Jaintias, all other hill tribes belong to the Tibeto-Chinese group. The Khasi and Jaintias speak Austric speech and the seven states are not bound by a common language.

Different geographical, economic and social factors have contributed substantially to the emergence of a centripetal force among the traditional inhabitants of India's North-East. The whole North-East India became a melting pot for various ethnolinguistic groups like Austro-asiatic, Tibeto-Chinese, Aryan etc. and a type of Mongoloid culture has been created in the region. But due to imposition of various social, economic and political gulf existing between different group of people, the centripetal force has now become weakened in the policy of North East India. The current trouble in the region is due to geographic isolation, long years of neglect and sudden exposure of relatively backward societies to the complexities of modern system imposed by the government of India. After independence huge investment through plan and non-plan funds were channalised in order to improve the quality of life among the inhabitants of the seven states of the region. In this connection the North Eastern Council is a regional planning body and it came into existence on First August, 1972. The Council allowed Sikkim to be its eighth member in December 2002 played a major role in recommending and getting various projects for improvement of means of communication, social and economic development. The development strategy of the region lies on mutual understanding of different states. The economy of North East India should be treated as a single economy with free inter-state flow of commodities. This development approach is essentially conceived as a special means to social ends. It has greater appeal to those who would like to achieve peaceful socio-economic changes.

North East India :
Basic Data-Ranking According to Area

States	Area
1. Arunachal Pradesh	83,743 Sq. km.

2.	Assam	78,438 Sq. km.
3.	Meghalaya	22,429 Sq. km.
4.	Manipur	22,327 Sq. km.
5.	Mizoram	21,081 Sq. km.
6.	Nagaland	16,579 Sq. km.
7.	Tripura	10,486 Sq. km.
8.	Sikkim	7,096 Sq. km.

Ranking According to Population

	States	Population (2001)	Population (2011)
1.	Assam	26,638,407	1,31,205, 576
2.	Tripura	3,191,168	2,36,71,032
3.	Manipur	2,388,634	4,27,21,756
4.	Meghalaya	2,306,069	3,29,64,007
5.	Nagaland	1,988,636	5,19,80,602
6.	Arunachal	1,091,117	6,13,82,611
7.	Mizoram	891,058	7,10,91,014
8.	Sikkim	540,493	6,07,688

Arunachal Pradesh : Capital Itanagar - Districts

	Districts	Area (sq. km.)	Population (2001)	Head quarters
1.	Changlang	46,629	124,994	Changlang
2.	Dibang Valley	13,029	57,543	Anini
3.	East Kameng	4,134	57,065	Seppa
4.	East Siang	4,005	87,430	Pasighat
5.	Lohit	11,402	143,478	Tezu
6.	Lower Subansiri	10,125	97,614	Ziro
7.	Paum Pare	2,875	121,750	Itanagar (Yupia)
8.	Tawang	2,172	34,705	Tawang
9.	Tirap	2,632	100,227	Khonsa
10.	Upper Siang	6,188	33,146	Yingkiong
11.	Upper Subansiri	7,032	54,995	Daporijo
12.	West Kameng	7,422	74,595	Bomdila
13.	West Siang	8,325	103,575	Along

Assam : Capital Dispur (Guwahati) - Districts

	Districts	Area (sq. km.)	Population (2001)	Head quarters
1.	Barpeta	3,245	1,642,420	Barpeta
2.	Bangaigaon	2,510	906,315	Bangaigaon
3.	Cachar	3,786	1,442,141	Silchar
4.	Darrang	3,481	1,503,943	Mangaldai
5.	Dhemaji	3,237	569,468	Dhemaji
6.	Dhubri	2,838	1,634,589	Dhubri
7.	Dibrugarh	3,381	1,172,056	Dibrugarh
8.	Goalpara	1,824	822,306	Goalpara
9.	Goalghat	3,502	945,781	Golaghat
10.	Hailakandi	1,327	542,978	Hailakandi
11.	North Cachar Hills	4,888	186, 189	Haflong
12.	Jorhat	2,851	1,009,197	Jorhat
13.	Kamrup	4,345	2,515,030	Guwahati
14.	Karbi Anglong	10,434	812,320	Diphu
15.	Karimganj	1,839	1,003,678	Karimganj
16.	Kokrajhar	3,129	930,404	Kokrajhar
17.	Lakhimpur	2,277	889,325	North Lakhimpur
18.	Morigaon	1,704	775,874	Morigaon
19.	Nagaon	3,831	2,315,387	Nagaon
20.	Nalbari	2,257	1,138,184	Nalbari
21.	Sibsagar	2,668	1,052,802	Sibsagar
22.	Sonitpur	5,225,2	1,677,874	Tezpur
23.	Tinsukia	3,476	1,150,146	Tinsukia

Manipur : Capital Imphal - Districts

	Districts	Area (sq. km.)	Population (2001)	Head quarters
1.	Bishnupur	496	205,907	Bishnupur
2.	Chandel	3,313	122,714	Chandel
3.	Churachandpur	4,570	228,707	Churachandpur
4.	Imphal East	—	393,780	Porompat
5.	Imphal West	1,228	439,532	Lamphel
6.	Senapati	3,271	379,214	Senapati
7.	Tamenglong	4,391	111,493	Tamenglong
8.	Thoubal	514	366,341	Thoubal
9.	Ukhrul	4,544	140,946	Ukhrul

Meghalaya : Capital Shillong - Districts

	Districts	Area (sq. km.)	Population (2001)	Head quarters
1.	East Garo Hills	2,603	247,555	Williamnagar
2.	East Khasi Hills	2,603	660,994	Shillong
3.	Jaintia Hills	3,819	295,692	Jawai
4.	Ri-Bhoi	2,448	192,795	Nongpoh
5.	South Garo Hills	1,850	99,105	Baghmara
6.	West Garo Hills	3,714	515,813	Tura
7.	West Khasi Hills	5,247	294,115	Nongstoin

Mizoram : Capital Aizawl - Districts

	Districts	Area (sq. km.)	Population (2001)	Head quarters
1.	Aizawl	12,588	339,812	Aizawl
2.	Champhai	3,185.85	101,389	Champhai
3.	Kolasib	1,282.51	60,977	Kolasib
4.	Lowngtlai	2,557.10	73,050	Lawngtlai
5.	Lunglei	4,538.00	137,155	Lunglei
6.	Mamit	3,025.75	62,313	Mamit
7.	Chhimtuipui	3,957	60,823	Saiha
8.	Serchhip	1,421.60	55,539	Serchhip

Nagaland : Capital Kohima - Districts

	Districts	Area (sq. km.)	Population (2001)	Head quarters
1.	Dimapur	—	308,382	Dimapur
2.	Kohima	4,041	314,366	Kohima
3.	Phek	2,026	148,246	Phek
4.	Mokokchung	1,615	227,230	Mokokchung
5.	Mon	1,786	259,604	Mon
6.	Tuensang	4,228	414,801	Tuensang
7.	Wokha	1,628	161,098	Wokha
8.	Zunheboto	1,255	154,909	Zunheboto

Tripura : Capital Agartala - Districts

	Districts	Area (sq. km.)	Population (2001)	Head quarters
1.	Dhalai	2,522	307,417	Ambassa
2.	North Tripura	2,825	590,655	Kailashar
3.	South Tripura	2,152	762,565	Udaipur
4.	West Tripura	2,997	1,530,531	Agartala

Sikkim : Capital Gangtok - Districts

	Districts	Area (sq. km.)	Population (2001)	Head quarters
1.	East	954	2,44,790	Gangtok
2.	North	4,226	41,023	Mangan
3.	South	750	1,31,506	Namchi
4.	West	1,166	1,23,174	Gyalshing

2

Physical Feature

North East India is characterised by hills, plateaus, mountains intermontane plains, piedmont plains and river valleys. The most prominent physical feature is in the narrow Brahmaputra valley with the Arunachal Himalaya to the north, the Mishmi and Miju Hills to the east, the Patkai Naga-North cachar Hills to the southeast, the Karbi and, the Meghalaya plateaus to the south, Southeast of the north Cachar Hills is the Barak plain of the Surma valley. The Naga Hills extend to the south into the highlands of Manipur and to the southeast info the Mizo Hills and the adjoining Hills in Tripura and then into the alluvial plain of Bangladesh. The southern margin of the Meghalaya plateau overlooking the Surma valley is remarkably abrupt while the northern slope facing the Brahmaputra valley is gentle.

The North East India region is physiographically not a homogenous unit and the present configuration of this region has taken shape during geologically recent time. But the ultimate result of various geological events took place through the geological past. The geological set up of this region has been possible through the works of geological survey of India, geologists of the Burma Oil Company, the Assam Oil Company, Oil India and the Oil and Natural Gas Commission. From such works it is known that North East India consists of very ancient Archaean and Shillong series rocks exposed in several parts of the Garo, Khasi, Jaintia and Karbi Hills. These rocks are similar to rocks exposed in the rest of the peninsular in Bengal and Bihar of which this was a part at one geological time. All these old rocks form the basement for very much younger Tertiary sediments in upper Assam. But the basement for the other Tertiary sediments of

Nagaland, Manipur, Mizoram and Tripura is not definitely known. The Arunachal Himalayas show a southerly fringe of soft upper Tertiary rocks like sandstones forming the sub-Himalayan belt. These rocks are oversidden by Permo-Carboniferous coal bearing Gondwana sediments. The rocks like dolomites, quartzites and the associated Abor volcanics etc. are mostly confined to the Lesser Himalayas. Then came the great Himalayas with the Dalings and the crystalline rocks.[1]

A large part of this region was a landmass upto the formation of the Himalayas about 2,000 million years ago. Then the eastern part of the Khasi Hills, the Jaintia Hills and the Western part of the Karbi Hills became a basin of sedimentation in which sandstones and shales of the shillong series were deposited. Due to tectonic reasons these were later uplifted and became a landmass. The whole region including upper part of the Brahmaputra valley remained a landmass till Permocarbaniferous period. Then, nearly 250 million years ago in the Arunachal Himalayan region to the north and to the south and west of the Karbi-Meghalaya Plateau, sedimentation began and basins were formed. In such basins were deposited the coal-bearing sediments of the Gondwanas, marine in the Arunachal Himalayan region and fresh water west of the Garo Hills. The famous Buxas series of rock groups-ortho-quartzites and shales, and dolomite limestones were deposited on the margins of the same landmass at about the same time. Along with the Buxas group there was a plateau of volcanism as indicated by the Abor Volcanics in the undivided Siang districts of Arunachal Pradesh. These sediments were also uplifted and became landmass during the Triassic times.

One important tectonic feature is the formation of a flat levelled surface by an area to the south which experienced

---

1. M.V.N. Murthy. "An Outline Geomorphological Evolution of Assam Region", *Proceedings of the Pre congress Symposium and Field-Study Meeting on the Physical Geography of Eastern Himalaya and the Meghalaya Plateau,* IGU Gauhati, Nov. 1968.

peneplanation. The southern margin of the Khasi Hills experienced plateau volcanism by the end of Jurassic Times. This event took place through east-west features, along which the southern block sank and the northern block rose. After the ceassation of volcanism, deposition of Upper Cretaceous sediments took place due to the invasion of the sea on the southern block about 110 million years ago. Again during the Eocene times, about 60 million years ago the area reached stable shelf condition and during that time fossiliferous calcareous formation deposited.

A large part of the Meghalaya and the Karbi Plateau became the basins of fresh water sedimentation during palaeocene times and the Therria sandstones were deposited this way. The environmental conditions at that time were favourable for the formation of layers of limestones and coal-bearing sandstones. The younger Sylhet formation is an example of such environmental conditions. It may be mentioned that the Garo Hills, the Jaintia Hills and the Karbi Hills remained a landmass till Mid-Eocene time when sedimentation began and the uppermost limestone layer began to be deposited when the areas sank. During middle Eocene time the sea invaded to the maximum extent and at that time upper Assam became an area of sedimentation. Sedimentation continued in the submerged part of the south Garo Hills, in the southern margin of the Khasi Hills and the southeastern part of the Jaintia Hills, during the late Ecocene time. There was no sedimentation in the Karbi Hills which stood as high ground. At that time a large sea covered the greater part of the Myanmar as well as the eastern margin of Assam, Manipur, Mizoram and the eastern fringes of Bengal.

During Oligocene period, to the east and southeast a long depression developed in the sea floor which opened out to the south and covered present day Nagaland, Manipur, Barak Plain, Tripura, Mizo Hills including Arakan Yoma. This depression was sinking and the extent of sinking equalled the thickness of sediments brought to the sea floor and so the depth of the sea remained constant and shallow. When the sinking stopped the sea was filled up and swampy condition prevailed where luxuriant vegetation grew and their decayed remains eventually formed the coal field of Makum. The oil fields of Assam like Nahorkatiya, Moran, Rudrasagar, Lakwa, Geleki etc. are found in rocks formed abit earlier than the formation of coal layers.

About 25 million years ago i.e. during lower Miocene times sedimentation continued uninterruptedly in the Garo, Khasi and Jaintia Hill which then uplifted to become a landmass. The Karbi Hills including its adjoining area became depressed and Surma sediments were deposited. The upper part of the Brahmaputra was still under water during Middle Miocene times (20 million years ago) and the northern margin in the Himalayan area also became a basin of sedimentation which contain rock fragments like jasper and epidote. Then after Miocene times upliftment took place on a large scale and the Patkai mountain uplifted with some folding.

During the Pliocene times (10 million years ago) the Himalayan source area was uplifted and in the Patkai-Naga Hills area earth movement resulted in thrusting. The Himalayan region was also uplifted forming the mountain chains. About one million years ago i.e. in the Pleistocene period upward movement continued which indicated by the river terraces with boulders in the area and the old alluvium exposed in the Brahmaputra valley and elsewhere. The river Brahmaputra has had a complicated evolutionary history. It is an antecedent river which has cut through the Himalayan, concomitantly with the rise and the river must have had its present configuration during the pleistocene and recent period.

The geomorphologicaly evolution of the North-Eastern region of India is one of uplift and sinking in various parts during the past 100 million years. Such events have produced the present physical features of the region. The major physical features are the Archaean plateau, the Tertiary hills and mountains and the alluvial plains. The Meghalaya plateau with its Karbi Anglong outcrops is believed to be the oldest part formed during the Precambrian period. The other parts such as the Brahmaputra valley, Cacher plain, Arunachal Pradesh, Nagaland, Manipur and Tripura were formed between 25 and 50 million years ago. The northern part of the region is a continuation of the Himalayan Mountain system, while the southern part consists of the Tertiary Hills and Mountains and the Western central part ie. the plateau of Meghalaya is considered to be an outlier of the peninsular India. The intervening areas between the Himalayas and the Meghalayas are covered by the alluvial deposits of the river Brahmaputra and its tributaries. The lowland Cachar or Barak plain is simply an extension of the Surma valley which is located south of the Meghalaya plateau, while the Brahmaputra valley is an extension of the Indo-Gangetic trough. The gradient is rather low with about 15-20 centimetres per kilometre. That is why flood plains and water logging areas are extensive in both the valleys.

The landforms of North East India have been evolved since Archaean to Recent times. Richard E Murphy has divided the landforms of North East India on the basis of both genetic and empirical factors and his physiographic divisions and sub-divisions are given below :

1. The Plateaus : Meghalaya Plateau, Karbi Plateau.
2. The Hill and Mountains : Himalayan Mountains Region, Inner Himalayan Region (Glacial and Periglacial) Lesser Himalayan Region, Eastern Hills, Dibong-Lohit Knot. Patkai-Tirap-Nagaland-North Cachar and Manipur Hills, Mizoram-Tripura Range and Valley country.
3. The Plains : Brahmaputra Plain, Bhabar-Tarai Belt, Northern Built-Up strip, Brahmaputra Flood Plain, Southern Built-up Strip, Southern Foot-hill zone, Intermontane and piedmont plains, Manipur Basin, Barak Plain, Tripura Plain.

Braodly speaking North East India may be divided into five physiographic units on the basis of lithology, age and mode of evolution (Fig. 2).

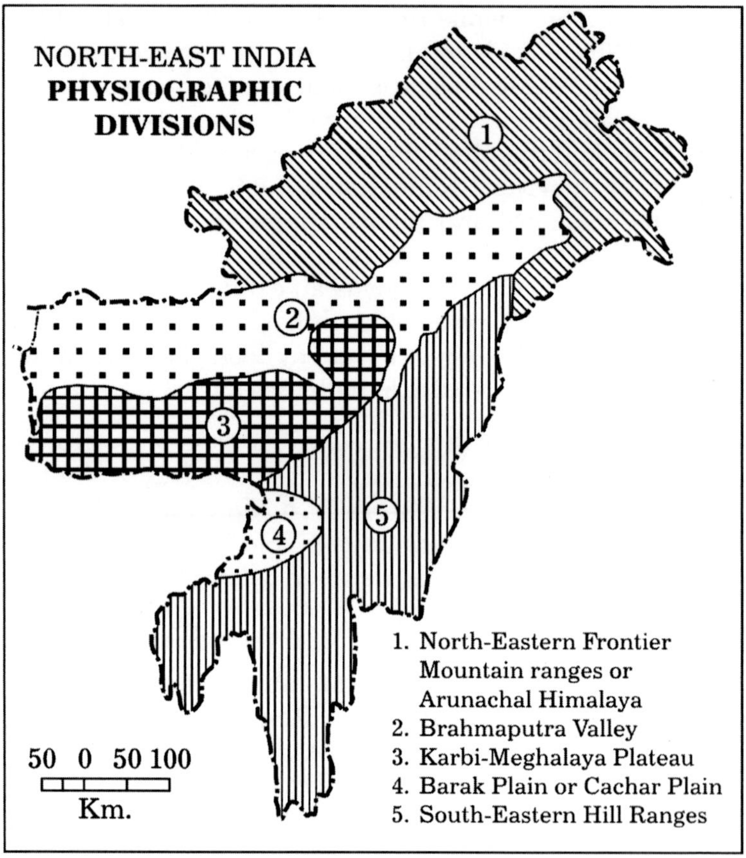

Fig. 2 : Physiographic Divisions

The Physiographic divisions of the region are :

1. North-Eastern frontier mountain ranges or Arunachal Himalaya.
2. Brahmaputra Valley
3. Karbi-Meghalaya Plateau
4. Barak Plain or Cachar Plain
5. South-Eastern Hill Ranges

1. North Eastern Frontier Ranges or Arunachal Himalaya : This region extends from the eastern border of Bhutan ie. the Dhansiri river to the syntxial bend at the northeast of the Mishmi Hills. The Brahmaputra makes a hairpin bend here and cuts across the mountains before flowing into the plains of Assam. Arunachal Himalaya is divisible into several section : Aka Hills (Hrussors Hills) from Dhansiri to Dikorai river, the Dafla Hills from Bharali river in the West to Ranganadi in the east, the Miri Hills in the North of Lakhimpur district, the Adi Hills (Abor Hills) between Dihang and Dibang and Lohit rivers. The Namcha Barwa is the highest peak (7,756 m) in the region and is located in the Mishmi Hills. The other high peaks of Arunachal Himalaya are Kulkangri (7,544 m) and Chomo Lhari (7,344.2 m) There are several glaciers including an important lake named Yegrongtso in this region. All the three sections of the Himalaya, the Siwalik (outer Himalaya), the Lesser Himalaya and the Great Himalaya are not well represented here. The Siwalik formations are not continuous like the western part of the Himalaya. Perhaps large part of the formation are washed away by the turbulent rivers of the region. The forested lesser Himalayas (1,200m – 3,000m) are intercepted by deep and steep sided river valleys. In most cases they cut vertically down into steep gorges and narrow valleys and flow towards Assam to meet the river Brahmaputra. The Great Himalayan region (above 3000m) are rising above the snowline to about 6000m on the northern border of the region. The whole region is extremely rugged, highly dissected with limited level space. The southern edge of the Arunachal Himalaya is very much abrupt. It rises from the Brahmaputra plain with abrupt slope whereas the northern edge facing Tibet is comparatively gentle. The turbulent rivers of the region carry huge loads of silts and these are deposited on the piedmont region giving to what a called alluvial or piedmont apron. Such feature are seen all along the foot hill region of Arunachal Himalayas.

2. Brahmaputra Valley : Hemmed in between the North-Eastern frontier Hills, Patkai and the Naga Hills and the

Karbi-Meghalaya Plateau, the Brahmaputra valley occupies a most significant part of the physiography of north East India. The valley is an alluvial plain formed by the deposition of sediments brought by the river Brahmaputra and its numerous tributaries. It extends from Sadiya in the east and Dhubri in the west. The Brahmaputra valley is very extensive, it is about 720 km long and 96 km in width on the average. The Brahamputra valley is narrow where the river is encountering a gnessic country right from the Karbi Hills and very much extensive in the undivided Lakhimpur district. The valley has been built by the deposition of aluvium, about 170.0 metres thick upon a sag created during the period of Himalayan upliftment. The main stream and its numerous tributaries flowing from either side are mainly responsible for supplying the alluvial debris from the elevated parts from the northern and southern sides.

The Brahmaputra valley on the whole has a gentle slope from east to west. Sadiya, situated at the head of the valley has an altitude of 135 metres, Dibrugrah 104 metres, Guwahati 51 metres and Dhubri 34 metres.

The northern margin of the Brahmaputra valley is characterised by abrupt slope and merges with outer rampart of the Arunachal Himalaya. The valley is bordered in the north by a narrow belt known as *bhabar* which are deposited coarse sands and pebbles brought down from the Himalayan region by the swift flowing mountain streams. Except during the rainy season, these are marked by dry river courses in which the water of the smaller rivers sink underground. Generally the large rivers flow on the surface of the bhabar belt. The water which sinks underground in the bhabar reappears on the surface where the plains begin. This water converts large areas along the rivers into swamps and the swampy, illdrained forested lands are known as Tarai. The southern margin of the valley is less precise and gradual. The western side of the valley of open and merges with the Ganga valley. Thus is Brahmaputra valley is the eastern most continuation of the Indo Gangetic trough.

On either side of the Brahamputra river there lies the flood plain which supports a series of swamps and beels. Most of the north-bank tributaries lose their tracks in such water features and flow sluggishly towards the Brahmaputra river through their sub-parallel courses. The flood plain also contains riverine sandy areas (Chars) and numerous temporary and semi-permanent sandy islands on the river bed of the Brahamputra.

The flatness of the Brahmaputra valley is broken by the presence numerous low hills which are seen along the gneissic country right from Tezpur and Karbi Hills to as far west as Dhubri. All these low hills are the outlying parts of the Meghalaya Plateau, because they consist of the similar kind of Metamorphic rocks. Beyond Tezpur and Silghat up along the valley is monotonous plain without any hills. This mounonous plain is known as upper Brahmaputra valley and the lower part of the valley which is borken by low hills is called the lower Brahmaputra valley.

Along the foothills of the south bank of the Brahmaputra valley some river terraces are seen in the Dihing valley near Margherita and Dapha valley. Here three terraces in different heights at 42 m, 48 m and 75 m respectively are recognised.

The extensive flood water of the river Brahmaputra and its tributaries has given rise to the formation of permanent marshes known as beels. Dipar, Bildara, Roumari, Satdala, Kapla, Kodomani, Chalchala, Bangalmari, Barbeel, Garangabeel, Chatabeel, Mohmari etc. are examples of such marshes. Many beels have formed as a result of the formation of ox-bow lakes by the rivers.

3. **Karbi-Meghalaya Plateau :** The Karbi plateau is known as the outlier of the Meghalaya plateau and structurally the area is a continuation of the Meghalaya plateau or abode clouds named by Professor S.P. Chatterjee in 1932. This plateau was studied in detail by him and published in the name and style as Le plateau de Meghalaya in 1936, Paris. Geologically the whole Meghalaya Plateau including the

Karbi Anglong region of Assam is a detached part of the penisular India. It is separated by the Malda gap which resulted of river erosion of the Ganga and the Brahmaputra. Thus the landscape evolution of the plateau is closely linked with the Indian peninsula and its landscape story consists of different types of erosion, sedimentation, folding, intrusions, movements of land and sea and emissions. The core of the plateau is an ancient mass of gneiss, schists and granite which have been exposed in the north but hidden in the south beneath Cretaceous and Tertiary deposits and a Mesozoic trap known as Syllet trap. The whole plateau was under sub aerial erosion from the Cambrian to the Jurassic period. It contains within its face the marks of Peneplanation which range from Precambrian to recent and sub-recent periods. The peneplains are at varying altitudes of 1860-1920m around Shillong, Latkor peaks 1440-1500m and 1410m in Unkhrah valley. The length of the plateau from the river Dhansiri in the east and Singimari river in the west is about 420 km and the width in 40 km on the average. The whole Meghalaya plateau is almost surrouded by the plain of Brahmaputra, Surma and the Kopili rivers. The southern margin of the plateau overlooking the Surma valley is remarkably abrupt while the northern margin facing the Brahmaputra valleys is gentle.

The plateau may be divided into four parts : Western Meghalaya or the Garo Hills, Central Meghalaya or the Khasi Hills, Eastern Meghalaya or the Jaintia Hills and the Karbi plateau or the detached part of the Meghalaya. The Garo Hills extends over the area of 7770 sq. km. The Moheskhola Adaguri range is the demarcating line of the Garo and the Khasi hills. The most important physical features of this part are the Tura range and the Simsang valley. The general elevation of the Garo Hills is comparatively low. The highest elevation is being recorded at Nokrek peak (1418 m) on the Tura range. The other important hills are Arbela range and Tura range. The Khasi Hills consists of several micro-physiographic units like the undulating hills in the north, western track, central upland southern face of the upland, the valley in the south and the southern belt of low hills. Just away from the Brahmaputra valley, the hills are gentle and low. They are separated from the more higher central upland by an important fault line. Above 488 metres most of the hills are conspicuous by their flat top character. Towards the Garo Hills the central upland slopes down and this tract is transitional in character between the Garo and the Khasi Hills. The central upland is the most important physiographic unit of the entire plateau. Several traces of erosion cycles are preserved in this part. The central plateau gently slopes southwards for a short distance for about six km and then rises very steeply upto the plain. The southern face is very much affected by fluvial erosion and has given rise to three platforms, namely Langkydrem plateau, the Cherrapunjee platform and the Mawsynrma platform. The southern part of the central plateau, because of repeated uplift, has been denuded by the river like Uni-Reas, Umngriand and Um-Rilang at different times. The valleys of these rivers are characterised by two stages, namely old stage in the upper parts and the youthful stage in their lower parts which shows the rivers are of antecedent type. From Jadukata to some distance towards Dhalaiganj the belt of hills are low. In most cases they are broken by tiny plains and some of them lie in isolation.

The Jaintia Hills forms a contiguous part of the Khasi Hills consisting of northern undulating hills, Jowai upland and the southern escarpment. There are more flat lands in the Jaintia Hills than that of the Khasi Hills. The general height of this part of the plateau is in between 1250 and 1750 metres. The Jowai upland acts as a watershed between the Brahmaputra valley and the Surma valley.

Karbi plateau is the detached part of the Meghalaya plateau. It is mostly separated from the Meghalaya plateau by the degradation of the Kopili and its headstreams and from the Naga Hills by the Dhansiri and its headstreams. The central part of this dissected Karbi plateau is higher with an elevation of about 1360 metres. In most cases the hills follow south-west to northeast trend and their ridges are not sharp.

4. Barak Plain or Cachar Plain : The major part of the Surma valley lies in the then East Pakistan, now Bangladesh. The area of this plain within India is about 7000 sq. km. On the north of the plain is abruptly demarcated by the Garo Hills. The southeastern boundary has a different character. Long spurs of hills project from both Tripura and Mizo Hills interspersed with broad valleys and low hills. There is a monoclinal fold and its floding has given rise to alternate rows of hills and valleys. The river Barak flows through the middle part of the plain sluggishly in meandering course forming series of swamps and ox-bow lakes. The flood waters accumulate in the depression giving rise to many marshes which dot the country side.

5. Southeastern Hill Ranges : This region includes the Patkai, the Naga, the Barail range, the highlands of Manipur, The Mizo Hills and Tripura ranges. This hilly tract is the southern extension of the eastern Himalayan region and is characterised by relatively low relief. Most of the ranges have north-south alignment and run parallely alternated by deep valley occupied by mountainous streams The general elevation of the ranges is 915 m from the sea level. There are a few notable peaks namely Saramati (3827 m) and Japvo Peaks (2914 m) in the Naga Hills and Noi-Isong (3777 m) at the syntaxial bend. The Blue mountain which is located in the Mizo Hills has the height of 2158 m. The whole region is very much unstable and falls into an important seismic zone and as a result of this, the area is criss-crossed by several faults and strikes. The most important which are Naga thrust, Haflong-Disang and Dawki-Tear thrust. The hills of the region are separated from one another by narrow steep sided valley. Generally the valley bottoms are conspicuous by the presence of gravels, boulders and other transported materials. The valley side ridges are clothed with tall vegetation, while the peaks of the ridges are covered by grassy vegetation.

3

Climate

North East India is mostly dominated by monsoon climate which implies a climate with cool dry season in December to February, a hot season from March to June, a hot wet season from July to September and a retreating monsoon season from October to November. The climate shows little modification of the standard monsoonal type, the hot season being shorter than usual, average temperature is lower than the rest of the country because the region receives higher amount of rainfall.

The climate of the region is controlled by some important factors like location, the Himalayan and other physiographic features, the great air-currents of winter and summer, western disturbances pre-dominance of maritime air mass, mountain and valley winds of the region and extensive local water bodies. All these factors exert their sizable impact in modifying the climatic conditions of North East India.

India is cut-off from the rest of Asia by the lofty Himalayan mountains and that is why the Indian monsoon is quite distinct from the rest of the continent. The northeastern part of India is situated on the southern foot-hills of the Himalayas. The Meghalaya plateau which separates two important river valleys, rise gradually from 300 metres in Garo hills to about 3000 metres in Naga hills towards east. The Surma valley including the Barak plain faces the Bay of Bengal. The undivided Cachar district is bordered by the Meghalaya plateau, the hills of North Cachar, Mizo and Tripura on its north, east and south but is open to west facing the Bay of Bengal. Thus clouds brought by the south-west monsoon get intercepted by 1800 metres high ridge of Khasi and Jaintia hills causing instability and heavy rainfall on the southern

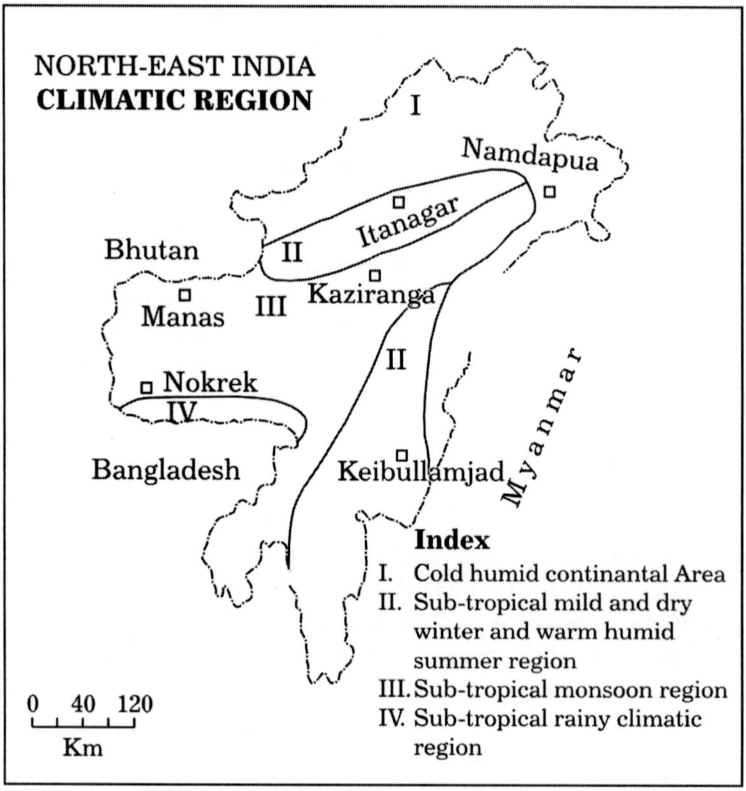

Fig. 3 : Climatic Regions

face of the range. The rain-bearing cloud which passes over the ridges of the Meghalaya plateau precipitates in the Brahmaputra valley and intensity of rainfall depends on the strength of the wind and angle at which they meet the orographic barrier. Generally the rainfall decreases on lee-ward side of the Khasi and Jaintia hills and increases towards the foothills of the Himalayas. There is a depression at the eastern end of the Himalayas which permits northeast monsoon during the end of the winter season influencing on the precipitation of the Brahmaputra valley. Rainfall on the western part of the valley causes from the rain bearing cloud that passes over the Garo and Khasi and Jaintia hills and in the central region (undivided Nagaon district) which is surrounded by Karbihills, Meghalaya plateau and Naga hills form a rain-shadow area. Thus the undivided Nagaon district is the driest and the Khasi and Jaintia hills are the wettest areas of the region. In general hilly areas receive more rainfall than the plains. Intensity and distribution of storm precipitation are dependent on the nature of atmospheric pressure created by the migrating air masses. Generally during the break monsoon period a westerly wave crosses the region towards plains, and the hills of North East India receive heavy rainfall. Similarly the low pressure formed over the Bay of Bengal, if moves north-westerly direction may cause heavy rain along its track and increases intensity in North East India. Besides formation of land-lows and upper air trough at the head of the Bay of Bengal produce heavy rainfall in different parts of North East India.

According to the Indian Meteorological Department, there are four seasons in India namely Northeast monsoon season (December-March), South-west monsoon season (June-September), the transitional hot weather (April-May) and the transitional period of retreating south-west monsoon (October-November). These four seasons are also felt in North East India.

1. **Cold Weather season (December to February) :** Foggy morning, sunny noon and clear night are the characteristic features of weather in the season. January in the coldest month for all the states.

This is the season of highest temperature contrast, ranging 18°C at Guwahati (plain), 9°C at Cherrapunjee (plateau) and 2.4°C at Ziro (Arunachal Himalayas). In this season, the natural scenery though gives an impression of landscape with dry soils and trees with old leaves, is however, enjoyable with seasonal flowers of various colour seen around. The cool but pleasent weather is usually interrupted by driving showers associated with western disturbances.

2. **Southwest monsoon or the Rainy season (June to September) :** This is the period of heaviest rainfall, June being the rainiest month of the year with an average monthly

rainfall of 40 cm. The amount of seasonal rainfall varies from 122 cm in Goalpara, 287 cm in Kokrajhar, 135 cm in Nagaon 245 cm Karimganj, 100 cm in Karbi-Anglong district of Assam, 185 cm in Arunachal Pradesh 180 cm in Meghalaya 130 cm in Mizoram and Tripura and 170 cm in Nagaland and Manipur. Though on certain days of heavy downpour temperature falls down considerably, yet when clouds disappear temperature rises to a fairly high degree within a short time. Here in most of the part of North East India, monsoon bursts towards the end of May or in early part of June followed by incessant rains sometimes for week together and lower June temperature is itself due to cooling effect of the rains.

3. The Transitional hot weather season (April-May) : The temperature rises considerably in late March and remains same to the middle of April and rises further in late April and May. The highest mean daily maximum temperature (32°C) is recorded in April. Generally the mean maximum temperature during summer ranges between 21°C and 32°C and the mean minimum temperature varies from 10°C to 21°C. Day temperatures in March are also sufficiently high to make the weather unpleasant and warrant the use of fans. Unpleasant dust winds (the Nor's wester) during this time often visit this region. Sometimes destructive storms which are known as 'Bardaichila' in Assam also visit many parts of North East India and this considerably lowers down the temperature. At the end of this season, the western disturbances disappear, but weather is in association with thunder-storms followed by rain.

4. The Transitional period of retreating southwest monsoon (October-November) : During this period the low pressure system becomes weaker resulting gradual decrease in the southwest monsoon. The temperature also decreases gradually. The range of diurnal pressure becomes more and more pronounced, the nights becoming relatively cold. The relative humidity decreases and the sky remains clear most of the time. The mean maximum temperature ranges between 29°C and 19°C and mean minimum temperature varies from 18°C to 8°C. Similarly the rainfall is not more than 25 cm except on the windward side of the Cherrapunjee range and at the foot of the Arunachal Himalayas. This season is characterised by relative calmness of atmosphere. The period of the retreating monsoon season is also known as Autumn. The natural landscape in the entire north-eastern region offers an impressive look with its green surroundings. Fogs begin to appear late in the evening and early in the morning during this period.

Temperature Pattern

Generally high temperature gradient is found to occur between the highlands and plain. In both the Brahmaputra valley and Barak Plain, temperature diminishes towards the highland areas. In the month of August 18°C isotherm encloses the area around Shillong which accounts for the lowest mean daily minimum temperature. This area is regarded as one of the coldest parts of North East India. The Western part of Manipur including Barak plain of Assam show minimum temperature of about 22°C.

During winter the mean daily minimum temperature is high in the areas covered by 12°C isotherm. Such areas are found in the Western part of Meghalaya, southern part of Dhubri district and the eastern most part of the Brahmaputra valley. Similarly the mean daily minimum temperature isothern of 40°C covers shillong and Imphal region indicating these areas to be coldest parts of North East India. Generally snow covers many places like Tawang, Langju etc. along Indo-China border.

Rainfall Pattern

Northeast India is an area of high rainfall. A large part of Meghalaya plateau, parts of North Cachar hills and Barak plain are enclosed by the isohyet of 300 cm and so these are high rainfall areas. Rain occurs less towards the western part of the valley and Arunachal Pradesh. The central part of Assam, southern Nagaland and Manipur are enclosed by the isohyet of 200 cm. Hojai-Lumding area of Nagaon district and Diphu region of Karbi Anglong district are the areas of scanty rainfall compared the other parts of northeastern India. This zone of scanty rainfall is known as rain shadow zone of Meghalaya plateau. The windward side of the Meghalaya plateau receives more rainfall on which Cherrapunjee is located. Thus Cherrapunjee is the wettest station experiencing 1087 cm average rainfall. The rain bearing wind is dried out as it descends leeward side of the plateau and so less rainfall occurs in the rain shadow area as mentioned above. Heavy orographic rains occur by the moisture laden air mass moving towards Arunachal Himalayas.

Classification of the Climates

The Climate of the Indian sub-continent have been classified by W. Koppern, C.W. Thornthwaite, Kendrew and Stamp. Their works reflect some of the main climate regions of India as they appeal to the people and their divisions are significant. North East India has several climates rather than a single monsoon climate. The climatic types of this region can be identified on the basis of temperature, rainfall, humidity and northerly and south westerly winds. The controlling factors as mentioned earlier, are location, physiography, the alternating high and low pressure cell of north-west India and the Bay of Bengal, the predominance of warm and moist maritime (MT) air masses, the local mountain and valley winds and the extensive local water bodies. Following Koppen, Thornthwaite, Kendrew-Stamp North East India can be divided climatically into four main climatic regions: Cold humid continental region, Sub-tropical mild and dry winter and warm humid summer region, Sub-tropical monsoon with partially dry winter, Warm and humid summer climatic area and Sub-Tropical rainy climatic region with very heavy monsoon rains.

I. Cold humid continental climatic region : The Cold humid continental climate occurs on the highlands of Nagaland, Manipur and Mizoram at an altitude of 2000 metres and continue up to 5000 metres. This is Dfc Climate characterised by shorter summer, over four months below 10°C and cold humid winters. During winter some areas are covered by snow and growth of plants is restricted to a few month till snow melts. The productivity of plant life is handicapped by low temperature and strong winds. The alpine and sub-alpine vegetation are confined to such areas and animal life is also limited.

II. Sub-tropical climate with mild and dry winter and warm humid summer region : This is Cwg climate with dry winter (wettest month 10 times rainfall of driest). The climate of this type is mainly found in southern part of Arunachal Pradesh, western Nagaland, large areas of Manipur and Mizoram. The entire climatic belt is covered by tropical evergreen, tropical semi-evergreen and tropical moist deciduous forests.

III. Sub-Tropical monsoon region : This climatic type is characterised by warm humid and mild but partially dry winter. It occurs in the Brahmaputra valley, the northern part of Meghalaya plateau, Barak plain and Tripura. The region is marked by heavy monsoon rains. The tropical moist deciduous and dry deciduous forests cover the lower part of the Brahmaputra valley, Tripura, northern part of the Meghalaya plateau and north Cachar hills.

IV. Sub-tropical rainy climatic region : This climatic region is marked by very heavy monsoon rainfall. The climate is Cwm type which occurs in the southern part of the Meghalaya plateau. Mawsynram, a village of this region records the highest rainfall in the world with 1,392 cm Typical rain forest occur in this region which resemble Selvas in having a large variety of plants and animals.

4

Hydrology

W.G. Moore defined hydrology as the science that treats of water, especially in relation to its occurrence in streams, lakes, wells and snow and including its discovery, uses, control and conservation. In fact hydrology is the science of the occurrence and cycle of water on the surface of the earth. There are many forms and ways in which water occurs and so hydrology can be divided into several branches. The branch of hydrology which deals with water in the atmosphere is usually called hydro-meteorology; with water as it flows over the earth's surface-potamology; with water in natural or artificial reservoirs-limnology; with ground water-geohydrology; with soil moisture-pedohydrology[1]. Some parts of hydrology are closely interrelated with other science like meteorology, hydraulics, physical geography etc., and as a result many boundaries and interdisciplinary fields exist. Generally precipitated water which is not absorbed into the soil is retained on the surface of the earth. If suffient slope and depth is attained, it runs off, creating overland flow and this overland is gradually concentrated in rivulet, small streams creating through which water flows into permanent rivers. These are also fed by sub-surface and ground water flow. The term 'drainage' refers to such process by which water is discharged from a surface area through various forms of streams, rivers, canals etc. due to gravity towards lower levels.

Drainage of North East India

The high mountains with rugged terrains and high

1. J. Nemec, "Engineering Hydrology", Tata Mcgraw Hill Publishing Co. Ltd. New Delhi, 1973, p. 14.

monsoon rainfall in the region contribute to the dense drainage network in the northeastern region of India. The entire region consists of parts of five important river basins : the Brahmaputra basin, the Surma-Barak basin, upper part of the Chindwing basin, upper part of the Kaladan basin and upper part of the Karnafuli basin.

The Brahmaputra is the largest and most important river basin of the Northeast India. The river has a catchment area of 580,000 km^2 and it flows through the southern part of China, India and Bangladesh for a total length of 2,880 km. Over Indian territory the Brahmaputra river traverses a distance of 918 km through the states of Arunachal Pradesh and Assam. In Arunachal Pradesh the river flow through Himalayan terrain while in Assam it runs over alluvial plains, thereby forming the extensive Brahmaputra valley of Assam. This valley is about 720 km long and 80-90 km wide. The Brahmaputra river system in India, with a vast and complicated network of tributaries covers a catchment area 195,000 km^2 that span over several states like Arunachal Pradesh, Assam, Nagaland, Meghalaya, Sikkim and West Bengal (Fig. 4).

The Chinese part of the Brahmaputra river is known as the Tsangpo. In the prehistoric past the Tsangpo had flowed from east to west. But then the gradual upliftment of the Himalayas changed the direction of the Tsangpo and eventually its final capture by the headward erosion of the Siang-Dihang brought it to its present courses. Thus the Tsangpo is an antecedent river and it is older than the Himalayas. In 1762 Chi Cho Nen, a Chinese geographer fixed the source of the Tsangpo the Tamchok Khambab mountain on the eastern flank of the Lanchen Khambab range of the Kailash mountains. So the Tsangpo is also known as the Tamchok Khambab river and the source of the river is the great glacier called Chema Yangdung. This glacier covers the southern flank of the Kailash range at an elevation of nearly 5150 metres, between latitude 30°31'N and longitude 82°10'E. Many headstreams like the Kubi, Chema Yangdung, Angsi

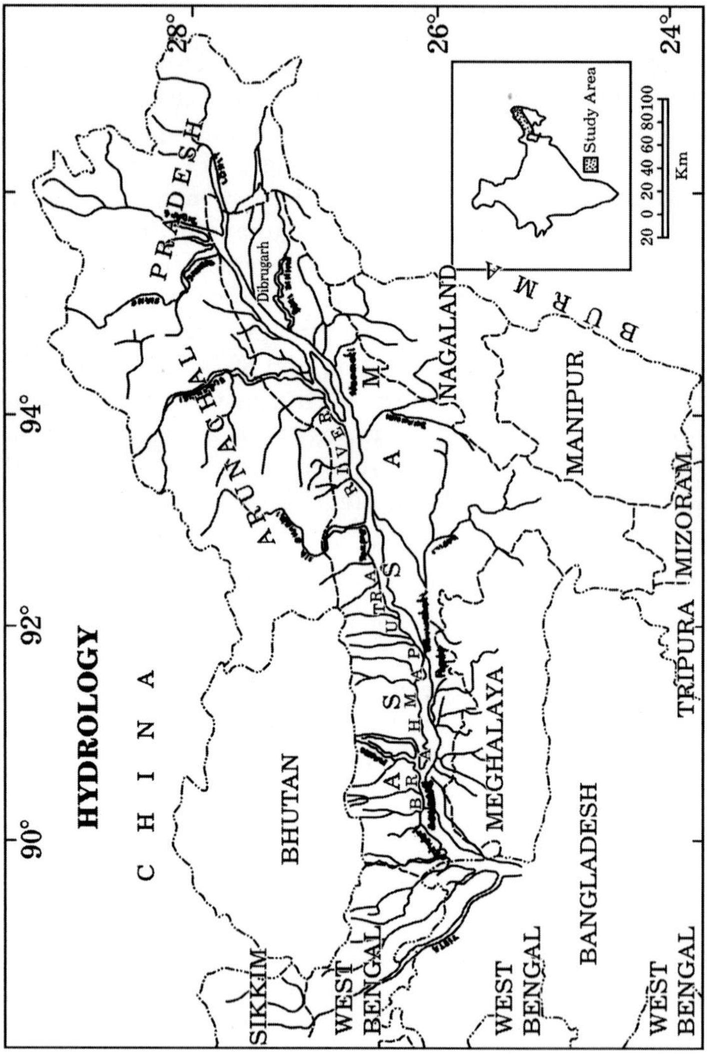

Fig. 4 : Hydrology

and Mariumch roll down the frozen glacial slope to give birth to the Tsangpo. The Tsangpo does not cut any deep channel for the flow of water on the cold Tibetan plateau. In spite of its immense elevation the Tsangpo is a sluggish river and it is navigable south of Lhasa. The bed of the river lies about 4910 m above sea level at Trandom, 400 m at Shigatze, 270 m at Gyalasingdon but at Sadiya it is only 147 m. The Tsangpo, while flowing in an easterly course meets its first Tibetan tributary, the Raga Tsangpo on its left at Lhatse Dzong ant at Shigatse another tributary named Nien-Chu-Ho joins this Tsangpo on its right. Then the Tsangpo is met on its left by the La-sa Ho and from here the river becomes broad. Travelling nearly 680 km from the meeting point of La-sa Ho, the Tsangpo takes two more tributaries namely. the Yarlungchu and Tarlungchu before turning southward and reaching Tse-La where the Niyangho meets the Tsangpo. Tse-La lies on the border zone at the northern edge of Arunachal Pradesh. The river becomes narrower from the point and at Pe, it tapers down to only 600 metres. The Tsangpo cuts a course through a succession of great, narrow gorges between the mountainous complex of Gyala peri (7150 m) and Namcha Barwa (7756 m), the highest peak of the Eastern Himalaya, then the Tsangpo flows southward and enters India in the Upper Siang district of Arunachal Pradesh. In Arunachal Pradesh the river Tsangpo is known as Siang or Dihang. The river debouches into the plain at Pasighat and then meets two other rivers, namely Dibang and Lohit. From this meeting point the river flows through the entire length of Assam in south-westerly direction in the name of Brahmaputra, ultimately it runs to meet the river Ganga through Bangladesh. A large number of tributaries join the Brahmaputra river from the north bank and the south bank.

Some important north bank tributaries are the Burisuti, Subansiri, Ranganadi, Buroi, Borgong, Jia-Bharali, Gabharu, Belsiri, Jia-Dhansiri, Noanadi, Nanoi, Barnadi, Puthimari, Baralia, Nona, Pagladiya, Buradiya, Tihu, Kaldiya, Beki, Manas, Buriaie, Champamati and Sonkosh. Some of these tributaries are huge rivers and carry huge amount of water.

Among the large tributaries the Subansiri originates from the Trans-Himalayan belt, the Jia-Bharali, Manas and Sonkosh originate in the Greater Himalayas and other tributaries have their origin in the Lesser Himalayan zone. The Subansiri is the largest tributary of the Brahmaputra with a catchment area of 37000 sq. km of which 1000 sq. km lies in Assam. The south bank tributaries are relatively smaller than those of the north bank and the important tributaries are Dibang, Lohit, Burhidihing, Desang, Dikshow, Jhanji, Bhogdoi, Dhansiri, Kopili, Digaru, Kulsi, Dudhnoi, Krishnai, and Jinjiram. The tributaries like the Burhidihing, Disang, Dikhow and Dhansiri originate from the Naga-Patkai ranges. The sources of the Kopili, Digaru, Kulsi, Krishnai, Jinjiram etc. lie on the northern part of the Meghalaya plateau. Most of the south bank tributaries flow for a long distance in their lower courses sub-parallel to the Brahmaputra river before discharging into the main stream.

The Brahmaputra basin falls under a strong monsoon regime, receiving an average annual rainfall of 265 cm, nearly 60-70 per cent of it occurring during month of June to September. So the heaviest rainfall of the summer monsoon occurring in the basin produces the strongest effects on the Brahmaputra and its tributaries. The rainfall within Indian part of the basin varies annually from 175 cm in the plains of lower Assam to 640 cm in the ranges of Arunachal Himalayas. Floods of varying magnitudes occur in the Brahmaputra valley during the rainy season due to such heavy rainfall. High intensities of rainfall along the foothills bordering the Brahmaputra valley and peaking of tributaries at the confluences within a very short period of time eventually give rise to high flood level of the Brahmaputra river causing flood below the foothill region. The heavy monsoon rains of very high intensity erodes, the steep and fragile slopes of the Himalayan watershed composed of young Tertiary sediments with an admixtures of cobbles and boulders. Thus, the Brahmaputra becomes heavily sediment-laden and carries an alarming volume of sediments. At Pandu, near Guwahati, the Brahmaputra carries an annual average suspended load of 344.5 million tons, over 95 per cent of which is transported between May and October. So a river like the Brahmaputra with such gigantic water and sediments discharge magnitudes when additionally loaded with heavy summer rain obviously becomes capable of creating flash floods.

The Barak is the second largest river in Northeast India. It originates from the southern slope of the Mt. Iso on the Nagaland-Manipur border in Senapati district. The river flows in a westerly and southerly course to Tipaimukh in the south-western corner of Churachandpur district of Manipur where it takes a sharp U-turn to the north and forms the boundary between Assam and Manipur. Then it turns to the west and flow across the middle of the plain till the river reaches Kandigram in Karimganj district. Here the Barak bifurcates into two branches, namely the Surma in the north and Kushiyara in the south on entering Bangladesh. The total length of the Barak river from its source to its confluence with the old channel of the Brahmaputra near Bhairab Bazar (Bangladesh) is about 396 km. The Barak basin covers an area of 41,000 km^2 and it includes southeastern part of Meghalaya, southern part of the Barail range, Cachar, Hailakandi and Karimganj district of Assam, northern and western parts of Manipur, northern part of Mizoram southwestern part of Nagaland and northern and eastern parts of Tripura. The Barak receives a large number of small tributaries like the Jiri, Chiri Madhura, Jatinga etc. flowing down from the southern slopes of the north Cachar hills and the Irang, Makru and Tuivai etc. from the western part of Manipur. The Surma-Barak river system also receives important south flowing tributaries like the Jadukata, Umew-umiam, Myngot Shella etc. from Meghalaya. The Barak river receives the Dhaleswari, Katakhal, Sonai etc. from the northern part of Mizoram. The Longai is a 152 km long tributary of the Kushiyara river and it rises from the Tampai hills of Tripura, then flows through a northerly course towards Karimganj. Besides, there are many beels and marshes which play an important role in the physical setting of the Barak river basin.

The Chinduwin river of Myanmar covers the southeastern part of Nagaland and northern part of Manipur and the head stream Tizu forms a basin of 6000 sq. km. Similarly the eastern margin of Manipur is drained by the head streams of the Khampat and Yuu river which cut the Patkai range to meet the river Chindwin of Myanmar.

The southern part of Mizoram is drained by the river Kaladan and its headstreams. The Kaladan covers it basin area of 9000 sq. km. Similarly the western margin of Mizoram and southern part of Tripura are drained by the river Karnaphuli of Bangladesh covering a basin area of about 500 sq. km.

Thus the entire northeast India has some networks of complicated river system. The plain of the region, namely the Brahmaputra, Barak and Manipur plain are flat over which the rivers flowing sluggishly creating a large number of beels, swamps, marshes and ox-bow lakes. The total length of the major rivers in North East India is about 19,468 km. The Brahmaputra and the Barak basins covers about 86 per cent of the total geographical area of the region. But the river basins are geologically and seismologically unstable and hydrologically dynamic and that is why only 10 per cent of the annual flow is reported to be economically harnessable.

5

Natural Vegetation and Forest Resources

The natural vegetation cover of North East India has been modified by clearing for cultivation and unregulated grazing. As a result the forest is practically absent in some plain areas, much of the lower hills and plateaus. Generally woodland is practically confined to the foot hill regions, riverine strips and villages. The floral landscape is rarely marked by an absolute preponderance of one of two species. The plants like sal, palm, bamboos, reed and tall grass of savannah type cover the greater part of the region in a hotch-potch fashion and the natural vegetation is far from taking the place of assemblages. The floristic affinities of North East India are mostly with the Malaysian realm.

At present North East India has less forest cover than it was earlier and during the last two decades, the vegetal cover over the region got depleted at an alarming rate. Vast deforestation of vegetal cover leads to the problem of silt in the river beds and causing flood. These are some of the important aspects of vegetal cover of this region.

The distribution of forest type is determined mainly by climate. In Northeast India rainfall is more significant than temperature, except in the Arunachal Himalayas. Soil factor is of secondary importance, thougth it plays a major role in controlling the distribution of species. A major part of each state of the region is occupied by mountainous terrain and hence altitudinal variation is an important determinant of climate and soil conditions in all the seven states of the region. Due to wide altitudinal, climatic and edaphic variations, several types of forests ranging from tropical wet evergreen to alpine types are seen in different states of Northeast India.

The Indian vegetation has been classified by H.G. Champion as early as 1936 and the biotic modification has been done by G.S. Puri. A revised survey of forest types was done by H.G. Champion and S.K. Seth in 1968. Following all these works, the forests of Northeast India can be classified into the nine major types : tropical wet evergreen forests and its sub-types, tropical semi-evergreen forests and its sub-types, tropical moist deciduous forest, high altitude coniferous forests, temperate broad leaved forests, mountain wet temperate forest, alpine forest, bamboo forest and grassland.

Tropical wet evergreen forests are naturally best developed in areas with over 203 cm of rainfall and short dry season. These forests occur up to 900 m above sea level and are found in Eastern Assam, part of Barak plain, Southeastern Arunachal Pradesh, Northeastern part of Nagaland and Northeastern Manipur. These forests are sub-divided into two distinct sub-types : south bank tropical wet evergreen (Dipterocarpus) and northbank tropical evergreen (Nahar, Jutulri) forests. The south bank type is mostly found between 150-600 m altitude and occurs in Tirap, changlang and part of Lohit district on the south. The forest type is characterised by its unique structure and composition with commercial timber species like hollong (Dipterocarpus macrocarpus), Makai (Shorea assamica) hollock (Terminalia Myriocarpa), Sam (Artocarpus Chaplasa), Nahar (Mesua ferrea). The forest type is also associated with climbers, lianas and epiphytes. The north bank type occurs along the semi-evergreen forest in association with teak (Tectona grandis), hollock (Terminalia Myriocarpa), shilikha (Terminalia Citrana), Nahar (Mesua ferrea) etc. These tropical rain forests are very dense and lofty, the upper storey reaching 37-46 m with individuals of about 70 m. On the drier side of such forests it is bordered by the semi-evergreen, which in turn merges with tropical moist deciduous. The tropical semi-evergreen type occurs all along the foot-hills and river banks upto an elevation 600 m in all the states of the region. This type is generally common in parts of Assam, Arunachal

Pradesh and Manipur containing teak (Tectona grandis) and sal (shorea robusta) mixed with Terminalla myriocarpa, Bombax Ceiba, Canarium strictum, Gmelina arborea etc. This forest type is also subdivided into two distinct sub-types namely low hills and plain semi-evergreen forest containing dominant species like terminalla myriocarpa, Stereospermum Chelonoides, Canarium strictum etc. and riverine semi-evergreen forests occurring river banks, riverine plains and swamp. The dominant species are Terminalla myriocarpa, Duabanga grandiflora, Albizia Spp. etc.

The tropical moist deciduous forests are monsoon forests and form the natural cover in several areas of most of the states of Northeast India with a moderate rainfall of 101-203 cm rainfall. Generally the trees remain leafless during February, March. The dominated trees are hollock (Terminalia myriocarpa), Khokon (Dubanga grandiflora), Shilikha (Terminalia Citrana), bahera (Terminala belerica), Champa (Michelia Champaca), Gamari (Gmelina arborea), Sal (Shorea robusta) and economically these are most important forests of this region.

High altitude coniferous forest belt is known as sub-tropical pine forest. It occurs at 1000-2000 m elevation with rainfall of 100-254 cm zone. The dominated tree in Pinus Kesiya and other species are pinus Wallichiana, Abies spectabilis, Alnus Quereus, Betula etc. This forest type is found in Arunachal Pradesh, Meghalaya, Nagaland and Manipur Temperate broad leaved forest occur in Arunachal Pradesh above 2000-2500 m and they have association of Quercus Michela, Acer, Castanosis, Rhododendron etc. Mountain and wet temperate forests also occur in Arunachal Pradesh above 2000 m. These are mixed species of fir (Abies spectabilis), Oak (Quercus Spp), Pine (Pinus Wallichiana) etc.

Alpine forests are found to occur above the tree line between 4000-5000 elevation in the Arunachal Himalayas. These areas are covered with snow and growth of plants is restricted to a few months when snow melts. So there is no tall trees but the vegetation is largely a dense shrubbly forest of Rhod odendron nivale, R. anthropogon, R thompsoni etc. The plants are mostly crooked and tend to branch low down on the bole.

The bamboos are grasses and these are found throughout Northeast India up to 2000 m altitude. The common bamboos of the region are Bhaluka (Dendrocalamus longispathus), Mawlak (Melocana bamboosoides), Hill-Jati (Oxytenthera Parvifolia), Rawthia (Teinostachiwm dulloa) etc. Generally bamboos are grown as undergrowth in tropical evergreen forests and moist deciduous forest. In the hills bamboos grow mostly in jhummed areas. The bamboos are the most useful plants of Northeast India. These are used to make huts, basketry, mats, sticks, furniture, household and agricultural implements. Generally the leaves are used for fodder and the stems and rhizomes are burnt. It is also exploited as a raw meterial for paper making industries.

Grasslands form an important feature of natural vegetation in the riverine areas and higher elevations of the region. Scattered patches of grasslands occur in all the states of the region. The important species are saccharum spontaneum, Imperta Cylindrica, Neyrandia spp, Paspalum spp, Jhysanoloena maxima etc. Some grasslands are seen through recurring annual fires at higher elevations and excessive grazing at lower elevations. These are also found in upper reaches at pine belt.

All the nine types of forest as mentioned above are found in different parts of Arunachal Pradesh. Only three dominating types, namely evergreen forests, deciduous and swamp forest are seen in Assam. Similarly the forest types of Manipur are montane sub-tropical, wet temperate and semi-evergreen forest. Tropical, sub-tropical and temperate forests types are common in Meghalaya. In Mizoram tropical wet evergreen, tropical semi evergreen, montane sub-tropical and sub-tropical pine forests are found. The important forest types of Tripura and Eastern Himalayan Bhabar Sal, tropical evergreen, moist mixed deciduous, low alluvial savannah woodland and moist bamboo brakes and the forests of Nagaland are mostly evergreen and coniferous types.

The forests of Northeast India can also be divided on the basis of legal status and ownership pattern into four categories: reserved, protected, unclassed and other which is illustraed in the following table. The major chunk of forests in Northeast India are under the unclassed forests which are either owned by the communities, village durbars and individual families. This was done for better exploitation from man and animals.

Table - 5.1
Forest areas (Sq.km) in North-eastern India as per Legal classification, 1997

State	Reserve forest	Protected	Unclassed	Other
Arunachal Pradesh	1337.0	0.8	3791	25.3
Assam	1727.7	337.3	1005.8	—
Manipur	137.7	417.1	960.6	
Meghalaya	71.0	1.2	779.2	
Mizoram	904.8	164.7	524.0	
Nagaland	100.4	—	762.1	
Tripura	386.9	—	244.6	
Total	**4,664.9**	**921.1**	**8,067.2**	**25.3**

Forest Resources : Forest is a renewable if it is used sparingly. Generally a forest takes a long time to develop into stable ecosystem and it is a living resource. Forest of vital importance in increasing the effectiveness of rainfall by checking runoff, maintaining the water-table and increasing humidity in the atmosphere by transpiration.

The economy of Northeastern India is dominated by forests and these forests provide number of products like timber, fuel, food, fodder, shelter, fibre, orchids and medicinal plants. Nearly half of the total population and three-fourth of the population of the rural area still depend on the said forest products.

The region produces large quantities of timber which are used for making houses, furnitures and forest based industries. The important timber species are sal, teak, champa, kakko, tata, kathal, bogipama, gurjan, hollong, hollock, gomari, nahar, bonsom, pine, oak, bonak etc. Similarly important plywood species are semul, hollong, am, bonak, hollock and gogra. Some important constructional species are bogipoma, hollong, lamptai, gomari, nahar, champa, bonsom, makai etc.

Bamboos form an indispensable forest product which centres into almost everything in daily life. In fact it is interwoven with the life and culture of the people of the region. The bamboo shoots are used for food, mature bamboos are used for making huts, fence, mats, toys, utensils and the wide usefulness of the bamboo plant is attested by the ubiquity with which it is grown in village groves. It provides an important resource for expanding paper industry.

Besides timber and bamboo, the region is very rich in non-timber and non-wood forest products or minor forest products. Such products have enormous economic, ornamental and medicinal value which include cane, broomgrass, mushrooms, oil yielding plants etc. Honey and wax are also extracted from the forests every year. A variety of medicinal plants are found to occur different parts of the region. Some important medicinal plants are Taxus baccata, Tinospara cordifolia, vinch rosea, Strychnos nux vomica, Dichora, febrifuga, Hodgsoni heteroelia, Dioscorea prazerai etc. Some of these plants are used by the local people to get relief fever, headache and other diseases.

Some forests are also a source of essential oils, gums, dyes and resins. Madhuca Spp and Lindera spp. are oil seed bearing trees. The important oil yielding plants are Aquilaria agallocha Chenopodium spp, Cinnamomum spp, Cymbopogon spp, Geranium spp, Piper spp. etc. The Pinus Spp, Canarium strietum Macaranga spp. are used for the extraction of gum and resin. The edible fruit bearing trees are Aegle Marmelos, Artocarpus integricolia, Dillenia indica,

Emblica Officinallis, Parkia roxburghili etc. Besides a number vegetables like dioscoree and topioca, mushrooms are also grown in many forests. These forests are also home of many animals, insects, birds etc.

The forest cover of North-East India had been assessed by the government at 1,64,043 sq. km of the total geographical area of 2,55,083 sq. km. The legally notified forest area and the forest area based on the imagery survey are 53.62 and 64.31 per cent respectively in 1997. In the states of North-East India the heaviest demand on forest is for fuel woods and agricultural lands. Due to increasing population and subsequent food pressure over limited agricultural land, forest land is being brought under cultivation. These two factors are mainly responsible to reduce the area of forests in the region. The process of deforestation is a serious threat to the economy and future environment in the region. The forest area of the states like Assam, Manipur, Meghalaya and Mizoram have been reducing at an alarming rate and the amount shrinking is given in the following table. The table - 5.2 is a warning and call for action. According to the National Forest Policy, 1952, one third of the country's total geographical area i.e. 33 per cent should be under forest and 60 per cent of land should be under forest cover in the hilly region of India. It is to be noted that the forest areas of the plains of North East India are considerably below the national norm. Except in Tripura, the forest cover of the other six states has shown consistently decreasing trend between 1991-1997. Tripura was the only states in North East India showing a gain of 11 sq. km. in forest cover whereas all the other states of the region registered decrease in forest cover, highest loss being in Assam to the tune of 927 sq. km during 1991-1997. The general loss of forest cover for the whole region was 1734 sq. km. during the period 1991-1997. Besides the two major causes as mentioned earlier, shifting cultivation, illegal timber felling, forest fier, diversion of forest lands for development activities and encroachment of forest lands are some other causes of degradation of forest and decrease in forest cover in the region. 'This depletion forest is causing major ecological

Table - 5.2

Changes in Forest cover between 1991-1997 in North East India

State	Geographical Area in Sq. km	Forest Cover as Assessed FSI (Sq. km)				Changes between Years (Sq. km)			Actual Forest cover as percentage of geographical area
		1991	1993	1995	1997	1991-93	1993-95	1995-97	
Arunachal Pradesh	83,743	68,757	68,661	68,621	68,602	–96	–40	–19	81.90
Assam	78,438	24,751	24,508	24,061	23,824	–243	–447	–237	30.40
Manipur	22,3271	17,685	17,621	17,558	17,418	–64	–63	–140	78.00
Meghalaya	22,429	15,853	15,762	15,714	15,657	–106	–55	–57	69.80
Mizoram	21,081	18,853	18,697	18,576	18,775	–156	–121	+199	89.10
Nagaland	16,579	14,321	14,348	14,291	14,221	+27	–57	–70	85.80
Tripura	10,486	5,535	5,538	5,538	5,546	–13	nil	+8	52.90
	2,55,083	**1,62,777**	**1,65,142**	**1,64,359**	**1,64043**	**–635**	**–783**	**–316**	**64.31**

damage. In fact during the last few decades, there has become a rapid degeneration of forest resouces in the region which threatened the economy and ecology of North East India requiring the intervention of the Supreme Court of India.

A report prepared by the World Wildlife Fund was published in the Assam Tribune on February 24, 2005, that the Northeastern region's forest as the "second richest in the world". According to the report, the North Bank Landscape covers approximately 14,000 sq. km. of the Himalayan foothill region north of the Brahmaputra river, which include parts of Assam, Arunachal Pradesh, North Bengal and Bhutan. This area comprises a major part of the Indo-Burma global biodiversity hotspot. It may be pointed out that a plot which had 107 plant species within 200 sq. metre is second only to the number of species recorded in Sumatra. Two teams from World Wildlife Fund, the Forest Department of Assam and Arunachal Pradesh, Wildlife Institute of India and Botonical Survey of India carried out the appraisal of Vegetation and large mammal habitats. The survey identified the North Bank Landscape as a prime habitat for several endangered species including the Asian elephant, tigers, leopards along with the diverse range of plant species. Wildlife expart Andreq Gillison described this North Bank Landscape as "extraordinary....... and a jewel in the crown of Indian Forests'. In order to conserve the rich biological diversity of this jewel in the crown of Indian forest, all the state governments of North East India, Government of India including North-Eastern Council and village communities must take steps at their respective levels. Many of the associated problems of the North Bank Landscape, can be solved if forest resources are exploited on the basis of sustainable development and sustained yield management must include economic, ecological and social objectives for sustainable development and welfare of the societies of North East India.

The National Forest Policy of India, 1998 is now in force. Its formulation has been timely and certainly a marked improvement over the policy of 1952, which emphasisted on increasing the area under forest cover to 33 per cent or one third of the countrys total geographical area and 60 per cent in the hills. The need for such a fresh forest policy, 1998 was long felt in India, It seeks to achieve a set target of 33 per cent of the country's total geographical area by 2012. India should have that quantum of its total land area under forest cover, but it is today no where near in the region of the fixed 33 per cent. In the first few years of its formulation, the Union Forest Ministry could scarcely achieve anything spectacular in terms of green cover increase in India. It may be mentioned that in 1999 forest cover increased only marginally to 19.39 per cent as against 19.27 per cent in 1997. Thus the growth rate is very low ie. only 0.12 per cent at the end of a full one year. This is a dismal showing in the sector of national forest cover scenario.

The Government of Assam has of late formulated a forest policy developing a common approach to management both environment and bio-diversity. It was long-over due in the context of the constantly threatened environment in Assam. The new policy, 2004 which is the first of its kind, seems to be a comprehensive, thoughtful one because the policy has considered almost all major environmental concerns like flora and fauna, wildlife, soil fertility, water, air etc. The policy provides a comprehensive strategy for environmental conservation and improved support system for livelihood for the people living in the fringe areas of forest and thereby seeks to overcome the two major environmental problems— degradation of biodiversity and forest cover. The guiding principles of the policy are- protection of the mega diversity with the involvement of communities and increasing and conserving forest cover through scientific sustainable forest management practices pinpointing the requirement for traditional knowledge and understanding of the local ethnic communities. According to this pro-people policy, the forestry programme should pay special attention to associate the local people closely as partners in management, in the protection, regeneration and development of forest as well as to provide gainfull emoployment to groups of people living in and near forests. The existing contractor system of the Forest Department should be replaced by the institutions such as tribal village council, cooperative and other institution. In order to avoid the exploitation of such poor people, there should be proper marketing development, fixation of minimum price for important forest product and mechanism for dissemination of information. It also include eco-tourism and set up to regulate tourism activities in areas of protected zones and scenic spot in Reserve forests. The new policy of the state laid down maintenance of environmental stability through preservation and restoration of ecological balance wherever needed, conserving natural heritage of Assam by preserving the remaining natural forests checking, soil erosion in catchment areas of rivers, increasing forest cover in the forest deficient areas and meeting bonafide livelihood needs for the poor people including tribals. The aim of this policy should be to insure progressive sustainable development of the state. In keeping with the National, North East India and Assam Forest Policies, joint forest management practices should form the basis of forest management in the state.

6

Geology, Soil Types and Mineral Resources

As discussed earlier Northeast India geologically is diverse in structure and age. Landmasses from Precambrian to Tertiary origin are found in this region. Except the Meghalaya and Karbi plateau which are considered as the continuation of the ancient Gondwana landmass (over 600 million years), the other folded hills and mountains of Arunachal Pradesh, Nagaland, Manipur, Mizoram, Tripura and the rest of Assam are of Tertiary period. Generally the alluviums of the plains of the region belong to Quarternary period. There are several structural features like folds, faults, lineaments, thrusts, traps etc. including several rock formations. These formations contain many minerals like coal, petroleum, sillimanite, limestone, clay, uranium in substantial quantities. The region is situated in the mergin zone of two tectonic plates, namely, the Indo-Australian and Europe-Asian plates and hence seismically Northeast India is very active. The occasional earthquakes in the region indicate that the earth movement has not ceased.

The northern and central parts of Karbi-Anglong, the isolated hills along the both banks of the Brahmaputra river between Dhubri and Tezpur are composed of Precambrian crystalline metamorphic rocks. The Eocene sediments of the Jaintia group extend along the southern side of the Karbi Anglong and the Disang Group cover parts of North Cachar Hills. The sediments of Oligo-Mio-Pliocene cover the southern part of the Karbi Anglong, the North Cachar, the hills of Barak plain and the northern foot hills of the Naga-Patkai range. Generally the Quarternary sediments form the older and Newer alluviums of high level terraces, the red bank soils and the recent alluvial deposits of the Brahmaputra and Barak plains.

The Precambrian Group or the basement rocks are composed of quartzo-feldspathic gneiss and these are overlain unconformably by the sediments of the Shillong Group. The Tertiary sediments comprise successively the Jaintia and Disang Groups lie on the weathered platforms of Precambrian age. The Desang Group are restricted to a narrow strip to the south of Haflong-Disang fault. The geosynclinal facies of upper Assam are known successively as Nagaon, Baragolai and Tikak Parbat formations and the Baragolai formation is associated with several oil sand horizons. The shelf facies of the Barail Group cover a large part of North Cachar Hills and the southeastern part of the Karbi Anglong. This group consists of coarse sandstone, shale and carbonaceous shale with minor coal seams. These are overlain by the Surma Group covering an extensive area in the Barak plain and the North Cachar Hills. The Surma formations are overlain by the Tipam Group of lower arenaceous facies and upper argillaceaous facies. The Tipam Group occupies a 300 km. long strip from Longtang to Digboi which includes several oil-sand horizons in upper Assam. The Dihing Group is overlain by the Quarternary formation and the group is associated with older alluvium of higher terraces. Besides the recent alluvial deposits cover extensive areas of the Brahmaputra valley and Barak plain.

The basement of the Meghalaya plateau is a gneissic platform of Archaean age. The basement formation is a gneissic complex of quartzo-feldspathic gneiss, sillimanite-quartz-mica schist, amphibolite and dolerite. Overlying this gneissic complex is the Shillong Group with dominant quartzite, phyllite, schist and conglomerate. This formation was first intruded by the Khasi Greenstone and later by Mylliem Granite. Then along the southern margin of the plateau Sylhet Trap basalts have come and rested over the eroded Precambrian basement. The ultra-basic complex in the Sung valley of Jaintia Hills contain phosphate and atomic minerals. Besides, there are other formations like Shella and Kopili formation of shale-sandstone-marl, Simsang formation of siltstone-sand, stone-sand, Baghmara formation of feldspathic sandstone-pebble canglomerate-clay and Chengapara formation and these rock formations are overlain by the older and the younger alluvium.

The rock formations like the Disang, the Barails, the Surmas and Tipam formations also occur in the state of Manipur. Some of these formation, namely the Barails and the Surma Group are extended to Mizoram. In Nagaland the rock sequences are well represented by the Disang, the Barail and the Dihing Group of Assam. Similarly the rock formations of Tripura are represented by Surma, Tipam and Dupitila formations. According to the Geological Survey of India, the rocks of Arunachal Pradesh belong to the formations of Tertiary, Gondwana, unfossiliferous sediments and metamorphic rocks. Generally the Tertiary rock formations are found from Bhutan border to the East Siang district, Gondwana deposits occur in the Ranga valley. Unfossiliferous dolomites, quatzites and shales occur in Tenga, Kameng, Subansiri, Kamla and Siang valleys. The parametamorphites and gneissic rocks are found to overlie the Abor volcanics, dolomites and quartzites in the upper part of Siang valley, The Mishmi area is made up largely by granodiorite-diorite rocks.

Soil Types

Generally the term soil refers to the loose surface material which has distinctive layers or horizons resulting out of disintegration and decaying of the mantle of rock or regolith over a long period of time. In 1932 Z.J. Schokalskya classified Indian soil in the framework of Russian Pedological principles. The Soil Survey of India was set up in 1956 and a great deal of useful work has been done by this organisation. A Soil map in Hindi was published in 1957 by The National Atlas of India. Different types of soils were shown in India. The soils of Northeast India are very complex in their characteristics and properties. So classification of soils into different types is a very difficult task. However, on the basis of works as mentioned earlier, the soils of Northeast India have been classified into three types : (1) Red loam soil,

(2) Laterite soil, (3) Alluvial soil. These are developed under varied conditions of geology, topography, climate and natrual vegetation.

1. **Red Loam Soil :** The red loam soil is a typical example of soil derived from rocks like granites, gneisses, diorites etc. which are relatively richer in clay-forming minerals but poorer in silika. Generally weathering of this type of soil is evident by the high percentage of clay, alumina and iron oxides present in it. Weathering is usually responsible for the removal of a large percentage of lime and liberates iron-oxides which give its red colour. These soils are highly acidic in nature and formed in-situ on the parent rock materials. Red loam soils are suitable for cultivating fruit-trees, especially oranges, and other crops like rice, potato can also be grown with irrigation. The red loam soils occupy entire areas of Mizo Hills, most parts of Manipur, Naga Hills, Karbi Anglong, most parts of Meghalaya and Arunachal Pradesh and some parts of undivided Cachar district.

2. **Laterite Soil :** Laterite soil is a layer of deposits resulting from the deep weathering of rocks in humid tropical climates. The laterites have been formed under wet and dry conditions of the tropical climates. The high temperature and rainfall cause removal of silica and alkalis from the weathered area leaving a matrix of iron and aluminium in the form of a thick red clay. The clay is plastic when wet but hardens once exposed to dry atmospheric condition: This type of soil is deficient in potash, phospheric acid and lime. The soil has heavy loams at lower part, but in the upper part it is thin, course and stony. So the leterite with loams and clay produce good crops and thinner part is unsuitable for growing crops. The laterite soils occur in northern part of Meghalaya, North-Western Nagaland, parts of Cachar district and few areas of Nagaon district.

3. **Alluvial Soil :** The soil deposited by a river along its course is called alluvial soil. This type is sub-divided into two categories— old alluvial soil and new alluvial soils. The old alluvial soil is more clayey and less Kankary composition.

Such soils are found to occur above the annual flood level and are more acidic. So these are suitable for tea cultivation, sugarcane, fruit and vegetable. Generally this sub-group is found in an elongated narrow patch between the foothills of the Bhutan Himalaya and the north bank plain (Western part) of the Brahmaputra valley. A narrow belt of old alluvial soil is also found between the foothills of Meghalaya-Karbi plateau, Nagaland and the south bank plain of the Brahmaputra valley. The alluvial soils are less acidic, often neutral and in some cases alkaline. They are found to accur in the riparian tracts of all the plains of Northeast India and are subject to annual floods and renewal. The soils are rich in lime and potash and very much responsive to manuring and irrigation. Hence such soils are suitable for cultivation of rice, jute, mustard, pulses and vegetable.

Mineral Resources

Mineral resources provide a base for the economic development of a region. Through geological survey has not yet been undertaken due to poor accessibility and difficult terrain conditions. Except oil extraction no serious effort has been made by the government for mineral extraction. So industrialisation as well as employment generation in all the states of Northeast India have been still lagging. However, during the last four decades, deposits of coal, natural gas, limestone, dolomite, sillimanite, iron, manganese, chromite, aluminium, copper, lead, zinc, phosphates, potash, mica etc. have been reported. Some deposits of metallic minerals and uranium are also available according to a recent survey.

Coal : Coal is carbonaccous rock consisting of altered remains of plants in association with mineral water. It is generally used for railways, power generation, cement industry, brick industry, paper, tea, steel plants chemicals and for domestic consumption.

Coal deposits of Northeast India are found in there distinct units— (1) Namchuk-Namphum coal belt of Arunachal Pradesh of Tertiary age (2) Schuppen zone of

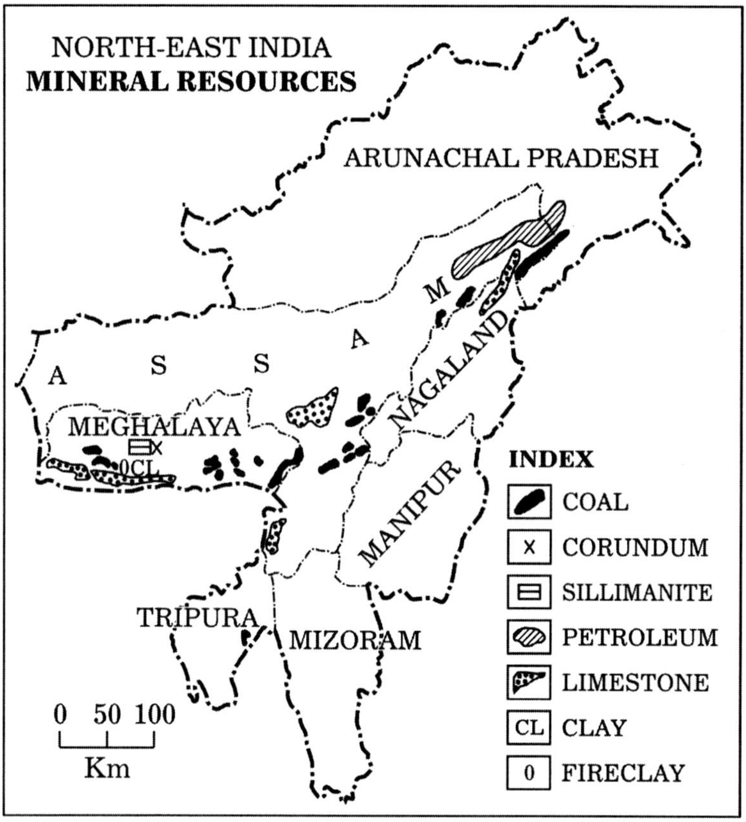

Fig. 5 : Mineral Resources

upper Assam, Nagaland and Arunachal Pradesh, and (3) The periphery of the Meghalaya-Karbi Plateau. Coal is found to occur in West Siang and Tirap district. Existence of good deposits of coal have been reported by GSI near Kharsang. The main coal seams occur in the lower member of Tikak Parbat formation. The Namchik-Namphuk coal field belongs to this formation.

The main coal producing horizons of Assam are the Tikak Parbat and Boragolai formations and the major coal fields are Dilli-Jaipur and Makum. The thickness of these coal seams are ranging from .03 m to 12 m with 42 to 60% fixed carbon. It is reported that inferred reserves of coal in 28 million tonnes in Dilli-Jaipur and 20 million tonnes in the

Makum coal field. Tertiary coals also occur in the Lower Sylhet formation of Jaintia Group. The main collieries of this belt are Koilajan, Sheelvetta (Karbi Alonglong), Dilthor, Khota Arda and Garampani (N.C. Hills). Some important characteristics of Assam coal are : moisture contents varies from 2 to 3%, ash varies from 0.8 to 79.6%, sulphur 1 to 4%, fixed carbon 29.6 to 65.5% and the calorific value varies from 5240 kcal/kg to 15000 kcal/kg.

High sulphur sub-bituminous coals are found in Meghalaya which occur in Garo, Khasi and Jayantia Hills associated with Shella Formation of Jaiantia Group. The important coalfields are East and West Darranggiri, Siju, Balhpakram, Pyndengrei, Langrin, Mawlong-Shella, Laitryngew and Bapung.

In Nagaland coal is associated with the Barail formation and coal fields are mainly found in Mon Wokha, Mokokchung and Tuensung districts.

The coal mining industry of the region is over a century old. At present coal reserves are found in four states, namely Assam, Meghalaya, Arunachal Pradesh and Nagaland and mining activities are confined to Assam and Meghalaya only. The total coal reserve of the entire Northeast region is 909 million tonnes of which 431 million tonnes are under proved category, 109 million tonnes under indicated category and 369 million tonnes under inferred category.

Oil and Natural Gas : Northeastern region is one of the major on-shore oil producing regions of India and oil is found in the Timpam sandstones of the Miocene age. The existence of oil was first recorded by Lieutenant R. Wileox at Sapkhong in the Burhi-Dihing valley in 1825. After one or two short-lived attempts at oil mining between 1879 and 1883 in the coal measures near Jaipur and Makum, oil drilling was transferred to the Digboi area in 1888. Production at Digboi began in 1892 and this field has proved to be very long-lived oilfield found in an east-west aticline in Miocene sand stones, shales and clays. In 1900 an oil company opened a refinery at Digboi and since then the company has continued exploration in the area under licence. Large reserves of oil and natural gas have been discovered at Naharkatia-Hugrijan and Moran area which are developing in partnership with the government, to supply new refineries at Noonmati, Barauni, Bongaigaon and Numaligarh by pipeline.

After Independence the oil industry has made some headway and it is divided into three segments, namely, (1) oil exploration and production, (2) refining and marketing, (3) petrochemicals and downstream units. A national undertaking, known as the oil and Natural Gas Commission has been setup in 1956 and since then the organisation has been searching out new oil fields with a good deal of technical collaboration from Rominia and Russia. It may be stated that the Naharkatiya - Hugrijan area in the Dihing valley has the reserves of 45 million tonnes of oil and 210 billion cubic metres of gas. In 1959 Oil India Limited was set up to promote public participation in both oil exploration and tempo of development.

Besides Assam, oil deposits are found in Arunachal Pradesh, Tripura and Nagaland. The important oil fields of Arunachal Pradesh are Kharsang in Tirap district and Kumsai in Lohit district. Mankiyanagar is the major oil field of Tripura. In North East India the oil companies drilled 1412 development wells of which 1376 are in Assam, 20 in Arunachal Pradesh, 11 in Nagaland and 5 in Tripura. Majority of production comes from Assam and only marginal contributions come from Arunachal Pradesh and Tripura. The Oil India Limited and Oil and Natural Gas Commission Produced 170.56 Million Metric Tonnes of crude oil and 64.34 Billion cubic metres of gas till April 1, 2001 in Northeastern region of India. The crude oil produced in the region is being supplied to four refineries, namely, Digboi, Numaligarh, Guwahati and Bongaigaon refineries through pipe lines.

Limestone : A large reserve of limestone is found in the states of Assam, Meghalaya, Arunachal Pradesh, Nagaland and Manipur. The total reserve estimated at 5,000 million tonnes.

The deposits of Mawmlwh and Mawsmai and Meghalaya, Dillai Parbat of Assam are being exploited for cement manufacture. Limestone deposits also occur in Siju, Shella-Bholaganj and Lumshang-Nongkhlieh belts of Meghalaya, Garampani-Umrangs area of Assam, Tidding area of Arunachal Pradesh, Nimi and Wazeho areas of Nagaland and Ukhrul-Hundung, Lamui, Khanggol, Paoye and Kasam areas of Manipur.

Sillimanite : Sillimanite is a refractory material and practically the whole of India's sillimanite supply comes from the Sanapahar area of Meghalaya. This area accounts for about 90 per cent of the total production of sillimanite in India. The total reserve of Sillimanite in Meghalaya is estimated at 25,000 tonnes and the annual production is about 2100 tonnes. Sillimanite is used for making some kinds of ceramic wares and refractory bricks. It is considered to be one of the best as refractory materials.

Clay : Clay is usually found in the alluvial tracts of Assam. It is generally used for the making of bricks and tiles. Fire clay occurs in association with coal seams in Koilajan area of Karbi Anglong and parts of upper Assam. China clay (Kaolin) is found in the Dora river of Lakhimpur district. Fuller earth occurs in Bhutan Khuti and white clay is found in the Nambar river.

Besides first grade uranium has been found in many places like Domasiat, Syndai, Sohra, Mawsynram, Mawkyrwat, Nangkulang and Maweit in Khasi and Jaintia Hills. High grade dolomite occurs in Dedza and Rupa areas of Arunachal Pradesh. Small occurrences of copper are found in Nungaw, Kongal, Ningthi etc. in Manipur, Siang, Kameng. Subansiri and Lohit districts of Arunachal Pradesh. Banded hematite-magnetite is found in the Chandar Dinga Hills in Kokrajhar district. Nickel-Cobalt bearing magnetite and nickeliferous chromite occur in a belt of Tuensung district of Naga Hills. Base metal sulphides occur sporadically in Meghalaya and Arunachal Pradesh.

From the above discussion it may be stated that North East India possesses a number of minerals in substantial quantities and some minerals occur in small quantitites, without much commercial importance at the moment. There are certain problems which are in the way of full utilisation of available mineral resources for industrial development of this region. Due to non-availability of capital, remoteness and lack of infrastructure etc. and inability to use existing mineral resources within the region by the existing industries are the major factors which stand in the way of development of mining industry at the moment.

7

Environmental Problems in North East India

In India environment was either a non-issue or a very minor issue which went unnoticed upto about 1950. But today India including most countries in the world have a full-fledged Ministry on environment that indicates the gravity of the situation. The protecting and promoting environment are now burning issues of the world. Environmental problems are two types, natural like earthquake, landslide, flood etc. and anthropogenic or man made which include pollution of air, water, soil and deformation etc.

Seismicity of North East India : Seismically North East India is very active. Seismicity relates earthquake and the region is an earthquake prone area. North East India has experienced a large number of earthquakes of tectonic origin. Records indicate the occurrence of destructive earthquakes in the region in 1548, 1598, 1601, 1642, 1660, 1696, 1714, 1869, 1882 and in 1897. In the 20th century, destructive earthquakes took place in 1918, 1923, 1930, 1932, 1938, 1943, 1947, 1950 and in 1988. It may be mentioned that the two major earthquakes of 1897 and 1950 caused major changes in the configuration of physical landscape by faulting, fracturing, subsidence, upheaval and landslides, river regimes including the Brahmaputra and the Surma river systems.

It may be mentioned that North East India is located in the subduction zone of the two giant tectonic plates, namely Euro-Asian plate and Indo-Australian plate. The Indian plate is moving towards north and is overriden by the other. Due to this many tectonic features like thrust, fold, fault, lineament, synclinorium etc. are found in the region. Geotectonically the region is very complex and the Indo-Myanmar border region, Arunachal Himalayas and the

Meghalaya plateau seismically more active than the Brahmaputra valley, the Surma valley and the Bengal region.

Among recorded earthquakes, the most severe, was one which took place on June 12th, 1897. This earthquake covered on area of 45,32,000 sq. km. from Rangoon in the South East to Kangra in the North West, from the Himalayas to Masulipatam and highly affected areas account 78,000 sq. km including the towns of Shillong, Sylhet, Rangpur, Guwahati, Goalpara, Dhubri, Tura, Barpeta, Mangadai, Tezpur and Rangapara. The epicentre of 1897's earthquake located on an area (25°0'N latitude and 90°0'E Longitude) and the shock of it was so severe that on the Tezpur Balipara railway the permanent way between Sessa and Rangapara is said to have been shaken level with the plain and the rails were bent and twisted out of position. The Chedrang and Samin faults were created by this earthquake. A tectonic lake, named Chand dubi was formed in 1897 earthquake.

The earthquake of August 15, 1950, with epicentre at Rima, a small township of Arunachal Pradesh has greatly influenced the courses and characters of the river of North East India. The courses of several rivers including the Subansiri and the Brahmaputra have undergone changes and the beds of many rivers have become shallow due to the deposits of debris brought down after landslides in the hills. After the earthquake of 1950, floods have become a common phenomenon in the plains of North East India. The surface relief of certain area changed considerably, necessitating to dismantle of the rail link in the Dangari-Saikhoaghat, Ledo-Range Ring and Moran-Khowang sections.

Landslide : The downward movement of a large mass of earth including rocks from a mountain or cliff is known as landslide or landslip. It is generally caused by rain water soaking into the land on a steep slope. Heavy rainfall saturate the slope and make it unstable and more mobile. Landslide is also caused by an earthquake. Extensive landslides on the Tertiary mountains and hills and loosening of the soils, subsidence and fissuring of the ground, river beds, changes in river courses are some of the outcomes of the earthquakes as described above and heavy rainfall. The terrain of recent origin of the Arunachal Himalayas, Nagaland, Highlands of Manipur and Tripura, Mizoram and North Cachar hills are highly susceptible to easy degradation by climatic, weathering and hydrological factor. So landslides are common in these areas during rainy seasons.

Land is degraded and unfit for plant growth due to soil erosion, desertification, shifting cultivation and development activities. Deforestation, overgazing, over cropping, improper tilling, occurrence of flood and the process of desertification result in soil erosion. Jhuming or shiffing or slash and burn agriculture degrades and disturbs soil stability. Development activities like construction of roads, rail tracks, canals, industrial estates, urbanisation, mining etc. are responsible for land degradation. In this connection it may be mentioned that the ecology in and around greater Guwahati in totality has now been destroyed by clearing of vegetation, hill cutting for earth and blasting of rocks by the vicious circle. It is reported by the Newspapers on July 25, 1999 that faulty policy decisions, rapacious denudation of the forest cover on the hilly areas, indiscriminate cutting of hills and encroachments hill slopes aided and abetted by local politicians have together resulted in the tragic death of ten persons in a major landslide in the Kahilipara colony bazar hill side area on 24th July 1999. Since then similar type of landslides have been taking place every year during the rainy season in Guwahati region.

Flood : Floods are extremely dynamic features of the natural environment, especially in the humid tropics. Due to the natural of relief features, unstable hills and loose soils, heavy rainfall and a variety of newly-emerged causes, North East India has been exposed to seasonal floods, particularly in its plains and foothills. The high intensity of monsoonal rains and devastating landslide coupled with erodibility of rocks, steep slopes and high seismicity constitute the major natural causes of the two important river systems of the region, namely the Brahmaputra and Barak system (Surma system).

In North East India floods are the combined result of natural and anthropogenic factors like urbanisation, deforestation, construction of buildings, bridges, barrages, reservoirs and landuse changes. Thus due to a variety of newly emerged factors in addition to those generally recognized, floods in both the Brahmaputra valley and Barak plain attained extremely large magnitude, high frequency and extensive devastation. It is mentioned earlier that the great earthquake of 1950 which heavily disturbed the topography and the drainage system of the Brahmaputra and its tributaries had increased the frequency and intensity of floods. The Brahmaputra basin has an area of 17.45 million hectares which are distributed in the states of Arunachal Pradesh (8.14 million hectares), Assam (7.06 million hectares), Meghalaya (1.17 million hectares) and Nagaland (1.08 million hectares). About three quarters of the plains of Assam is flood prone. The ferocity of the floods in Assam has been considerably increased since 1988. In that year (1988) floods affected 4.22 million hectares of land, 21 districts, 7740 villages and damaged 155522 houses and killed 125 human lives. Simarly in 2002 floods affected 3.30 million hectares of land, 22 districts, 6560 villages and damaged 19827 houses and killed 42 men. In July 2004 the wave of floods has shot up to 50 lakh people in 5,223 villages in 23 districts of Assam, the death toll has shot up to 21 persons and the government of Assam has opened 1,296 relief camps to shelter the affected people. Besides, 5800 kilometres of roads 836 bridges were damaged in floods in Assam last year (2004) and an amount of Rs. 755.34 crore would be required to repair the damage.

The flood problem has now become more serious due to recently emerged man made causes. The flood control measures adopted in the river basins since the early fifties and during the first five year plan about 1500 km of embankments along the banks of the Brahmaputra and some of its important tributaries including the banks of the Barak and its tributaries were unscientifically constructed. Besides such poorly managed flood control measures, large-scale human occupation of flood plains, reclamation of swamps, destruction of wet land have aggravated the flood situation of the river basins of the region. The existing flood control activities are of a short-term and ad-hoc nature and so these are not at all successful in withstanding the flood hazards in Assam. Dredging of the rivers has also proved impractical and embankments constructed for controlling floods now create a worse flood situation in the plains of North East India. So Management of flood plains and reduction off flood hazards need to be approached through properly planned designed. The management of flood is very complex problem which needs a multi-disciplinary approach to combat flood damages.

Anthropogenic Environmental Problems : The natural environment is now in danger of getting damaged beyond repair, the social, political and economic environments are also as an indirect consequences, getting increasingly susceptible to ills and human culture is under the threat of collapse. The environmental hazard is a resultant of overpopulation, rapid industrialisation and increased number of vehicular traffic. Over population means the presence of more population in a given area than can be supported adequately by the resources available in that area. It is a major cause of all environmental problems. In 1789 Thomes Rober Malthus published an essay on the principle of population and in that essay he argued that population tends to increase geometrically, whereas food supply can only be increased arithmetically and population always increases until it reaches the limits of subsisence after which it is checked by war, famine and pestilince. In this connection it may be mentioned that North East India shelters 38.5 million population or 3.74 per cent of the population of the country, but the region can hardly produce 2.8 per cent of India's total food grains. If such imbalance continues in near future than the revolution of Malthusian Nightmare will take place in the region in the form of famine, malnutrition and epidemics. Urbanisation expresses the growth of towns and cities at the expense of the countryside with which are spatially and functionally knit together. In the developing countries it is associated with ecological degradation, desertification, war, famine etc. and McGee coined the term pseudourbanisation to describe the phenomenal growth of such towns and cities of India and other South Asian countries on the face of mounting unemployment, lopsided occupational structure, mushrooming of squatter colonies inadequate transport and civic services.

North East India is still the least urbanised region within the country, but the urban population of the region is increasing at a much higher rate as compared with the country as a whole. The urban population of North East India was 4,59,875 in 1951 and the same increased by 12 times to 59,72,078 in 2001. This reflects a net movement of people from rural to urban areas and the massive population movement from outside North East India including Nepal and Bangladesh. A huge influx of rural migrants to the towns and cities indicates the lack of employment opportunities in villages and small towns. Such migration of rural people to urban areas has led to massive demand in food, housing, transport services and other civic amenities. The poor section of urban dwellers are additionally disadvantaged because they are forced to live on marginal lands like steep hill sides and along water courses. Thus the general quality of the urban habitat as well as the lives of the urban dwellers in North East India is rather bad. Though this problems is not so acute as in the Northern India, it is to be taken seriously with purpose full plans of remedial measures.

The most important challenge of environmental pollution in the urban and industrial areas has been the auto-fumes emission. For example vehicular emission is becoming problem in the city of Guwahati. In 1971 the population of Guwahati was 2.92 lakh which rose to over 8 lakh indicating growth of population more than 380 per cent in 2001. similarly the number of both motorized and non motorized vehicles has alarmingly increased and at present about 3 lakh motor vehicles plied on the roads of Guwahati. The vehicular emission survey (Assam Pollution Control Board, 1999) indicated more than 80 per cent of diesel vehicles and 53 per cent of vehicles in the city violet the standard emission limit and these vehicles throw a high collective dose of air pollutants. Considering the problem and to understand the status of the vehicles plying on the roads APCB has carried out several rounds of Vehicles Emission Survey at important cities and towns like Jorhat, Dibrugarh, Sibsagar, Tinsukia, Silchar, Moran and Bongaigaon and found that the condition of engine, carburetor, fuel injection system etc. of diesel, petrol or two or three wheelers are not satisfactory.

The throwing out of garbage and soild wastes has become a problem of many areas of India. It is estimated that at least half a bucket of garbage-left over of cut vegetables, empty polythene bags, paper, worn-out clothes, plastic bags, glass bottles are thrown out from an average Indian household. There are about 10 million families in India and they account for as much as 50 million bucket of solid waste every day. Every cubic metre of such garbage can foster about 750 flies and the lack of management of garbage has been responsible for several diseases.[1]

In the urban areas of India, the disposal system is mainly landfill. There is no garbage recycling process in the cities and industrial areas of India. Garbage are seen to dump in land fill sites in low-lying areas, road sides and along the river banks which become the breeding ground for disease-bearing bacteria. It may be mentioned here that the river Bharalu passing through the heart of the Guwahati city may cause a serious health hazard to the people according to a study conducted by the Pollution Control Board of Assam. The water of the river gets contaminated because almost all the drainage channels of Guwahati are connected with the river while in some places the garbage is dumped in the river.

Generally the poor people, trapped in web of poverty are forced to live in the slums of the towns and cities of North East India. There are about 90 slum locations in Guwahati

---

1. Seshgiri, N., 1994, "Pollution", New Delhi, National Book Trust, India, p. 8.

and nearly 22 per cent of the total population live in such slums. The slums of this city are the legacy of the unprecedented growth of population since 1951 and the haphazard expansion of the city within the post independence period. Similarly there are 32 slum areas in the city of Shillong and these are distributed in Shillong Municipality, Shillong Cantonment, Mawlai, Nongthymmai, Madarting and Pynthorumkhrah.

There are no garbage bins either in Guwahati or in Shillong to put away the rubbish and no municipal vans come to clear the garbage. So the slum dwellers deposit rubbish on the road sides, drains or outside their house. So it is natural that there are high incidence of diseases including viral infections in the slums of the towns and cities of North East India. Such incidence of diseases are the results of environmental hazards like contaminated water, unhygienic disposal of human waste and poor facilities for disposal of garbage.

Deforestation : Deforestation is one of the outcomes of various developmental activities in India. The factors like population pressure, heavy exploitation for immediate gain instigated by industrialists and traders have caused a substantial reduction of forest areas in North East India. Besides forest fire, encroachment, squatting and settlement, flood, soil erosion and for accommodation of the increased population, urbanisation and industrialisation, opening of roads, railways, irrigation works, hydel projects etc. have taken a heavy toll of the forest areas. Reduction of forests have also been caused by extraction of coal in the forests of Garo Hills, Jaintia Hills, N.C. Hills, Jeypore reserved forest and exploitation of oil and natural gases in upper Assam and Arunachal Pradesh. Dwindling of forest areas in the region have been discussed in Chapter-5 natural vegetation.

Rampant poaching and theft of forest products are the root causes of deterioration of habitat quality. Man made forest areas with commercial species are now included in recorded forest area. Such areas are not suitable for wildlife habitat. North East India comprises 51 types of forests ranging from tropical rain forest to alpine vegetation. These forests are the habitats of thousand of wild lives which include 14 species of non human primates and most important of them are hoolock gibbon, stumptailed macague, pigtailed macague golden langur, honuman langur and rhesus monkey, rhinoceros, pigmy hog, swamp deer, Asian wild buffalo, feral horse, elephant, Royal Bengal tiger leopard, golden cat, fishing cat, Gangetic dolphin, other crocodile, 958 bird species etc. The forest lands and national parts of Assam are under the grip of encroachers. Apart from large-scale encroachment internally, some reserved forests of Assam are being encroached externally by other states like Nagaland, Arunachal Pradesh and Meghalaya. The Supreme Court has issued an order that eviction in all the Reserved forests in Assam must be cleared by September 2002; but the eviction operation failed to give desired results.

It is estimated that about 6,000 sq. km of forest lands including reserve forests and National Parks are under the grip of encroachers. All the protected areas, namely 5 National Parks and eight Wild-life Sanctuaries have varying degrees of illegal occupation of encroachers as shown in the following table - 7.1.[1]

Table - 7.1

Name of National Parks and Wild life Sanctuaries	Total Area of the Park/ Sanctuaries in kilometre	Percentage of encroach-ment
National Parks		
1. Kaziranga National Park	430	8
2. Manas National Park	500	7
3. Nameri National Park	200	11
4. Orang National Park	78	9
5. Dibru -Saikhowa National Park	340	7

1. Mahanta, T.R., "Assam's Forests and Forest Administration : Past and Present", The Rhino, Vol. IX : August, 2004. p. 5.

Sanctuaries

1. Barnadi Wild Life Sanctuaries	26	8
2. Nambar Life Sanctuaries	37	12
3. Laokhowa Life Sanctuaries	70.13	13
4. Garampani Life Sanctuaries	6	10
5. Deepar Beel Life Sanctuaries	4.14	10
6. Sonai-Rupai Life Sanctuaries	140	10
7. Pobha Life Sanctuaries	49	10
8. Kochugaon Life Sanctuaries	214	10

The eviction operation was started by the conservator of forests, central Assam Circle, Guwahati and in the process only 15335 hectares of Reserve forest lands have been cleared of encroachment because of intervention of local politicians, the eviction operation could not make it success.

North East India has been identified as one of the 18 hot spots of biological diversity in the world. A strategy for its conservation is taken through a network of protected area and the present position for the whole region is shown in the following table - 7.2.

The coverage of the protected area network is only 5% of the geographical area which is not representative and falls short of the target of 10% suggested by the Wildlife Institute of India. These biodiversity rich areas have been under severe attack due to population pressure, industrialisation, urbanisation and commercial exploitation.

Table - 7.2
Protected Areas in North East India

State	Geographical Area (km^2)	Sanctuaries No.	Sanctuaries Area (km^2)	National Park No	National Park Area (km^2)	Total Area (km^2)	% of protected area to geographical area
Arunachal Pradesh	83,743	9	6,177.45	2	2468.23	8645.68	10.32
Assam	78,438	8	990.58	2	930	1,920.58	2.44
Manipur	22,237	1	184.85	2	81	265.85	1.19
Meghalaya	22,429	3	34.21	2	267.48	301.69	1.34
Mizoram	21,089	3	560.00	2	250.00	810.00	3.83
Nagaland	16,579	3	24.41	1	202.02	226.43	1.36
Tripura	10,486	4	603.62	0	—	603.62	5.75
Total North East India	**2,25,083**	**31**	**8575.12**	**11**	**4,198373**	**12,773.85**	**5.00**

Source : National Action Plan on Biodiversity, Ministry of Environment and Forests, GO1, New Delhi, 1997.

8

Population

North East India is a landlocked region and is surrounded by hills and mountains on three sides and the western side is bordered by plains. So literally it is boxed by China, Myanmar, Bangladesh and Bhutan and the region is connected with the mainland by a narrow corridor of the Himalayan foothills. The corridor is subjected to occasional disruptions due to heavy rain and floods. Thus the geographical location of the region has been responsible for its isolation.

But in spite of its geographical isolation, earlymen of different ethnic stocks having diverse socio-cultural backgrounds entered into the region from different directions at different stages and made the region as their permanent abode. The Brahmaputra and the Surma river systems were also the vital agents in the colonisation of the region and the evolution of composite agricultural society. The Austro-Aisatic linguistic groups are believed to be earliest settlers of North East India. The Khasis and Jaintias of Meghalaya of today are of this linguistic group. They were followed by the Mongoloids who linguistically belonged to the Tibeto-Burman group. They are distributed over the hills and plains of the region and can be divided into two main linguistic branches-Arunachal branch and Assam-Burmese branch. The tribes of Arunachal such as Hrusso, Sherdukpens, Khowas, Apatanies, Nissis, Adis, Mishims, Khamptis, Noctes, Wanchos etc. are the members of the Arunachal branch. The Bodos, Nagas and the Kuki-Chin speakers are of Assam-Burmese branch. These Mongoloids were referred to as Kiratas in the Mahabharata, Vedas and Puranas. While the migration of the Mongoloids to the Northeast was a continuous process, it is believed that after the incoming of the major Mongoloid groups, there came the Caucasoids in succession from the western direction. This is a major racial group of the region which is divided into many types and sub-types. Another group of migrants belonging to the Siamese-Chinese branch came to this region from the Shan Plateau in the thirteenth century through the north-eastern routes. They established a kingdom in Assam which persisted till the coming of the British in 1826. Broadly speaking the Caucasoids or the Indo-Aryans entered from the west, The Austro-Asiatic from the east and Mongoloids from the north, east and to a certain extent from the south lay the region with a composite pattern of cultural synthesis and evolution and infact the whole North-Eastern region of India became a melting pot a different ethnic groups.

During the British regime the construction of railway and motorable roads and the opening of tea gardens in Assam opened new avenues of employment which led large number of people to migrate to this region from other parts of India, Bangladesh and Nepal. These new migrants created many socio-economic problems besides disturbing the original ethnic strucutre of the settlements. The present tea garden and ex-tea garden labourers which form a sizable section of the contemporary Assamese population are descendants of certain Australoid groups who came to Assam from Bihar, Orissa, Madhya Pradesh.

The post-independence period witnessed some important event which led to a remarkable change in the demographic as well as settlement structure of North East India. The territorial boundary of the region has changed from time to time. Thus after partition of India, the Muslim Majority district of Sylhet was transferred to the East Pakistan (Bangladesh) following a referendum in the district. The Nagas were given a state 'Nagaland' in 1963. An autonomous state of Meghalaya was created which subsequently made into a separate state in 1972. Similarly Arunachal and Mizoram were created as Union Territories in 1972 and these two units also gained full statehood in 1987. Just after independence due to discrimination against the religious minorities by the rulers in East Pakistan, there resulted in large scale migration of Bengalee Hindus from the country to Assam. Again during the war of Liberation of Bangladesh a total of 10,00,000 refugees took shelter in Assam. While many of them returned to the native places following the liberation of Bangladesh about 1,00,000 of them are believed to be stayed in Assam. This has now been a never ending process and its effects led to the change of demographic and settlement pattern of the whole region.

Growth : Since independence, the political map of Assam including North East India has undergone many changes and its present seven states, namely Arunachal Pradesh, Assam, Manipur, Meghalaya, Mizoram, Nagaland and Tripura have been formed from the erstwhile composite Assam, princely states of Manipur and Tripura. The population data of the last 100 years of all these states are not available and the total population from 1901 to 2001 of the region and the states is shown in the following table - 8.1:

Table - 8.1
Population of North East India
(1901-2001) (000 Persons)

Census	Arunachal Pradesh	Assam	Manipur	Meghalaya	Mizoram	Nagaland	Tripura	North-East India
1901	—	3290	284	341	82	102	173	4272
1911	—	3849	346	394	91	149	230	5059
1921	—	4637	384	422	98	159	304	6004
1931	—	5560	446	481	123	179	382	7172
1941	—	6695	512	556	153	190	513	8619
1951	—	8029	578	606	198	213	639	10281
1961	337	10837	780	769	266	369	1142	14500
1971	468	14625	1073	1012	332	516	1556	19582
1981	632	19897	1421	1336	494	775	2053	26608
1991	865	22414	1837	1775	690	1209	2757	31547
2001	1091	26638	2388	2306	891	1988	3191	38495

Source : Census of India 1991 : Final Population, Total Brief Analysis of Primary Census Abstract, paper 2 of 1991 and Census of India 2001.

It may be stated from the above table that population figures for Arunachal Pradesh are available only from 1961 onwards. Higher growth of population is the most important demographic feature of the region. The population of North East India was only 1 million in the year 1831 which grew by four times to 4 million in 1901. The population of the Northeastern states increased gradually from 1901 to 1941. When India exprienced a decrease of population by 0.31 per cent during 1911-21, Assam experienced an increase of 20.48 per cent, Manipur 10.92 per cent, Meghalaya 7.21 per cent, Mizoram 7.90 per cent, Nagaland 6.55 per cent and Tripura 32.59 per cent. But from 1951 onwards the rate of increase was higher. The high rate of increase is primarily due to influx of the immigrants from inside and outside of India. The increase of population during the last five decades is tremendous and this rise in population figure in the region is atributed to both natural increase and immigration. It is observed that during each decade about 5 to 7 million people have been added to the population of the region. The total population of North East India was 3,84,95,089 in 2001.

The most important aspect of population trend of the region is the marked differences in spatial growth for instance, the population of Assam has increased 9 times from about 3.3 million in 1901 to about 27 million in 2001. During the same period the population of Manipur grew by 8 times from about 3 lakhs to 24 lakhs. The growth of Tripura was 16 times from about 2 lakhs to 32 lakhs, Nagaland by 20 times and Mizoram by 11 times during 1901-2001.

The decadal growth rate of the hilly states of North East India was much more than the national average in 2001. The decadal growth rate of Tripura was 34.30 per cent in 1981-91, but it was 15.74 per cent in 1991-2001.

Similarly the average annual exponential growth rate of North East India was 2.0 per cent during 1991-2001. This growth rate is much more than the national average ie. 0.07 per cent for the same period. The decadal and average annual exponential growth of population for the decades 1981-91 and

1991-2001 of the states of North East India are shown in the following table - 8.2.

Table - 8.2

States	Decadal growth rate in per cent		Average annual exponential growth rate in per cent	
	1981-91	1991-2001	1981-91	1991-2001
Assam	24.24	18.85	2.2	1.7
Arunachal Pradesh	36.83	26.21	2.8	2.3
Meghalaya	32.86	29.94	2.5	2.6
Manipur	29.29	30.02	3.3	2.7
Mizoram	39.70	29.18	4.5	2.6
Nagaland	56.04	64.41	3.1	4.9
Tripura	34.30	15.74	3.0	1.5
North-East India	**27.45**	**22.02**	**2.5**	**2.0**

Source : Census of India.

Distribution and Density of Population : The Northeastern region of India presents the complexitites of the eastern Himalayan ranges, Indo-Myanmar hills of Nagaland, Manipur, Mizoram and Tripura and the senile plateau of Meghalaya-all encircling the Brahmaputra valley. According to Spate and Learmonth this valley of Assam is a ramp-valley forced down between the Shillong plateau (Meghalaya plateau) and the Himalayan thrusting. Such complex physiographic conditions have provided an excellent habitat for the tribes to continue with their primitive modes of economy and has forstered isolation to varying degrees to the numerous tribal groups. The Manipur plain, Assam valley and Tripura plain, Barak plain provide ideal environment for the settlement of agricultural communities. The hilly areas with excessive rainfull and luxuriant forests provide suitable habitates for the tribes who practise shifting cultivation as their chief means of living. The plains of North East India constitute 28 per cent of the total area which supports the

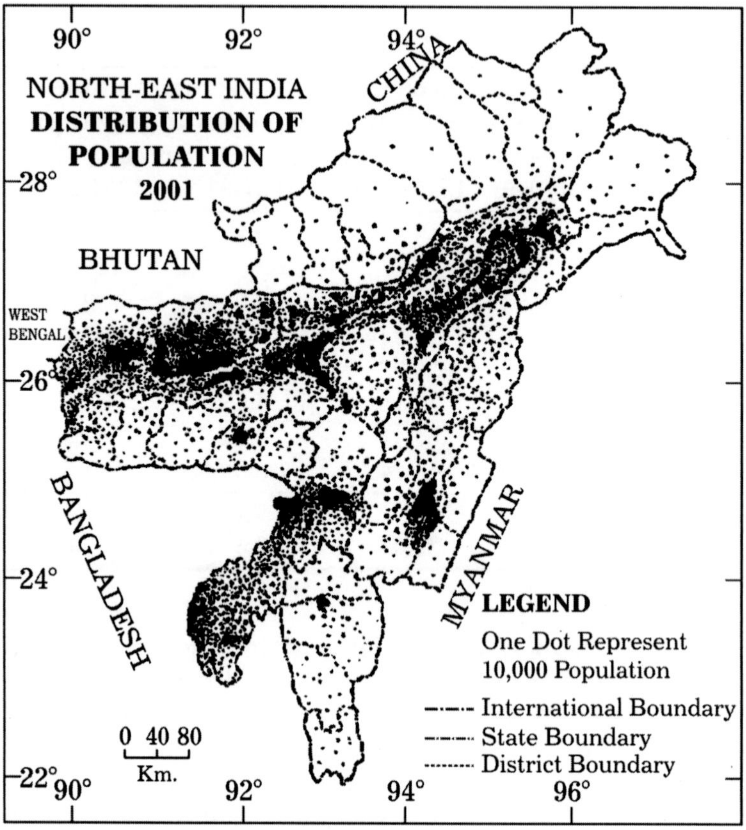

Fig. 6 : Distribution of Population

bulk of the population of the region and the hilly areas (72 per cent) being agriculturally less productive support very sparce population. Assam with its two fertile plains the Brahmaputra valley and Barak plain support nearly two-third of the total population (384,95,089 persons, 2001) of the region. Similarly level land, fertile soil and better transport and communication of population in the western part of Tripura and Manipur basin. Again in mining areas like Cherrapunji, Digboi, Naharkatia, Moran etc. The concentration of population is more. Besides population concentrations are found along the roads and railway including industrial and commercial area both in the hills and plains of the region.

The over-all density of population of North East India was 151 per sq. km in 2001 and 1991 the density was 123 persons per sq. km which was very less in comparison to national average of 324 (2001). This low density of population reflects the hilly topography with limited cultivable land, poor economy and under-developed transport and communication system. Assam ranks first among all the states of North East India in terms of density of population with 340 persons per sq. km. followed by Tripura (304), Nagaland (120), Manipur (107), Mizoram (42) and Arunachal (13). Arunachal is the only state which has the least density of population in the country. So three density zones can be recognised in the region. The density zones can be recognised in the region. The region of very sparse-population with below 50 persons per sq. km. includes Mizoram and Arunachal Pradesh, region of sparse population between 50 and 150 persons is constituted by Meghalaya, Manipur and Nagaland and the region of dense population above 150 is formed by Tripura and Assam.

There is a variation in the density of population within the states of the region. The density of population is highest in the district of Nagaon (604), followed by Dhubri (584) and Kamrup (579) and the lowest density is seen in North Cachar Hills (38) as per 2001 census in Assam. Similarly the plain districts of Manipur, namely Imphal East (555) and West (847) Thoubal (713) and Bishenpur (415) are very densely populated. The density of population in the East Khasi Hills district of quite high, while the upper Subansiri and Dibang valley district of Arunachal Pradesh have a density of population below 10 persons per sq. km.

Sex Ratio : As per 2001 census, the total male population was 1,98,74,535 and female population was 1,86,20,554 which was 51.63 and 48.37 per cent respectively. The sex ratio of the population of North East India was 937 females per thousand male which was more than national average of 933. Sex ratio was found highest in Manipur (978) followed by Meghalaya (975), Tripura (950), Mizoram (938), Assam, (932) Nagaland (909) and Arunachal Pradesh (901). Variations of such ratio are also observed. For example, Imphal west and Bishnupur districts in the Manipur basin recorded highest sex ratio, 1007 and 1003 respectively in 2001. It is observed that the sex-ratio is lower in Assam, Nagaland and Arunachal Pradesh which indicates that each of these states received a large number male population from outside the region who engaged in various civil, military and social services including trade and commerce.

It is to be noted that both birth and death rates are declining in the region. For example birth and death rates of Arunachal Pradesh were 3.68 per cent and 1.98 per cent respectively for the year 1971 and the same declined to 3.63 per cent and 1.51 per cent in 1989. Similarly the birth and death rates for Assam were 3.93 and 1.87 per cent in 1971 and these were declined to 2.7 and 0.97 per cent in 1999. Since the natural birth rates and death rates are quite lower, the overall growth of population in the entire region must be mainly attributed to immigration.

Literacy : The census of India accords literacy status to a person who could read and write with understanding in any of the languages and the effective literacy rate may be defined as that person who attains seven years of age and above. According to this definition the literacy rate of North East India was 65.77 per cent as against the national average of 65.33 per cent in 2001. Among the states Mizoram had the highest literacy ie. 88.49 per cent, followed by Tripura 73.66, Manipur 68.87, Nagaland 67.31, Assam 64.28, Meghalaya 63.31 and Arunachal Pradesh, 54.74 per cent.

There is a great variation of literacy rate between males and females in the region. In 2001 the male and female literacy rates were 72.99 and 58.02 per cent respectively. It was 75.85 and 54.16 per cent respectively for India in the same year. The low female literacy rate was due to women in many states of India used to marry at quite a young age. According to the International Institute for Population Sciences, Bombay, the percentage of those women marrying below the age of 20 years was still more than 60 per cent in many states of India including Assam. Thus the gap of literacy between the male and female disparity in literacy is not equal among all the communities of the region. For example, the caste Hindus constitute the overwhelming majority of the village Ichadagharia under Rangia Police Station of Assam. The position of literacy among the children upto the age group 6-14 was very good, ie. 100 per cent, but the numbers of drop out were higher among the female children than among the males beyond this age group (Survey period April, 2002). According to the Annual Report, Ministry of Human Resource Development, Goverment of India, 1994-95, The drop out rate at the primary stage was only 39 per cent but it increased to 77 per cent when they reached class X in Assam. Thus the problem of literacy get more complicated because the drop out rate were quite high in all the states of North East India (Table - 8.3).

Table - 8.3
Drop out Rates and Literacy Rates

States	Drop out rates from class I to class V 1994-95 in Per Cent	Literacy rates in Per cent 1991	Literacy rate in Per cent 2001
Arunachal Pradesh	60.52	41.59	54.74
Assam	39.05	52.89	64.28
Manipur	68.26	59.89	68.87
Meghalaya	32.06	49.10	63.31
Mizoram	57.58	82.27	88.49
Nagaland	31.65	61.65	67.11
Tripura	63.49	60.44	73.66

As mentioned earlier, the overall literacy rate of the states of North East India, except Mizoram is rather low. Such low level of literacy in the region may be due to existence of schools without adequate infrastructure, including physical facilities like drinking water, urinals etc. lack of awareness among the people, poverty, unintersting school curriculum and others. Substantial disparities in educational infrastructure exist in the plains and hills of North East India in the manner in which educational institutions operate. It is seen that pupil-teacher ratio also varies from low to high in different areas of North East India, which should be rationalised. The existing unintersting school curriculum should be modified with including new activities like basic computer knowledge, drawing, dancing, physical fitness, flower making, toys etc. The isolated areas of the plains and remote hills of the region demand more schools even though the number of school children is small. The improvement of education and literacy appears to be very difficult because the Government is spending less than 2 per cent of the total budget on education. Therefore the Government must increase the total annual budget on education.

Urbanisation : As per 2001 the total urban population of North East India was 59,72,074 which was 15.51 per cent of the total population in the same year. At national level it was 27.78 in 2001 The spatial distribution of urban population is highly uneven. Although Assam has the highest number of urban population, Mizoram with 49.50 per cent was the most urbanised state of the region Assam with 3,389,413 urban population recorded the least percentage of urban population (12.72%), followed by Tripura (17.02%), Nagaland (17.74%), Meghalaya (19.63%), Arunachal Pradesh (20.41%) and Manipur (23.88%), Thus the growth of urban centres and urban population in North East India is rather slow and insignificant. This is mainly due to its rural economy and a poor level of industrialisation. The urban population of North East India stood at about 6 million which came to be about 15.51 per cent in 2001. This accounts only 2 per cent of the India's urban population.

Urbanisation is a recent phenomenon in North East India and the leve of urbanisation in the region was less than half of the all-India level (Table - 8.4).

Table - 8.4
Level and growth of urban population 1971-2001

States	Urban Population		Urban population as Percentage of total	
	1971	2001	1971	2001
Arunachal Pradesh	17,288	222,688	3.70	20.41
Assam	12,9222	33,89,413	8.82	12.72
Manipur	14,1695	570,410	13.19	23.88
Meghalaya	147,170	452,612	14.55	19.63
Mizoram	37,759	441,040	11.36	49.50
Nagaland	51,071	352,821	9.95	17.74
Tripura	121,775	543,094	10.43	17.02
North-East India	18,46,980	59,72,078	9.43	15.51
India	**109,094,309**	**285,354,954**	**19.91**	**27.78**

Source : Census of India

In the last four decades, with the expansion administrative set up coupled with development of education and commerce some new towns have emerged in the hill states and other areas. Most of these towns are imposed administrative centres, with some trade and commercial activities. In fact urbansiation in North-Eastern states is not linked to broad based economic progress but to administrative and other factors including political and forced migration.

The 1991 census has given one lakh plus status to eight urban centres of the region, namely Guwahati (achieved such status in 1961), Shillong, Imphal, Agartala, Aizawl, Dibrugarh, Silchar and Jorhat and these cities continue to be large cities in North East India and others are small urban centres. The small urban centres have a predominately rural economic base and a substantial segment of its work-force being agriculture. Agriculture is a space consuming activity and it is labour intensive. It requires fertilizers, processing plants, distribution of depots and marketing facilities. The rural people require economic and social services. All these services and facilities cannot be provided everywhere. These may be provided in a rational manner in the small towns. Again the small towns appear in the hierarchy because there are different grades of demands from the villages, each having different thresholds of population and ranges of goods. Such an urban hierarchy should be properly developed without gap so that every area and everyone can get equal opportunities. These hierarchy of towns not only provide services for the increased production in the rural sector of economy but also provide new innovations and work as catalysts of social change.

9

Settlements : Rural and Urban Settlements

Population and settlement are interrelated. The term population as discussed earlier is the total number of inhabitants of a country as any unit of area. But settlement includes all forms of human occupance or occupied human dwelling places. Even an isolaled occupied hut is called a settlement. The term settlement usually indicates a community of dwellings and associated buildings ranging from a hamlet to a megalopolis. It may be noted that settlements tend to form where there is easy access to resources or services such as water supply, fertile soil, minerals, shops, commercial activities, industries and means of communication and transport.

All settlements-rural or urban, large or small form part of a system where interdependence and interrelation exist. The environmental conditions have cumulative effect on the growth and distribution of population and settlements system of North East India. This settlement system is typically the village system and its rural-social space intimately related with local, sub-regional and regional frameworks of nature, mainly ecological. The different social groups, interacting mutually within their ecological and territorial contexts and the resulting socio-cultural and economic problem are rural in origin. The setttlement system of North East India contains various kinds of spaces like territorial, social, cultural, ritual all leading with varied permutations and combinations to their morphological patterning.

Rural Settlements : North East India is a region of villages. They are arranged in remarkable variety of forms and patterns. The villages are related to marked changes in physical geography within relatively short distances and to successive movement of people, from adjoining countries and different parts of India since time immemorial. In 1901 the plains of North East India presented a panorama of extensive paddy fields dotted with tiny villages which lie hidden beneath the luxuriant belel-nut, coconut, plantain and bamboo groves. The villages in those days were not well defined units but groups of huts stood out clearly in the centre of the paddy fields. So it was difficult to indicate where one village ended and another began. It was recorded that in 1901 about two-thirds of villages were small hamlets with less than 500 inhabitants. According to Extracts from the Assam Census Report, 1881 there were 3,73,807 inhabitants which were distributed in 2,836 villages in the hill districts of region. The hill districts were Cachar Hill tracts, Garo Hills, Khasi and Jaintia Hills, Naga Hills, Civil and Military, Naga Hills tracts, Mizo Hills, Manipur and Tripura were not included in that report.

The post-independence period witnessed some important event which led to a remarkable change in the demographic as well as settlement structure of North East India. In the wake of partion a large number of Hindu refugees migrated into this region from East Pakistan (Bangladesh). Besides the region has made some progress in the field of agriculture, industry, medical aid, education etc. With the growth of human habitation more villages sprung up robbing the natural landscape. The former villages with undefined boundaries as described in the old Gazetteer, have gradually transformed into more homogenic units with amenities of modern living like drinking water, roads, hospitals, school etc.

The character of village sites varies from place to place in North East India. In the plains like the Brahmaputra valley, Barak plain, Manipur plain and Tripura plain the houses are built in large cluster or small cluster as per allocation of the agricultural land. Generally the old villages are almost invariably found on the bank of the rivers and in their neighbourhood. The exact site of such villages is decided on the basins of maximum accessibility and availability of perennial source of water. The river levees are by far the most favourite village sites in the plains of North East India. The central part between such levees is swampy and when the village site becomes more crowded due to the increase of population, the villagers build their houses further away from the river bank on artificially raised lands. Some immigrant communities are found to settle in the low lying rice and jute fields of the lower Brahmaputra valley. Large villages are often found where periodical markets are held and generally they are sited on the bank of the river.

In Arunachal Pradesh most of the villages are sited on the slopes of the hills and the proximity to water source is the principal factor in selecting site. The site selection and house construction in all the tribal areas of Arunachal Pradesh is ceremoniously observed in consultation with the village priest.

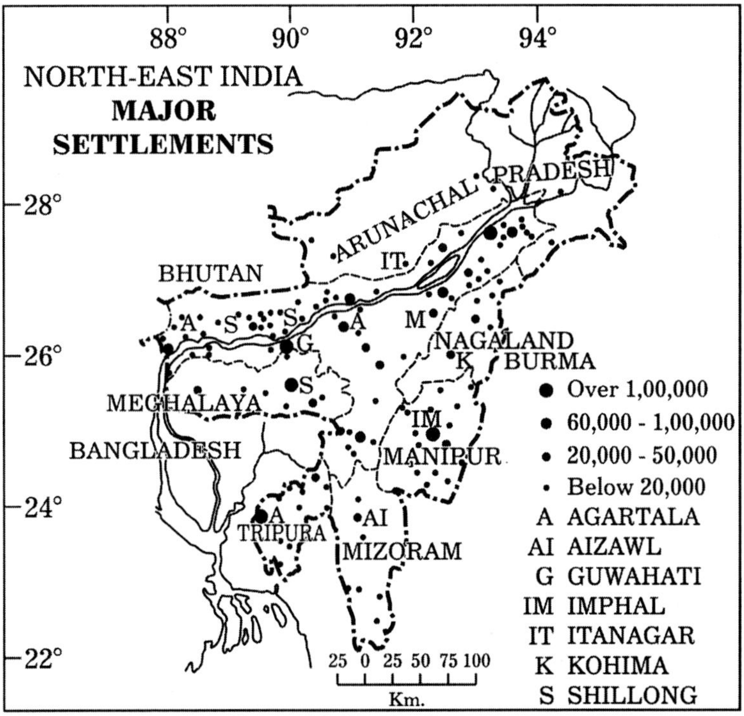

Fig. 7 : Major Settlements

In Meghalaya large villages are located on gentle to moderate slope and small villages and isolated hamlets are generally sited on moderately steep slopes and dissected terrain. Such sites possess some soil cover to permit cultivation. The Khasi villages are generally strongly fortified with stockades, ditches and stone wall.

In Nagaland villages are clustered. They are sited on both hill tops and hill slopes including ridges. Generally the Sema villages are seen on the hill tops and these are constructed for safety and self protection. For the same reason their villages are large and cultivated fields are seen on the hill slopes. The relief features of Mizoram are characterised by parallel ranges of hills with deep narrow valleys. The valleys are more wider in the western part and allow the growth of Settlements. The altitude of the eastern part is high and slopes are steep and hence the growth of settlement is retarted. In the highlands of Manipur and Tripura villages are found on the ridges or near the crest of the slopes. The location of the villages in different parts of North East India is influenced by physiography, availability of agricultural land, water features, transport facilities and other socio-economic factors.

According to 2001 census North East India had a population of 3,84,95,089 persons, of which 3,25,23,001 lived in rural areas and 95,72,078 in the urban tract. Obviously, the population of the entire region is mostly rural ie. 84.49 per cent and urban population is as low as 15.51 per cent. On the basis of population size, the rural settlements are classified into six orders. The lowest order of settlements having less than 200 persons is mostly distributed in the marshy tracts of the plains or forest covered areas of the hills. Surprisingly in Tripura there are about 40 villages of this order. This is perhaps due to recorganisation of village consequent largely upon the disturbed political environment in the state. The next higher grade having population of 200-499 are well distributed in the entire region with the exception of Tripura. The medium villages with population 500-999 form the third order settlements and they are well distributed in all the states of the region. The fourth order villages having population of 1000-1999 are not uniformly distributed. There are large number of such village in the Brahmaputra valley because in this area agriculture is permanent and the soil productivity is high. The fifth (2000-4999) and six order villages (5000 and above) are very few in the region except in Manipur and Tripura. The villages of Manipur and Tripura are generally large and populous because of creation of some administrative centre and also recorganisation of villages. The fifth and sixth order villages are multifunctional in nature with weekly or biweekly markets. Generally such large villages are rural urban centres or rural central places because they perform central activities like trade, transport, education, health and other social services, small scale industries apart from agricultural functions.

The percentage of population living in villages of various population sizes are not uniform in the region. It is observed that highest percentage of rural population lives in medium villages (500-999) and lowest percentage of rural population is very large village (5000 and over) and very small village (under 200) as in Assam. In Meghalaya and Arunachal Pradesh the majority of rural population lives in very small (under 200) and small (200-499) villages. In Tripura 45.61 per cent of rural population lives in large villages (2000-4999) and in Nagaland 30.57% of such population lives in villages of 1000-1999 persons. In Manipur and Mizoram the majority of rural population lives in small, medium and large villages.

Settlement Pattern : The spatial distribution and arrangement of settlement is known as settlement pattern. Earlier the geographers were concerned essentially with the study of patterns in terms of the relationship of the settlement to its physical setting and its historical evolution. Now they are more interested with a search for order in the spacing of settlements and their internal organisation. It has been observed that along with environmental factors other cultural factors like transportational lines, nearness to urban centres agricultural lands etc. influence the distributional pattern of rural settlements in North East India.

The dominance of small-sized agricultural villages and low agricultural settlements density have been observed in different parts of North East India. This is mainly due to poor resources for their subsistence. Such small-sized villages have needed larger areal base for their existence and as a result of this villages of the region are widely space. For example, the spacing of such villages in Assam is 1-2.30 km. 3.76 km. in Manipur, 1.69 km in Tripura, 4.85 km in Nagaland and 6.61 in Arunachal Pradesh. Usually, the rural settlements are classified into three types, namely compact, semi compact and hamleted according to their spatial arrangement of houses or occupance units. Compact settlement units indicate very close spatial organisation while hamleted types mean wide and loose spatial organisation. In the light of these facts, the settlements of North East India clearly fall into the following main categories :

1. **Strassendorf or Steet Villages :** These are linear types of settlements. They are formed when the attractive or restrictive forces encourage or discourage the growth in direction. These are the common forms of settlement in the Brahmaputra valley and the indigenous Assamese people live in linear villages where one of the axes of the village is markedly longer than the other. This is due to the influence of site. Generally two series of farmsteads face each other and stand on the main roads and river banks. Both natural and cultural forces in the sites are responsible for linear growth. The rectangular cluster settlement of the river levees becomes elongated along the high ground if the areas are liable to inundation. Where there is no danger of floods the advantages offered by the proximity of a river cause the elongation of the settlement. On the edge of the hills or on the points of different relief features such as low lands and low hills villages often develop a linear pattern, indicating the impact of restrictive forces of nature.

Roads and cart-tracts are the cultural features in the sites. Villages mostly lie on the main highways and cart-tracts. If these are important link with the central places of market towns the elongation may be striking. In the Brahmaputra valley such elongated pattern of settlement on both sides of the roads and river bank is the rule. This is more prominent in the relatively less populated districts of Dhemaji, Lakhimpur, Dibrugarh, Tinsukia, Sibsagar, Jorhat, Golaghat and Sontipur. Usually linear settlements have very low MC

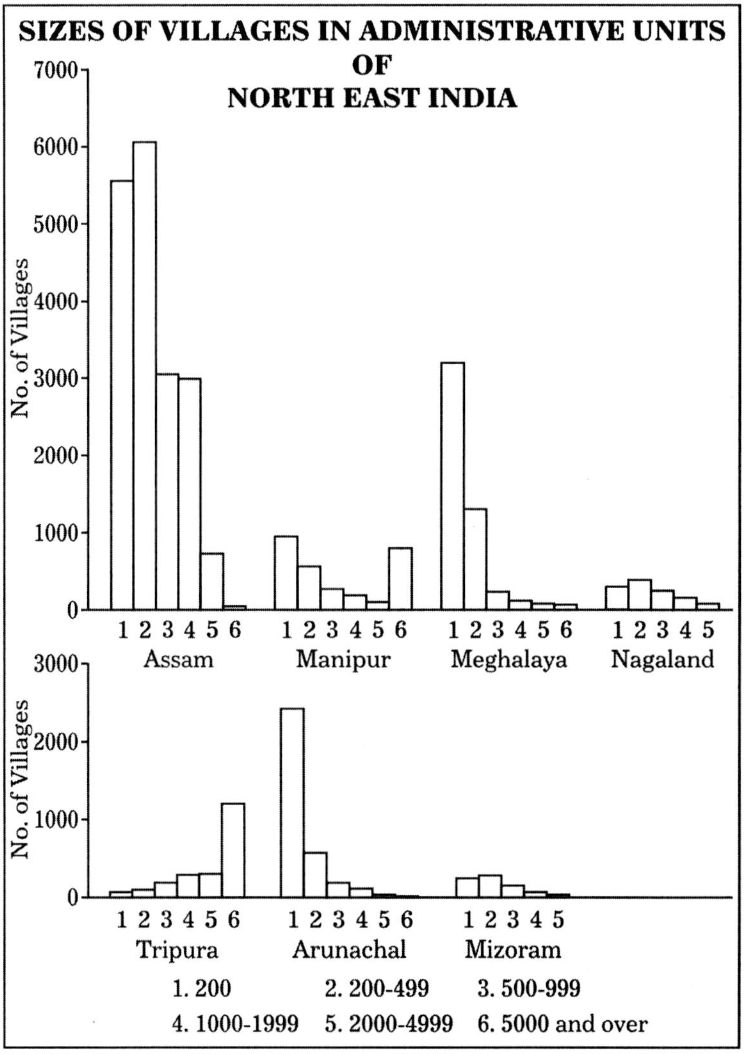

Fig. 8 : Sizes of Villages

values* (For example, Niz Chatia, Sontipur district MC=20.60; Dhighali, Dibrugarh district, MC = 19.12) which create many problems in fomulating some development plans for them.

Haufendorf of Clustered Type : In thickly populated parts of the plains of the lower Brahmaputra valley the Barak plain, Manipur basin and Tripura plain Haufendrof or irregular clustered villages is the rule. According to Meitzen there is a close, relationship between socio-ethnic group and the village plan including its types. Generally the clan settlements of the lower Assam plains are of such types. In Nalbari district including Rangia region of Kamrup district where density of population is very high rectangular pattern of settlements is frequently met with. Here the shape of the villages is roughly rectangular and reason for this pattern is the shape of the cultivated land which are some sort of rectangle with their boundary lines roughly running north-south and east-west direction. Footpaths and cart tracts run usually on the boundary of the cultivated fields which also confirm to the field pattern. Rectangular form of field requires a minimum turning of the plough and least strain on draught animals. Such a ploughable farm size accounts mostly for rectangular farm of the village. This is a heritage of the ancient past. Then this system has been culminating into Bigha system. Such a system of land subdivision may be comparable to that of Jori system of Japan and China. The compact type of settlements of the Brahmaputra valley are comparable to Haufendorf of Kanto plain of Japan.

Ciflik or Square Type : This type of settlement is highly concentrated around the margins of the Black sea. Ciflik or square type of settlement is also concentrated in the thickly populated parts of North East India having good network of roads. These are mostly lying at the crossing of roads and

---

* MC = 100. Aa/3.1416 (Dd/p)2, where Mc is the measure of circularity is shape, Aa is the actual area contained in the settlement unit, Dp distance between most distant point on the boundary of the unit.

the pattern is related to some geographic features which control the extension of settlement outside a square space. The restricting influence is often exerted by a thick orchard surrounding the village of tanks or roads.

Eschdorf or Semi-compact Type : This is intermediate between the compact village and the isolated farmstead. An Eschdorf settlement consists of some hamlets separated by small fields and is connected by a winding footpath or a cart-tract or a road. Such type of irregular settlement is seen in the Sub-Terai region of the north bank of the Brahmaputra valley including the foot-hills of the Arunachal Himalayas. The huts are distributed in linear and scattered manner where there is clearance of forests. Eschdorf or semi-compact settlements are also known as amorphous settlements.

2. **Marshufendorfer or Marsh Village :** Some linear villages are observed in the marshy tracts of the various plains of North East India. These are particularly seen from Sisi in Dhemaji district along the north bank of the Brahmaputra river up to Sareswar Bill near Dhubri. Similar types of settlements are also seen in the marshy tracts of Barak plain and along the bank of the Loktak lake of Manipur.

A special type of settlement is found in the 'Char' areas of the lower Brahmaputra valley. These areas are mostly occupied by the immigrants and their villages are located within the cultivated lands without following any road or river which results in the formation of nucleated and chaotic agglomeration of settlements. The immigrants introduce intensive type of agriculture, unknown to the indigenous people and they are mainly seen to settle in the riverine areas of Goalpara, Dhubri, Barpeta, Kamrup, Darrang, Marigaon, Nagaon and Sontipur district.

Dispersed Settlement or Streusiedlugen Type : Dispersed villages are the rule in the foothill plains and hill slopes and difficult terrain and turbulent drainage lines unfavourable for inter-village interactions and agricultural activities of the region. Such settlements are found in all the hilly areas of

North East India. Shifting cultivation has been the main source of livelihood for several tribes of the highlands of the region. An estimated 4,43,336 household earn their livelihood from his primitive type of cultivation and isolated settlements are common in areas of shifting cultivation with very limited civic amenities.

Latifundium or Estate Settlement : This is a special type of compact rural settlement which differs in certain fundamental from the typical agricultural village. It is associated with extensive tea estates where large number of hired labourers are necessary to carry on the ordinary works of a tea garden. In a typical tea garden there is usually a central core which contains the sumptuous factory and the residences of the officials together with the lines of huts of

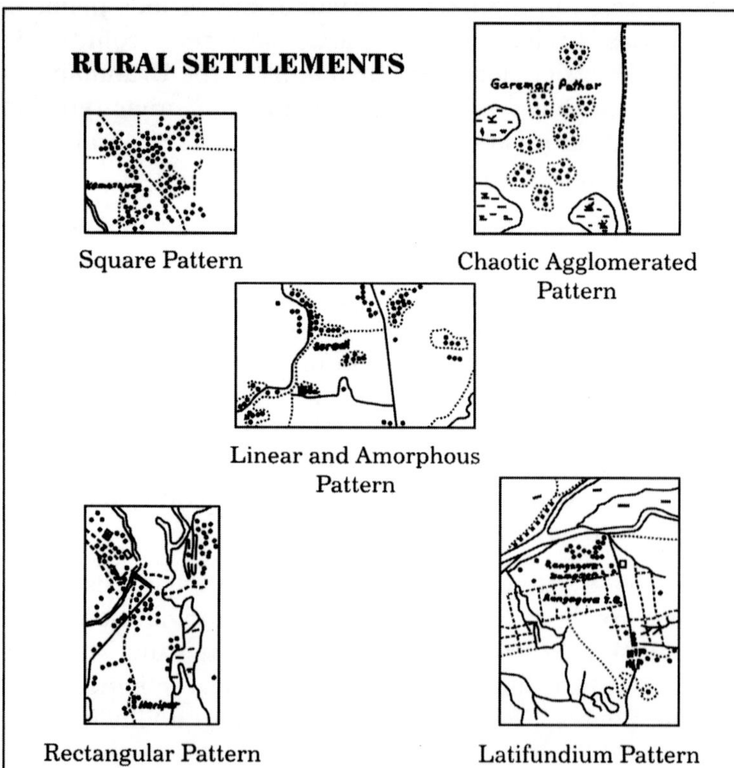

Fig. 9 : Rural Settlements

labourers, a school and hospital. This type of estate settlement is composed of buildings owned by the estate and rented to the labourers and settlement life is closely regulated by the estate authority. Such settlements are found in the tea gardens of Dibrugarh, Tinsukia, Sibsagar, Lakhimpur, Jorhat, Golaghat, Nagaon, Barak plains and Tripura.

Urban Settlements :

India is one of the most unurbanised countries in the world. Only 27.78 per cent of the total population (1,027,015,247) of India live in 4689 urban centres as per 2001 census. Thus the majority of the inhabitants of India (72.22 per cent) live in the countryside. Their primary occupation is agriculture and allied activities. But most of the country dwellers partake of services which require regular and frequent visits to those towns as mentioned above. In 1961 census, an uniform and somewhat rigid test was applied throughout India for an area to be recognised as an urban unit. The definition adopted in 1961 for an urban area was also followed in 1971, 1981, 1991 and 2001. This was spelt out as follows :

(a) All places with a Municipal Corporation or a Municipality of a Town Committee or a Notified area or a Cantonment.

(b) All other places which satisfied the following criteria : a minimum population of five thousand, at least 75 per cent of the male working population is non-agricultural and a density of population of atleast 400 per sq. km. According to this definition there were 4689 urban centres with 28,53,54,954 urban population in India in the year 2001.

In comparison of India, North East India is predominantly more a rural region and only 15.51 per cent of the total population live in about 200 towns. This low degree of urbanisation in the region is due to the fact this part of India has a subsistence agricultural economy and general lack of town founding industries. The development process in North East India started during the colonial rule with the export oriented tea plantation, exploitation of forest and mineral resources like oil and coal. These activities are still colonial in nature. The wholesale trade and commerce were and still are at the hands of outsiders and consequently investible surplus is siphoned out of North East India and as such it tends to prevent rather than help the formation of urban settlements. However, there has been a significant growth of urban population and urban centres in all the states of North East India during the last five decades. The creation of new states in the region and the consequent increase in the governmental expenditure and establishment of new administrative headquarters may explain this phenomenon.

North East India is physiographically not a homogenous region and as such the growth and distributional pattern of urban centres show significant variations within it. While the degree of urbanisation is more in the plain like Brahmaputra valley, Barak plain, Manipur basin, Tripura plain, due to better means of communication system and economic base. The higher rate of urbanisation is felt primarily by the smaller hill states like Manipur (100.3%) Nagaland, (56%) and Mizoram (117.2%). The rate of urbanisation in the small states of the region is not stable because it (urbanisation) is not linked to broad economic development. The rapid growth of urban population in these states is not because of any industrial growth or significant economic development but because of creation of new administrative centres and recorganisation of service centres consequent mainly upon recent political events.

The Brahmaputra and its tibutaries, the Barak river, Imphal river and Haora river, by virtue of the exceptional utility for agriculture, trade and commerce are well known and for the same reason large number of rural central places and towns have clung to their river banks since time immemorial - Guwahati, Tezpur, Jorhat, Sibsagar etc. are the old established historical towns of the Brahmaputra valley. Similarly Silchar and Karimganj are grown along the Barak river. Agartala is located on the bank of the Haora river and Imphal is sited on the bank of the Imphal river. Besides, roads and railways also play on important role in the location of urban centres in North East India. In the hilly areas of the region the general weakness of economy lies in their poor agricultural bases which fail to produce enough food materials for their growing population or raw materials for industries. In such areas the process of urbanisation has been developed in *Pari Pasu* with forest mining, transport, manufacturing and also power as in Meghalaya, Besides, service sector has been accentuated during the last three decades where job opportunities are created in the offices and educational institutions by the Government.

The British who came to occupy North East India built some trading posts, military garrisons and cantonments in a number of places. Along with these other British services, such as administrative, medical educational institutions, railways and telegraphs and postal services, banks etc. were added to the gathering points and these in due course were transformed into towns and potential urban centres. Most of the district and subdivisional head quarters such as Dibrugarh, North Lakhimpur, Golaghat, Silchar, Karimganj, Nagaon, Mangaldai, Barpeta, Goalpara, Dhubri, Tura, Kohima, Aizawl etc. were established during the British period. The introduction of railway during this period led to the growth of Rangia, Champarmukh, Furkating, Simaluguri, Mariani, Dimapur, Lumding, Rangapara, Tinsukia, Sadiya, Dibrugarh etc. grew up. It is also significant to mention that the urban centres like Palasbari, Haji, Sarthebari, Soalkuchi etc. grew up as centres of small scale industries while Digboi developed as an urban centre due to the extraction of oil.

In 1947 India become independent and since then due to gradual extension of motorable roads and means of modern transport and industrialization new market towns like Abhayapuri, Barpeta Road, Howli, Hojai, Lanka, Kharupatia, Lakhipur, Nazira, Tihu, Tangla, Bihpuria, Dergaon, Maranhat, Tura, Jawai, Dharmanagar, Kailashar, Udaipur, Jiribam, Moreh, Churachandpur, Lunglei etc. grew up. More recently some new service-cum administrative towns, such as Itanagar, Naharlagun, Pasighat, Tezu, Along, Ziro, Namsai, Roing, Khonsa, Bomdila, Kolasib and Dhiphu have been established in different states of the region. Cherrapunjee was the seat of administration during the British rule and remained more or less stagnant and now it has developed as a mining town. The other mining towns are Namrup, Duliajan and Margherita.

The urban centres of North East India do not exhibit any features what Christaller called marketing, traffic network or administrative principle. It has been observed that there are more people in town than jobs, socio-economic facilities like education, health, accommodation, finance and commerce etc. But inspite of having a low level of social services and economic facilities some towns like Guwahati, Shillong, Imphal, Agartala, Aizawl, Dibrugarh, Silchar and Jorhat are becoming important urban centres of innovation owing to their locational importance and accessibility. The modern city of Guwahati has been identified as the ancient Pragjyotishpura and the Ahom king made it the administrative headquarters of lower Assam. Modern Guwahati dates back to the British occupation of Assam in 1826 and it is from this date the city came to have due importance. Except few temples, an earthen fort and few tanks there are hardly any medieval remnants and ruins in Guwahati. It is to be noted that throughout the 19th century and also during the first four decades of the 20th century the growth of Guwahati was very slow. But, thereafter, both spatial and population growth of the city was rather rapid. During the World War II the Britishers used this city as their strongholds by establishing civil lines and contonments. The significant development during the British period was the establishment of the cantonment at Paltan bazar, opening new lines of transport and communication and improvement of old ones within the town which imparted and added to the city. This then was followed by the independence of the country and since then Guwahati has undergone a remarkable change and the present expansion of the city is the result of agglomeration of urban structures developed around multiple nuclei. The significant development which ever took place in the evolutional history of Guwahati were the establishment of the High Court, the Railway

Headquarters, the University Campus, the Engineering College, the Medical College, the construction of Saraighat bridge, oil refinery, military cantonment at Satgaon. The Industrial Estate, many central and State Government offices and institution etc. and all these were during the early sixties. Just after independence, a large number of refugees from the erstwhile East Pakistan came to settle here with their families. These factors coupled with an ever incresing stream of men from various parts of India came to Guwahati in search of employment which rendered a spectacular growth of urban population in Guwahati. In accordance with this economic and social background the population of Guwahati increaed rapidly during the modern period. During the decade of 1951-1961, Guwahati recorded and increase of population of 130.9 per cent i.e. from 43,615 (1951) to 1,00,707 (1961). It rose to 2,00,377 (1971) which, was 16 per cent of the total urban population of Assam. The temo of growth and the development of the city was further enhanced during the next few years with the setting up of temporary capital complex at Dispur near Guwahati. In 1971 about 20,000 people including their families came to Guwahati from Shillong along with shifting of Capital of Assam from Shillong to Guwahati. The site of capital complex has selected some road side villages with paddy fields all around near Goneshguri, Guwahati. The decision of shifting the capital of Assam from Shillong to this site was political and administrative and ecological consideration was not taken into account at that time which has now been proved to be be an ecological disaster. Guwahati, today extends by 27 km from the cantonment area of Satgaon in the east to Khanamukh in the West and about 12 km from the Brahmaputra in the north to Basisthasram and the National Highway By Pass No. 37 in the south. Thus the city covers an area about 300 sq. km. with a total population of 808021 as per 2001 census. Guwahati is linked by daily air service with Kolkata and Delhi besides daily air flights to Agartala, Imphal, Silchar, Tezpur, Jorhat, Dimapur, North Lakhimpur and Dibrugarh and the airport has now been given the status of international airport by the Ministry of Civil Aviation, Government of India.

Shillong, the provincial capital of Assam was also established by the Britishers. It was made summer capital of a new province of Eastern Bengal and Assam created in 1905. In 1909 Shillong was constituted a Municipality and in 1912 a seperate province of Assam was created and since then horizontal and vertical expansion have been taking place both within and outside it Municipal area. Thus shillong grew as a regional centre of governance, capital of erstwhile Assam and now most urbanised and capital city of the state of Meghalaya. The population of Shillong at that time of creation of Municipality was only 2147 in 1878. It increased to 38,192 in 1941. But after independence the town attracted more people and in 1961 recorded 1,02,398 persons. The growth of population has still been increasing and in 1991 it became 2,23,366 and in 2001 the same increased to 2,67,811 persons. Shillong is a multifunctional urban centre with administration, commerce and education as major functions.

Except Itanagar all the state capitals are class I towns with a population more than 2 lakh and they are multifunctional. Agartala has three major functions like service, trade and commerce and manufacturing. Imphal has functions like household industries, service and trade and commerce.

Aizawl, the beautiful capital of Mizoram has a unique history of its own. It originally belonged to the chiefdom of Khalkom, the North Lushai chief. A strong military post was constructed at Aizawl under captain Browne, the then political officer of Mizoram. The first bazar at Aizawl was opened in 1910 by Mr HWC Cole, the Superintendent of Lushai Hills. The local people brought their agricultural products and sold at whatever price they could bargain for. The first High School in Mizoram, known as Governement Mizo High School was established in 1944 and since then the town has been growing. The growth of population in Aizawl has been phenomenal resulting in congestion and the city has two major functions namely primary and tertiary activities. All the major urban centres can be viewed as system because of their inter relationship among the different categories of settlements of North East India. Guwahati system is characterised by the occurrence of higher order settlements with diversified functions within them. Imphal, Agartala, Shillong and Aizawl are regional systems with less intensive interaction amongst their rural and urban components and they are not well defined but oriented firmly towards Guwahati, the urban magnet of North East India.

The settlements in North East India are a sort of unplanned growth of their physical and cultural setting. They are still in primary stage of development on a account of their functional character, socio-economic condition and unscientific foundation of planning. So there is often a hiatus between the regional city and the towns on the one hand and the rural service centres and villages on the other. An examination of the settlement hierarchy in the region shows that there is a discordance between the major urban centres and villages. There is very little generative link between urban and rural sectors of economy in the settlement system of the region. The growth of cities and major urban centres is essentially a centre-down strategy of development in India and hence this strategy has no appeal for the 'bottom-up' or development from below. But small urban centres constitute some important elements in the development process for both 'centre-down' and 'bottom-up' strategy which are gaining currency everywhere. Most of the small urban centres are potential growth centres. These potential growth centres have a significant role in the face lift of the country side especially to their surrounding rural areas. But forcible shift of a activities and services from the major urban centres to the minor or small towns without having the required resource base and the infrastructural facilities should be avoided. It is to be noted that most of the small towns do not have strong economic base and they have poor linkages with the rural settlements. So economic viability and the future distribution of demand should be primary consideration for adopting a policy on planning for growth centres and regional development of North East India.

10

Agriculture and Landuse

The majority of the people of North East India live in villages and 85 of them depend on agriculture for their income and employment. But agriculture of this region is monsoonal type with characteristics features like fragmented and dispersed land holdings, primitive and outdated implements, heavy emphasis on grain crops, high proportions of agricultural employment and low per capita yield.

The most striking feature of agriculture of this region is the extremely fragmented uneconomic nature of arable lands. The size of holdings indicates the problems of population pressure on land as well as the influence of environmental and socio-economic factors on it. Generally small and fragmented land holdings are not suitable for application of modern machinery and for information of capital input. The average size of land holdings in Assam is reported to have declined from 1.47 hectares in 1970-71 to 1.24 hectares in 1995-96. In 1990-91 the average size of holding in the states of Manipur, Meghalaya, Mizoram, Nagaland and Tripura were 1.23, 1.77, 1.38, 6.82, 0.97 hectares respectively. The average size of Arunachal Pradesh (3.62 ha) was higher than the North East India average (2.44 ha). The agricultural census of 1970-71 defines holdings upto 0.5 ha as sub-marginal, those between 0.5 to 20 ha as medium and those above 20 ha as large holdings. In Assam there are very few large or medium holdings and 60 per cent of the operational holdings having less than one hectare account for 19 per cent of the total operated land in the state. In the hill state like Arunachal Pradesh the number of marginal holdings increase at a very rapid rate. Small-sized fragments are certainly uneconomic very rapid rate. Small-sized fragments are certainly uneconomic and pose serious operational difficulties. The reasons for fragmentation are mainly the laws of inheritance, land use, the land tenure system and increasing pressure of population on land created by the fact that a vast majority of the population of the region has to depend on agriculture in the absence of alternative occupations. The problem can be solved by implementation of land reform measures. The Assam consolidation of Land Holding Act, 1960 (amended in 1966), Land Revenue and Land Reforms Acts, 1960 Tripura and Manipur), the Jhum Land Regulation Act of 1970 in Nagaland, Land relations in Meghalaya and Arunachal Pradesh (guided by un written traditions and customary laws) are some of the important land reform measures of the differents states of the region. Effective implementation of land reforms is necessary in the interest of raising the productivity lands of the region.

It is natural that the fragmented nature of agriculture lands restricts the use of modern implements and farming is carried on in the traditional ways. Generally the method of cultivation in the plains of North East India is not very different in other parts of India. The power used in cultivation is derived from a pair of bullocks and human labour. The implements used for cultivation are wooden ploughs with iron blades, spades and steel hoes. Manures were not used earlier because of the abundant supply of fertile land in the areas. So the indigeneous farmers did not feel the necessity for improved farm practices in those days. Now with increasing pressure of population, the indigeneous farmers also began to use fertilizer but the use of it still to get currency. It is to be noted that the people of this region do not use cow-dung as fuel as is done in other parts of India.

The hill tribes of the region practise shifting cultivation or slash and burn cultivation known as Jhuming. In Jhuming farmers do not use any plough or bullock. Jhuming is a no tillage' method of fragile tropical soil of the hill slope which involves clearing of vegetation with axes, *daos* (large knives), hoes and iron-capped sticks. Rice, maize, millets, chillies, cotton, seasame, gourds etc. are grown in Jhuming areas. The land looses its fertility after 2-3 years of cropping and the farmers have to shift to another piece of forested land for growing crops. The abandoned Jhuming areas requires 3 to 15 years depending on the nature of land to recover its fertility and to be covered with vegetation. Jhum cultivation is very destructive because it involves destruction of extensive areas of vegetation every year affecting the environment. The destruction of forests on the hill slopes by Jhuming means the mass destruction of the habitats of insects, birds and animals too. A large number of hill people depend on shifting cultivation for survival. But due to increase in population, Jhum-cycles are now becoming shorter and as a result jhum field does not get adequate time for natural recovery. Jhuming at upper reaches of high hills enhances soil erosion which eventually converts the land into wastelands. The destruction of vegetation on such hill slopes by Jhum cultivation also cause heavy floods in the plains.

In Arunachal Pradesh about 54,000 families earn their livelihood from 700 sq. km. jhum-plots every year. Similarly in the highlands of Manipur, the area under shifting cultivation (annual) is 900 sq. km and the number families practising it is about 70,000. Annual area under shifting cultivation in Nagaland is only 190 sq. km, but the number of families practising this system of agriculture is quite high i.e. 1,16,046. A large number of hill tribes of Meghalaya, Mizoram, Tripura and Assam also earn their livelihood from shifting cultivation. An estimated 4,43,336 families of the entire North East India earn their livelihood from an annual area 3,869 sq. km Jhum lands. But all the tribes do not practise jhuming. In Arunachal Pradesh the Apatanis practise a scientific system of terrace cultivation. A section of Khasis also grow crops on the gentle slopes of the Khasi Hills embanked by earthen dykes. Similarly the Angami Nagas practise terrace cultivation with the help of skilfully engineered irrigation. The other hill tribes should also be encouraged to adopt such scientific system of terrace cultivation or efforts should be made to modify the existing jhum cultivation suitably in order to keep its adverse effects at minimum level.

Rice is the most distinctive and very important crop of the agricultural areas in North East India. The socio-economic welfare of the people of this region depends mostly on the success or failure of the rice crop. Despite the fact that a great variety of crops like rice, maize, pulses, rape and mustard etc. are grown, overwhelming emphasis is given on rice cultivation in the entire region. Rice covers about 68 per cent of the cropped area.

The output of agricultural products per unit of hectare or labour is quite low in the states of North East India in comparison with other states like Uttar Pradesh, Punjab, Haryana, Madhya Pradesh, West Bengal etc. At present, the agricultural products of the region could not meet the needs of her increasing population as the net area sown is only 14.6 per cent. It may be mentioned that the total foodgrain in North East India is less than its requirement and the yield per hectare is 10,344 kilogram. So the region has to import food grains about 1.5 million tons annually, huge quantity of animal proton and other consumer goods. The green revolution had started in India from the early 1970s but its impact was not felt in the region. The increasing pressure population requires expansion of agricultural land which can be made available either by decreasing the area under forest or by reducing the length of the fallow periods particularly in the hills. Both these phenomena are seen in the region. The rural work-force is also increasing with the rapid increase of population. In fact, the region is encountered with a serious threat for the fast growing labour force which cannot be employed in the present form of agricultural sector. For them new job opportunities may be created in non-farm sector.

The share of agriculture in the State Domestic Product is usually taken as an indicator of economic development. Generally developed economies are less dependent on agriculture. The economies of the states of North East India are underdeveloped and that is why the percentage share of agriculture in state domestic product is about 50 per cent. But in more developed states in India like Maharashtra it is only 16 per cent. In developed countries like U.K. and U.S.A. the national income derived from agriculture is only 3 per cent. Similarly the absolute number of people engaged in agriculture has been very high. For example, seven out of every ten persons in Arunachal Pradesh, Meghalaya, Nagaland and Mizoram depend on agriculture. Since the secondary and tertiary sectors of the economy are very poor to provide employment to the increasing working population causing thereby serious problem of unemployment, underemployment and disguised employment in all the seven states of the region. Thus agriculture is the dominant activity in the regional economy of North East India and about 8 million workers are directly engaged in agricultural works.

Type of Farming

Broadly speaking the type of farming in North East India may be grouped into three categories : (1) shifting hill cultivation, (2) sedentary peasant agriculture and (3) capitalist plantation agriculture.

1. **Shifting Hill Cultivation :** It is known as jhum cultivation in Assam hills and other hilly regions of North East India. Deciduous forests of the hill slopes are especially suited to this practice. Generally jhuming may initiate severe soil erosion. In some areas of the region jhuming is the only cultivation topographically possible. On abandoned jhum fields planting of rubber, coffee and other commercial trees are also seen. Instead of jhuming some tribes like Khasis, Angamis and Apatanis practise terrace cultivation which is more scientific. The terraces are generally irrigated by means of man made channels which distribute water over each step of terraces. Jhuming and terrace cultivation have been discussed earlier.

2. **Sedentary Peasant Agriculture :** This type is by far the most important and is the norm of India farming including the plains of Assam, Manipur, Tripura and in the small valleys

and lowlying areas of the hills. The agriculture of this type is mainly based on animal energy. It is associated with use of old worn-out implements including a pair of cattle. So it is bound to be less productive. This traditional method of agriculture may be replaced by modern agriculture based on inanimate energy i.e. machine and power. The sedentary peasant agriculture of the region suffers from low productivity, inadequacy of manure, absence of adequate irrigation facility and frequent flood. As in other parts of India agricultural operations begin with the arrival of the monsoons in the month of June. Two agricultural seasons are ***Kharif*** and ***Rabi***. The ***Kharif*** season begins with the onset of the monsoon and crops like rice, jute, maize etc. are grown in this season which are harvested in late autumn. ***Rabi*** crops like wheat, gram, rape and mustard etc. are sown after the rains and harvested in Spring.

3. Capitalist Plantation Agriculture : Plantations are mainly confined to tea with little coffee and rubber in North East India. Tea plantation was started by the Britishers by bringing labourers from the Chotanagpur Plateau region. Capital from multinational companies is frequently invested in the development of plantations. Tea is a plantation crop and it grows well in deep, fertile, well-drained soils. The plant requires a warm moist climate with an average rainfall of over 150 centimeters. Tea gardens are mostly confined to the Brahmaputra Valley, gently sloping hills of Assam and Tripura. The North East India contributes about 80 per cent of India's total output. Tea is the most important item of export and it is the second largest foreign exchange earner in India.

Major Crops and Their Distribution

The climate and ecological conditions are most congenial for the cultivation of varieties crops like rice, maize, pulses, oil seeds, wheat, millet, jute, cotton, sugar cane, rubber, coffee, tobacco, potatoes and several varies of fruits. Besides tea is grown extensively which is the most important plantation industry and needs separate treatment.

Rice : Rice is the leading and staple food crop of North East India. It occupies 3.4 million hectares of land in the region and production of rice amounted to 4.7 million tonnes in 1993-94. During this period the average yield per hectare was only 1396 kilogram against 1879 kg/ha in India.

Rice cultivation follows the rainfall lines and its producing area in the region coincides with the areas having rainfall of over 100 centimetres. It is dominant crop where rainfall exceeds 200 centimetres. The major rice-producing areas are the Brahmaputra Valley, Barak plain, Manipur basin and plains of Tripura, valley bottoms of the hills and jhum fields and terraces of the hill states.

The rice crop, as in other parts of India is grown either wet or irrigated crop or unirrigated crop in the low-lying areas. An upland variety is grown in the hilly areas under the usual method of jhuming. There are three varieties of rice grown in the plains of the region. They are autumn rice, winter rice and spring rice according to their harvesting season. The autumn rice is called Ahu in Assamese and is generally grown by the broadcast method. Winter rice or Aman (called Sali in Assamese) is grown by transplanting method. Under this method seeds are sown first on seed-beds in the months of May and June and transportation is done in the prepared wet fields in July and August. The Aman rice is harvested in November and December. A special variety of winter rice (called Bao in Assamese) is grown in the wet lands of Assam. This is sown in the months of March and April and is harvested in November and December. Spring or Boro rice is generally grown in the marshy areas during the dry season and is harvested in March-April.

Now a days the local varieties of rice have been replaced by high yielding varieties like ***Ranjit, Bahadur, Masare, Luit, Chilarai, IR-50, IR 36*** etc. The area under such varieties have been showing a gradual increase over the years.

Maize : Maize is a high yielding food crop. It is grown particularly in the hilly areas of the region and the hill states in the production of maize. Only small patches of land are devoted to maize cultivation in the plains of Assam, Manipur and Tripura and the larger areas are cultivated in the jhum fields. In 1958 the Ford Foundation Agricultural team visited India and advised the farmers to introduce new hybrid varieties. But in North East India only a section Naga farmers introduced hybrid varieties of maize in their fields. The area under maize was 10,700 ha and the production of maize was 1,28,400 tonnes in 1993-94.

Pulses : The pulses are of great importance in protein intakes and form the second important staple food after rice. The pulses include gram, arhar or tur, lentils ***(Masur)***, black gram ***(Matikalai)*** magu and peas. Pulses are grown almost all over the region as *Rabi* crops and Assam is the leading producer. The pulses are leguminous crops and are useful as cash crops on poor soils. About 1,48,000 hectares of land is under pulses which produce over 70,000 tonnes of pulse grains annually.

Oil Seeds : The major oilseeds, grown in this region are mustard and rape, sesamum, castor, linseed and groundnut cultivation of sun-flower and soyabean have also been introduced in the region in recent years. The area under different oilseeds is about 2,19,000 hectares and the annual production is about 3,00,000 tonnes. Assam is the leading producer of oilseeds and 90 per cent of the total area under different oilseeds in North East India is found in Assam alone. These are mostly ***rabi*** crops.

Wheat : About one-tenth of the cropped area in India is devoted to wheat and it is essentially a crop of North India. The crop requires fertile soil and cool and moist climate during the growing season followed by a warm dry climate at the time of ripening. The bulk of India's wheat is common breadwheat (Triticum Vulgare) which is typical of the alluvial soils of Northern India) This crop has been introduced in North East India after 1960s. But the area under wheat has not been increasing significantly and the wheat fields are mostly concentrated in Assam. The area devoted to wheat is about 93,000 ha and the annual production is about 1,26,000 tonnes.

Millet : Bajra and Jowar are the important crops belong to the millet family. These two crops are grown in the jhum fields of the hilly region of North East India. Bajra and Jowar are primarily the crops of fairly dry areas and poor soils. But in the hills of North East India millets grow well in areas with moderate temperature and moderate rainfall. The region has about 44,000 hectares under millet cultivation and produces about 35,200 tonnes annually.

Jute : Jute is cultivated for its fibre. It is a typical monsoon crop of Assam. Earlier jute was grown only for home comsumption. But after the inflow of peasant immigrants to the flood plains of the Brahmaputra valley, large-scale cultivation of jute started as a cash crop. After the partition of the country jute cultivation spread to other favourable areas of the region. Now this region produces about 9,41,000 bales of jute on 1,04,000 hectares of land.

Cotton : Cotton plant is raised from seed and it is aboriginal to India, grown and woven since time immemorial. It grows well in areas with temperature between 20°C and 35°C and moderate rainfall. The fibre plants thrives well in the drier parts of the black cotton soil zone of the Deccan Plateau. Ecological condition of North East India is not very suitable for cotton cultivation. However, some staple cotton is grown mainly in Garo Hills, North Cachar Hills and Karbi Anglong plateau. The region produced about 10,400 bales of cotton on 12,700 hectares of lands in 1993-94.

Sugarcane : India is the homeland of sugarcane and is the leading producer in the world. It grows well on fertile soil which requires high temperature and high rainfall. Except the areas of heavy rainfall and flood plains, sugarcane is cultivated in all the plains of North East India. But high concentration of sugarcane cultivated areas occur in the plains surrounding the Karbi Plateau. Earlier the crop was cultivated as a source of gur and malasses for domestic use and now the crop is grown for the production of sugar also. The region has 48,100 hectares under this crop.

Rubber : The rubber is a tropical plant which requires over 200 cm of rainfall for a long period, a constant humidity, high temperature and well drained soil. Such physical conditions are also available in North East India. Some wild rubber used to grow in several parts of the region in the past and Assam used to export a few tonnes rubber annually during the British period. In 1957 the Department of Soil Conservation again newly introduced rubber plantation in the abandoned jhum fields of Assam and since then rubber cultivation has been done in other states of North East India. Now the region produce over 1,200 tonnes of rubber annually on 34,000 hectares of land.

Coffee : Coffee was first cultivated on the foothills of Cachar in 1850 s which could not sustain due to some reasons. It has been reintroduced in 1954 and extended its cultivation to other states of North East India. It requires a rich, well-drained soil, a warm climate and moderate rainfall. Coffee cultivation is mainly confined to the depleted abandoned jhum fields. The total area under this crop is about 3500 hectares.

Tobacco : Tobacco is a winter crop which requires constant care and attention. It is grown all over the region. Earlier a small quantity of tobacco was grown for domestic use. Now Assam is the leading producer of tobacco. The total production of tobacco in the region is about 5,000 tonnes and the area devoted to it is about 7,900 hectares.

Potato : Like tobacco potato is also a winter crop. Most of the cultivable area of North East India is also suitable for growing potato. It grows well on the fertile sandy soils in the plains and red sandy soils with humus in the hills. The crop is not indigenous to India. It was introduced first in the Khasi Hills as early as 1830 and then its cultivation spread to other parts of Northeast India. Potato in not perishable like other vegetable and can be stored and exported. Therefore the increase of potato cultivation may reduce unemployment in the agricultural sector. In 1992-93 the region produced 6,88,900 tonnes of potatoes on 96,500 hectares of land.

Besides, several varieties, of banana, arecanut, betel vines, orange, coconut etc. are grown in different part of North East India. The annual production of banana is about 5,53,000 tonnes and that or areca nut is about 78,100 tonnes. These two products are also exported to other parts of India.

Tea : Tea means dried leaves and shoots from the evergreen shrub known as *Camelli sinesis*. There are two main types of teas : Indian tea which is allowed to ferment and China or green tea, which is only partially fermented. The wetter Bhutan Himalayan and Arunachal Himalayan slopes and their piedmont fans and old alluvial uplands offer ideal conditions for tea. When the East India Company began planting tea shrubs with Chinese seeds in 1834, a wild variety was found in the Assam Hills. At that time tea tree was mainly used as timber for door posts because of its strength and durability. The singphos also used to drink tea by using wild leaves.

Tea plantation in India has a colonial origin. A group of British planters formed a company at Nazira in 1840 for commercial plantation of tea at a large scale. In 1859 a second important tea company named Jorhat Tea Company was formed and to encourage tea plantations in Assam, the Government made some provisions for the settlement of waste land for tea cultivation. At that time the planters faced difficulties is securing labour force since local labourers were not available. The planters had to bring labourers from other parts of India (mainly from Chotanagpur plateau) in large number to cope with the expansion of tea plantation in Assam. By 1856, the plantation was started in Barrahagun, near Hailakandi and then it was extended to Tripura.

Tea cultivation may be placed both under agriculture as well as industry. Tea plantation is an industry because it is a processed and manufactural commodity, subject to excise duty. It is governed by both agricultural and industrial rules and regulations. Tea plantation is one of the oldest industries in Assam. It is labour intensive and an important cash crop of Assam. Covering the largest area of 2,30,978 hectares under estate farming 856 tea gardens of Assam, produce huge quantity of tea i.e. 461 million kilograms by employing quite large number of labourers. But the consistency of Assam tea has been declining in the world market due to growing competitive altitude amongst the tea growing countries of the world. The volume of tea sold through Tea Action Centre at Guwahati was 12.6 million kilograms in 2000-2001 against 145.1 million kilograms sold in 1999 accounting a fall of 15.5 per cent in sales.

Landuse : It means classification of land according to the use to which it is put. The primary division of the land in India as estimated by Surveyor-General in 1958-59 is shown in the following table (Table - 10.1).

Table - 10.1

Area	In Million hectares	Per cent
Forest	52.7	16.1
Not available for Cultivation	46.4	14.1
Permanent Pasture and Grazing	13.1	4.0
Misc-tree crop and groves	5.7	1.75
Culturable waste	20.6	6.3
Fallow, other than current fallow	12.3	3.75
Current follows	11.9	3.65
Net area sown	131.2	40.2

Due to exploding population the pattern of landuse as shown in the table - 10.1 has now been changed. The man-land ration in India now one of the lowest in the world which is about 0.41 hectare per capita. Similarly the per capita availability of forest land in India has been dwindled from 0.09 ha (1981) to 0.08 ha (1995). This is an alarming situation for the whole nation and so efforts are to be made to formulate effective landuse plans for different regions of the country.

Forest areas are generally protected, managed and controlled by the Forest Department of the Government. Lands not available for cultivation are the area covered by homesteads, roads, towns, villages, rivers, ponds etc. The areas fallow, other than current fallow prior to 1947 was termed 'cultivable waste other than current fallows'. About 8 million hectare of land were recorded under this head for Assam in 1946-47. Naturally it was misunderstood by the outsiders who thought large areas of cultivable land were lying waste in Assam. This notion was not correct and the fact is, due to high growth of population after independence and the consequent increase in demand, causes stress on land resources of this part of India. It is observed that the growing pressure of population requires expansion of the cultivated land either by decreasing forest land or by reducing the length of fallow period in jhuming. Both the phenomena are seen in North East India. The general land use pattern of the region for the years 1995-96 and 1998-99 are presented in table - 10.2

The table - 10.2 reveals that there exists difference between total cultivated land and total cultivable area which indicate scope for further expansion of agriculture in North East India. The states like Assam, Meghalaya, Mizoram and Nagaland appear to have enough scope for expansion of agriculture, whereas in other states, such as Arunachal Pradesh, Manipur and Tripura scope is marginal.

The economic structure of the states of North East India is dominated by agriculture and allied activities. But the land under cultivation in the region in only 16 per cent of its total geographical area. It varies from 2.5 per cent in Arunachal Pradesh to 7.2 per cent in Manipur, 9.4 per cent in Meghalaya, 4 per cent in Mizoram, 15 per cent in Nagaland, 36 per cent in Tripura and 45 per cent in Assam. The shifting cultivation is the common mode of agriculture in the hilly areas. It is practised by about 4,44,400 families over an area of 3,900 sq. km. This method of cultivation has given rise to problems of landslide and erosion, deforestation, loss of fertility of the soil etc. Flood, bank erosion and drought in certain areas are the main hurdles to the development of agriculture in the plains. Besides there is little crop diversification in the states of North East India. About 76 per cent of cultivated area is under food grains, 5 per cent under oil seeds and 3

Table - 10.2
Land Use Characteristics

States	Reporting area in 000 ha 1995-96	Forest 000 ha 1995-96	Total Cultivated area, '000 ha 1995-96	Total Cultivable area, '000 ha 1995-96	Percentage share of rice to total cropped area 1995-96	Average size of operational holdings, ha 1990-91	Yield of Rice kg/ha 1998-99
Arunachal Pradesh	5495	5154	213	293	48.9	3.72	988
Assam	7850	2012	2854	3229	63.6	1.27	1345
Manipur	2211	602	140	164	84.6	1.23	2290
Meghalaya	2241	937	272	1074	42.1	1.77	1420
Mizoram	2088	1598	109	445	59.6	1.38	1649
Nagaland	1546	863	325	626	61.4	6.82	1445
Tripura	1049	606	281	340	54.2	0.97	1939
India	**299875**	**68479**	**156024**	**183626**	**23.0**	**1.55**	**1926**

Source : Indian Agriculture in Brief, 2000, Ministry of Agriculture, Govt. of India.

per cent under fibre crops. The food grain situation in the region is nor good. According to ICAR estimates the requirement of foodgrain in the year 2000-2001 was 7,940 million tonnes while its production for the same year was only 6,346 million tonnes. Various institutions like Assam Agricultural University of Jorhat, Fishery College at Raha, Veterinary College in Mizoram, Home Science College in Tura, Horticulture College in Arunachal Pradesh etc. are coming up which should strength the agricultural infrastructure in the region. Perhaps the transfer of technology has emerged the biggest contraint in increasing agricultural productivity of the entire region. All these show the need of scientific land management for extension of agriculture in the region.

Agricultural Development

Throughout the post-independence period till today agriculture has been the mainstay of the regional economy and has provided a livelihood to the 85 per cent of the population of North East India. The percentage of agricultural workers among the main workers is higher than the national average. But the agricultural productivity in the region is much lower than national average. So the developemnt of agriculture in all states of the region is very important to strengthen economy of North East India.

During the first three plan periods, the increase in net sown area had been an important factor for an increase in the area of crops. generally the net sown area has been increased by reclaiming culturable waste lands. The scope for further increase in the cropped area lies mostly in improvements in cropping intensity. The factors which contributed to improvement in cropping are irrigation, fertilisers, appropriate crop rotations, selective mechanisation and short maturity crop varieties.

Irrigation : The artificial application of water to the land in order to grow crops or the improve yield of crops is known as irrigation. Water for irrigation comes from two main sources, namely surface water and ground water. Surface water is supplied by the rivers, lakes, ponds etc. Ground water is generally derived from rain water that has percolated down or from water that was trapped within the rock during its formation. Like other parts of Monsoon lands, Monsoons are very erratic in North East India and failure of rains plays havoc with unirrigated areas. Irrigation is important for higher and stable yields.

Table - 10.3
Surface and Ground Water Potential

State	Surface Potential mm³	Ground Water Potential mm³	Irrigation '00ha Major	Potential Minor
Arunachal Pradesh	366000	787	Not Estimated	266
Assam	558776	14820	970	1700
Manipur	19794	44	135	105
Meghalaya	67216	357	20	100
Mizoram	31291	not-estimated	not-estimated	80
Nagaland	14090	neligible	10	80
Tripura	7616	588	100	115

Source : Basic Statistic of North Eastern Region, 1995.

The Brahmaputra river basin and the Barak river basin cover about 86 per cent of the geographical area of North East India. The river basins are geologically and hydrologically unstable and only 10 per cent of the annual flow is economically harnessable. The whole region is very much prone to earthquakes of high intensities. All these phenomena make the region unfavourable for construction of large dams for the purpose of irrigation. The water potential of all the seven states of the region is presented on table - 10.3 and accordingly Assam has the highest surface water potential of 558,776 mm^3 while Tripura has the lowest surface water potential of 7,616 mm^3. Similarly the total ground water and surface water potential of North East India is 16.6 mm^3 and 1064.7 mm^3 respectively.

In North East India only 8.1 lakh hectares or 22.50 per cent of the total agricultural land is under irrigation which is less than the national norm of 25.55 per cent. Manipur has 46.4 per cent of its total agricultural area under irrigation, followed by Nagaland (40.5%), Meghalaya (25.9%), Arunachal Pradesh (21.4%), Assam (21.2%), Mizoram (12.3%) and Tripura (12%). Since 72 per cent of the area of North India is hilly, the development of major and medium irrigation projects is not economically viable. So various strategies like ground water extraction, creation of surface storage, water conservation tanks etc. should be undertaken for irrigation.

Fertilisers : The Indian farmers have been using cow dung, compost and other organic manures to restore soil nutrients since time immemorial. Fertilisers are the main input in increasing agricultural productivity. But the consumption of fertiliser in India is only 47 kg per hectare against 400 kg in Japan. In North East India the use fertiliser is very insignificant, only 2.5 kg per hectare. The rapid growth of population in the region has necessitated more supply of food and other products. All these call for an increase in the cropped area vertically through multiple cropping, rotation of crops as well as higher yields per hectare. All such agricultural development are facilitated by the use of fertilisers.

Tools and Seeds : Deep and perfect tilling of agricultural lands cannot be done by traditional methods and implements. Many new implements could much be improved and some new one like seed-drills, cheap threshing and winnowing appliances, better water-lifts, efficient can-crushers and oil-expellers are desirable. The use of tractors in a very limited scale has been introduced. These are beyond the means of most individual farmers, but can be made available by co-operatives. Selective mechanisation does the farming activities by reducing the time taken in harvesting, preparing the field for the next crop including sowing the planting of crops.

At present Indian agricultural scientists have made it possible to evolve varieties with a shorter maturity period, thus facilitating multiple cropping. The technological break through achieved by introduction of fertiliser-responsive high-yielding varieties since the mid-sixties. This forms a major element in the strategy of agricultural development. Recently some farmers of North East India have started using high yielding varieties of seeds for raising a few crops. The productivity of some important crops like winter and summer rice in the region showed encouraging results during 2000-2001 due to the intoduction of high yielding varieties of rice. For example the total area under HYV of rice which stood at 12.01 lakh hectares during 1996-97 has increased to about 14.50 lakh hectares during 2000-2001.

Animal Husbandry : The programme for the development of agriculture implies the improvement of animal husbandry which is badly managed. In India bullock is more important than cow and there are about five bullock to every four cows. The essential equipment of the Indian farmers are a pair of bullocks or buffaloes to do ploughing and the draw the cart and cows are reared secondarily to give milk. In North East India, particularly in Assam, each family has about three heads of cattle. But the quality of cattle is very bad. The yield of milk per cow per day is very poor. Similarly the local bulls are very week to drag iron ploughs. Nothing much was done for the improvement of animal husbandry earlier. Artificial insemination programme may possible help the success of livestock farming in the region. Recently the North Eastern Council has set up a number of cattle breeding centres for producing hybrid and pure bulls in the region. Besides, pigs, goats and poultry are reared by some tribals and non-tribal people of the region. Now various schemes have also been introduced to develop modern piggery, sheep farm and poultry farm by the all the state governments and some autonomouns bodies of the region. The fish production of the region is very poor. It is estimated that the region needs about 500,000 tonnes of fish annually, but the entire region could produce hardly 1,00,000 k tonnes a year. But the region, especially Assam, Tripura and Manipur have numerous water bodies to rear fishes, catering the demand of local markets. So efforts may be made to develop fisheries in the water bodies of the region.

11

Industry

In a narrow sense the term industry is confined to the production of goods i.e. manufacturing industry. In a wider sense the same term is used to describe the service industries, banking, transport as well as mining activities. Similarly the term industrialization is used to designate the growth of manufacturing industry. Generally agriculture, mining and services are excluded from it.

Industrialization has always been recognized as a major tool for economic development of a region. It is the principal component of the Secondary Sector and its main function is to provide work for the growing population to satisfy the demand for manufactured goods and to raise the standard of living by the per capital income of the region. Industry is responsible for converting raw materials into finished goods which is turn encourage the development of tertiary sector, like marketing, transport and servicing etc. The transfer of persons engaged in the primary sector to secondary and tertiary sectors are generally visualized as social changes brought about by industrialization.

India has been experiencing the acute problems of industrial development since long. In fact, there was no industrial policy of the government in the pre-independence period. An industrial policy was first announced by the Government of India only in 1948. Accordingly the Government was responsible for the planned development of industries their regulations.

Under the policy the industries were divided into four categories, namely (i) defence and strategic industries were to be the exclusive monopoly of The Central Government

(ii) basic and key industries were to remain with private undertaking (iii) twenty important industries including heavy machinery, machine tools, electrical engineering, automobiles etc. were to be in the private sector but subject to Government control and regulation and (iv) residual industries were to be run by private enterprise. This industrial policy was revised in 1956. Under this policy the industries were listed in either Schedule A (Central Government Owned) or is in Schedule B (State owned) and other industries which were not listed in Schedule A and B were left to the private sector. There were important restatements of industrial policy in 1970, 1977 and 1980 which to an extent modified the Industrial Policy statement of 1956. The Eighth Five Year Plan (1992-97) with a size of Rs. 7,98,000 crores was launched on 1 April 1992. The plan targeted a lower growth of 7.5 per cent in industrial production as against 8.5 per cent achived in the Seventh Five Year Plan period. But the Eighth Plan stressed in achieving efficiency of production by relaxing the industrial policy framework. The Ninth Plan (1997-02) targeted an annual Gross Domestic Product (GDP) growth of 6.5 percent on the base of 3.9 per cent growth in agriculture, 8 per cent in industry and 6.8 per cent in services. But agriculture recorded negative growth in three out of five years while the performance of manufacturing was far below the target. The loss of such growth momentum in India may be partly attributed to the declaration in the global economy in 2001.

The current strides in the direction of a liberal industrial policy need to be viewed against the backdrop of the recent changes in the global economic and political order. The industrial policy of the government is now imbued with a spirit of liberation and openness which the business and industrial community welcome. The government has liberalized many of statutory hurdles to facilitate the flow of foreign and indigenous capital to industry.

The North-East India is generously blessed by nature with its huge resources. The drainage area of the Brahmaputra basin is 194413 km^2 with an annual run off 537240 Mm^3 and that of the Barak basin and other are 78150 Km^2 and 59800

Mm^3 respectively. The total area covered by other water features like lakes, reservoirs and tanks are 91256, 51609 and 40706 hectares respectively. The total groundwater of the region is about 17 Mm^3 and in most cases it is contaminated with high concentration of iron, dissolved acides, toxic substances etc. Supply of such quality water to various consumers like Public Health, Agriculture and Industry requires scientific treatment for better uses.

Natural vegetation and forests are called 'green gold'. These resources contribute to the regional and national economy and also ameliorate the regional climate and maintain ecological balance (Ref. Chapter 5). The forests of the region are rich in timber, cane, bamboo, agar wood and medicinal plants and provide habitats for various types of birds, reptiles, herbivorous animals and their predators. These forests and animals of North-East India may prove to be very good attraction for the tourists and there are very good prospects to develop forest based industries including tourist industry in the region.

The region is blessed with excellent soil condition of difference types and a variety of crops like rice, wheat, maize, sugarcane, jute cotton and fruits such as pineapples, oranges, lime, banana etc. are grown on different soil types of the region. The chief plantation crops grown in the region are tea, coffee and rubber. The area under tea plantation is about 236475 hectares, coffee 44000 hectares and rubber 36080 hectares.

The work participation rate in Assam was 36.37 per cent, Arunachal Pradesh 47.46, Manipur 41.51, Meghalaya 43.06, Nagaland 44.20, Mizoram 49.36 and Tripura 31.36 per cent according to 1991 census and the national average was 37.64 per cent. Besides the rate of literacy is comparatively higher ranging from 54.74 to 88.49 per cent (2001 census) with a large number of educated men and women in all the states of North-East India. In spite of these advantages, the region is depending on foodgrains, pulses, mustard, oil, sugar, other products like fish, eggs, building materials like cement, steel and hardwares, electrical goods and other items of daily consumption. Thus North-East India is yet to experience economic development on a scale achieved by many other states of India.

Constraints of Industrial Development

The process of production in North-East India is still for self consumption and not for market sale. For example, agriculture and allied sectors are still based on traditional techniques. The major industries like petroleum refineries, coal, fertilizers, cement, paper mill etc. established in this region have not generated employment for the local people. The region has only 1.8 per cent of the registered factories providing employment only 1.7 per cent of the factory employees of the country. Except tea and petroleum industries which started and organized by Britishers in Assam, not much progress has yet been achieved in the industrialization of India's North-East. The whole region is still industrially backward while other Indian states having the same industries conditions have gone ahead.

The region which covers 7.76 per cent of the geographic territory of India has 12.98 per cent of the National Highways of the country. The distribution of railway per 100 square meters in Assam, Tripura and Nagaland are 3 km, 0.12 km and 0.08 km respectively which is quite inadequate and it is non-existent in Meghalaya, Arunachal Pradesh, Mizoram and Manipur. Power is the most important factor to start any industrial venture. The region has abundant hydel power potential, but only 0.03 per cent of the total potential hydel power is being utilized in the states of North-East India. It may be noted that the partition of India in 1947 virtually cut-off the whole North-East India from the rest of the country which made the region completely isolated from the mainstream economy. Because of partition North-East India has its 90 per cent of border with international countries like Bhutan, China, Myanmar and Bangladesh. It is only connected with the mainland by a narrow corridor of foothill land (chicken's neck) of northern part of West Bengal.

Thus the vast market of the then East Pakistan (Bangladesh) which was earlier open was made close after the partition of the country. The whole North-East India suffered a set back due to its forced socio-economic and political isolation thrust upon it. The economy of a country or a region should be an open economy for industrialization, but unfortunately this isolation stands on the way of industrialization of North East India. In recent years international borders are losing their rigidity and this region is also witnessing the emergence of a free market scenario and globalisation of economic zones. The recent development of Guwahati as International Airport, establishment of Customs clearance, export-import, banking and other infrastructural facilities would definitely go a long way in economic development of the region and its neighbouring countries like Bhutan, China, Myanmar and other Southeast Asian Countries and Bangladesh.

Besides the difficulty of transport and consequence lack of marketing facilities, inadequate finances, low level of local entrepreneurship and orthodox attitude towards industrial development are the greatest hurdle to the industrialization of the region. The local entrepreneurs of North-East India are not familiar with complex banking procedures. So they have not been able to take full advantage of the presence of various financial institutions and banks like **IDBI, SIDBI, IFCI, ICICI, UTI, LIC, GIC** etc. So an institution with special knowledge of the region and dedicated exclusively to its requirement is felt necessary. Besides industrialization also depends on the qualities of the people, their ability and desire to learn and apply better methods of production to their enterprise and the removal of all intuitional obstruction including red tape.

Present Status of Industries

The fineness and artistic skills of a wide variety of industrial products of ancient Assam including Manipur earned universal acclamation. Handloom products like Muga Mekhela and Riha, beautifully decorated blouse pieces, Eri

Chadar, fabrics prepared out of mulberry silk, working in metal, ivory, wood, leather, clay, cane, bamboo etc. were flourished in ancient Assam. During the Ahom period these industrial products reached a high degree of perfection. But during the British period the indigenous industries faced stiff competition from the mill made cheap goods, imported from outside and quickened. The decay of many cottage industries and brought others to a point of extinction. But these traditional industries were so deeply rooted in the substratum of the Assamese life which could save some cottage industries from the total annihilation. Weaving still continues to be an important occupation, especially of the women of the region.

As mentioned above handloom weaving is still very important in this region and there are about 1.3 million handlooms and about 1.5 million weavers in North-East India. The total production of these looms is about Rs. 1060 million which accounts for 6 per cent of the national output. Raw materials required for this industry are cotton, muga (golden silk), pat (pure silk) and eri (endi) and generally the cotton yarn and the greater part of the silk yarn are purchased from the markets. All the varieties of silk worms, namely endi, muga and pat mainly reared in Assam and partly in Tripura, Meghalaya, Nagaland, Manipur and Mizoram.

Several weaving training centers have been at different central places of the region. Sualkuchi and Raha in Assam are the most important centers of handloom industry for both cotton and silk and an excellent research centre has also been established by the government at Titabar.

There are about 5000 handicraft units engaging about 40,000 craftsmen. The main items of handicrafts are bamboo and cane baskets, cane furnitures, mats, wood-carving, terracotta, dolls, toys, gold smithy, brass work, ivory work, bell-metal work, coir industry, soap, fruit canning etc. There are 22 industrial estates in North-East India and they are distributed 12 in Assam, 5 in Tripura, 2 in Meghalaya and 1 each in Arunachal Pradesh, Nagaland and Manipur.

Most of the large and medium industries belong to agro-based, forest-based, mineral-based, chemical and engineering industry. The major agro-based industries are cotton ginning and hosiery mills, a spun-silk mill, a jute mill, few khandsari and sugar mills, a vegetable oil pressing mill, a few food processing several rice mills etc. The forest based industries include plywood industry, few match factories, 4 medium paper mills, and extraction of agar essence etc. Petroleum and natural gas, coal, limestone and sillimanite are important minerals in the region. Oil refineries, petrochemicals, cement factories and a few fertilizer plants have been set up in the region. The chemical industries include plastic industry, a few drug manufacturing units, carbon blocks and carbon powder manufacturing units.

Engineering industry includes a few workshops to repair machines of tea factories and train engines, a few iron rerolling mill and a few factories for production of Hume pipes etc. There are 166 large and medium scale industrial units in the region of which 118 are located in Assam 17 in Arunachal Pradesh, 16 in Nagaland, 7 in Meghalaya, 6 in Manipur and 1 each in Mizoram and Tripura. The condition of Mizoram and Tripura is very bad. In fact the growth of industries in the entire region is very discouraging.

Conclusion

The above discussion has given an idea about the industrial policy of the government of India, bases of industries, constraints to industrial development and the present status of industries in North-East India. The entire region is endowed by nature with abundant resources, but is still economically a backward region. The whole region is characterized by poverty, untapped resources and under utilized man power. The new industrial policy has so far failed to have any impact in the region and the region's efforts towards industrialization has not yet met with any outstanding planners. It is very difficult to adopt the pattern of industrialization in North-East India as found in rich and developed countries. So the main thrust of the development strategy for a poor region like North-East India should therefore be to establish small and middle size industrial units in selected sites in rural and semi-urban areas. Such industries can be established without separate building for factory, a large group of hired labour and costly sophisticated machinery. The majority of population in the region live in villages and over 70 per cent of the population dependes on their livelihood on agriculture and allied section. So the development of the industrial sector should be related to agriculture and allied activities. The food processing industry has a bright future in the whole of North-East India. Similarly the tea packaging may get a boost if the railway networks container services reach the region. There is a very important need for creating better transport and communication facilities for attracting investment by entrepreneurs in the States of North-East India. Now-a-days people of a particular region or a country are regarded as the basic resources for development and prime mover of economy. Thus training is an important component of human resource development strategy and such strategy should be oriented to the application of science and technology for improvement of job oriented courses in some institutes in North-East India. The industrial development strategy of the whole region lies on mutual understanding of different states. So the economy of the region should be treated as a single economy with free inter-state flow of commodities. This approach is essentially conceived as a special means to achieve peaceful socio-economic changes.

12

Transport and Communication

Till lately, there was no modern means of transport and communication in Assam or any part of North-East India. In early days people travelled on foot, or on horse back or elephant back or on bullock carts, and the mails were carried by runners. During the medieval period, the Koches and Ahoms built a number of roads in the Brahmaputra valley. Because of rugged terrain and wet climate road building was a difficult task. Roads became impassable during the rainy season. So most of the travellers chose the more convenient river routes. Boats were the important vehicles for the common man and rivers served as roads and highways in the plains of North-East India. Tame elephants were owned mainly by the upper classes for travel by land. The Brahmaputra served as the main artery in the communication system of the Brahmaputra valley. Large number of boats were sailing regularly in this river. The royal boats were numerous and even in so wide a river as the Brahmaputra regulation of boat traffic was found necessary to prevent collisions between royal boats and those of fishermen.[1] The river merchants or Saudagars of Assam used the river Brahmaputra and the Meghna as their trading routes. The Bay of Bengal was accessible through these two important rivers. The link between Assam and Bengal was maintained by water.

In 1837 John M. Cosh in Topography of Assam wrote that there were three overland routes namely Murshadabad-

---

1. P.C. Choudhury, "The History of Civilisation of the People of Assam to the Twelth Century A.D.", *Guwahati : Dept. of Historical and Aniquarian Studies in Assam,* 1959, p. 379.

Mauldah, Dinagepore-Rangpore-Bauugwah and Goalpara and there by the Brahmaputra, Dacca-Dumary-Puculoe-Jamalpore-Singymary and Goalpara and Sylhet-Chirra-Moplung-Nunklow-Ranneygodown-Cannymook and Guwahati.

Along the frontier of Bhutan and Assam there were as many seven dwars to interact the people of Assam with

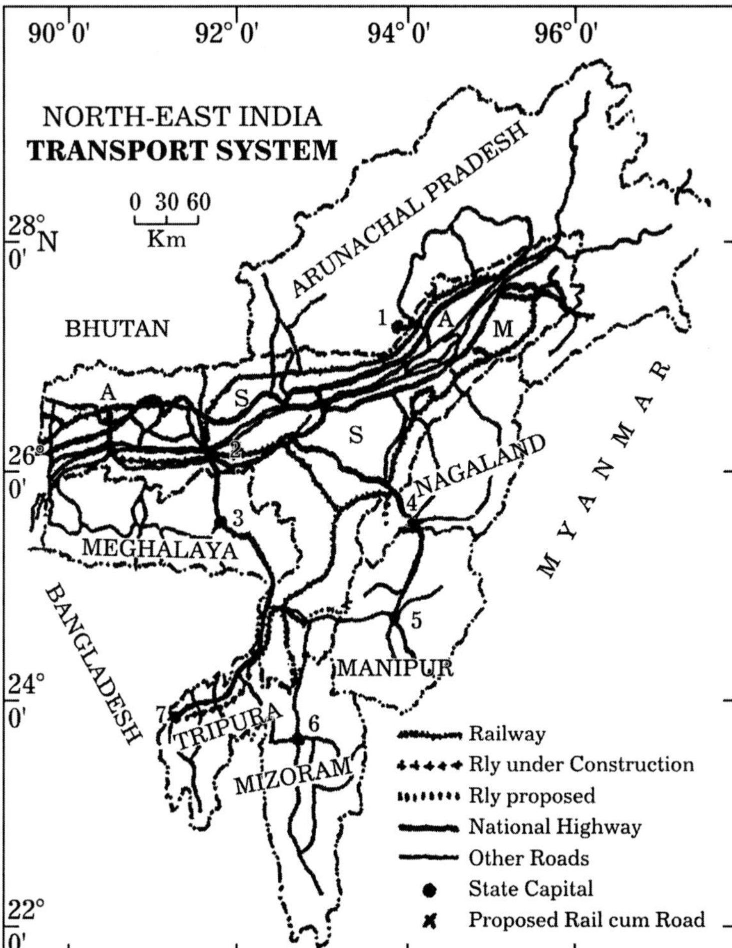

Fig. 10 : Transport System
1. Itanagar, 2. Guwahati, 3. Shillong, 4. Kohima, 5. Imphal, 6. Aizawl, 7. Agartala

Bhutanise. The important dwars were Bijni, Chappkhamar, Chappaguri, Banska, Ghaukolla, Kalling and Booreeguma. Besides, there were others Dwar's like Kerkaria, Kuriapera Dwar etc. towards east in the district of Darrang. These Dwars or mountain passes were connected by some land routes. Trades between Assam and Bhutan including Tibet took place through these Dwars. Rice, Tussa cloth (a kind of coarse silk cloth, manufactured by the Native Women in Assam) iron, lac, skin, buffalo horns were exported from Assam region. The imports from Bhutan and Tibet were Yak-tails, ponies, musk, gold-dust, blankets, knives, salt, chowries etc. Markets were held at above mentioned dwars and transactions continued for about three months. Chouna, Geogunshur, Udalgiri, Doimara, Daranga etc. were the important markets on the border of Assam. During the Ahom period, some officers called duaries were appointed by the Ahom Rulers for the management of the dwars. The Bhahmaputra valley was linked up with Myanmar through Manipur by land routes. An open road ran from upper Assam into Myanmar and thence to China. Sadiya town of the Brahmaputra valley was connected with Yunan by a 'silk route' and the Stilwell Road from Assam to Myanmar built by the British in the early part of the last century traces the path of the ancient silk route. During the reign of Koch king Naranarayan an important road was constructed connecting Coch Behar (West Bengal) with Narayanpur (Lakhimpur District, Assam) under the supervision of the king's brother. Gohain Kamala and was completed in 1547 A.D. This great road which still exists partly in known as the Gohain Kamala Ali. Several such Raj-Ali's or raised roads were also constructed by the different Assam Rajas in the Brahmaputra valley.

Waterways

In the past the Brahmaputra river served as the main artery in the communication system of the greater part of the region when roads and railways were not developed. In 1848, government steamers were deputed to ply between Calcutta (Kolkata) and Guwahati. The Indian General Steam

Navigation Company entered into a contract in 1860 to run a pair of vessels every six weeks provided the government boats were withdrawn from the line. At that time Guwahati received directly all the merchandise from outside the region. The raw materials flowing from all parts of North-East India also found a direct route through Guwahati to other industrial and commercial places of India. For this the Brahmaputra served as the main through fare, furnishing cheapest transportation. Jute grains, mustard oil and coal etc. were at first carried by trucks or by goods train and then these were sent to Kolkata by steamers while other consumer goods and heavy commodities which entered Assam and North-East India were carried from Kolkata to Guwahati also by steamers. This transportation system has been affected by partition of India after Independence because the downstream part of the Brahmaputra was included in the then East Pakistan (Bangadesh). However Guwahati still acts as an important river port for intra-state movement of goods. The inland steamer service connecting Assam with other parts of India was closed down in 1965 due to Indo-Pak hostilities. The earthquake of 1950 caused some geotectomic changes of the river Brahmaputra affecting the navigable channel in the upper reaches which resulted closure of river services by the Joint Steamer Companies from 1954 onwards. The construction of the Saraighat bridge across the Brahmaputra at Pandu in 1962 improved the overland road and railway transport system of the region affecting the water transport. For all these the River Steam Navigation Company went into liquidation and the Government of India set up the Central Inland Water Transport Corporation Limited in its place. The Government of Assam also set up a Directorate of Inland Water Transport under the Transport Department in 1959 to look after the development of waterways ferries and for training of inland water transport personnel. The Central Inland Water Transport Corporation and Inland Water Transport Directorate introduced steamer and ferry services at a number of places on commercial basis. Important ferry ghats along the Brahmaputra are Sadiya-Saikhowaghat, Dibrugarh-Sonarighat, Dihingmukh-

Sassikalghat, Nemati-Kamalabari, Tezpur-Silghat, Guwahati-North Guwahati, Dhubri-Fakirganj etc. and these ghats are seen to engage in transporting the passengers and local goods from one bank to the other bank of the river. Besides, the river Brahmaputra has several river ports like Dibrugarh, Disangmukh, Nemati, Silghat, Guwahati, Goalpara, Dhubri, Biswanath and Silghat etc. Similarly the important river ports of the Barak river are Karimganj, Badarpur and Silchar. Small country boats are generally used for navigational purpose in other states of the region at a limited scale.

Railways

Railways occupy a pride place in the Indian transport system and the first train ran between Mumbai and Thane in 1853. The total railway route of the country was 63028 km in 2001. The railway communication commenced in the region in 1880 and the first railway line was the Dibru-Sadiya line. It was constructed during 1882-1884 connecting the tea, timber, coal and oil producing areas of upper Assam with the river port of Dibrugarh. Then Jorhat Provisional Railway Line was constructed connecting the tea producing areas of Jorhat region with Kokilamukh steamer ghat in 1885. In 1895 Tezpur-Balipara narrow gauge line was constructed by a private company to afford an outlet to tea manufactured areas of the north bank of the river Brahmaputra through the river port at Tezpur. These railway lines were constructed to serve the needs of the local tea industry in their respective tea growing areas.

In 1897 Guwahati was connected with Jamunamukh of Nagaon district by a railway line and this extended upto Lumding after three years. The whole railway line was completed in 1903. It was one of the costliest and most difficult railway enterprise that had ever been undertaken in India. Several people had to lay down their lives during the construction of the railway line in thick forest areas. Then the railway communication from Chittagong to Old Cachar district of Assam was established during 1897-1904.

Before partition Assam was connected with the rest of India by the Bengal Assam Railway. The Eastern Bengal railway line from Kolkata was extended upto Dhubri in 1902 and then to Amingaon in 1910. In 1911 another railway line was constructed from Rangia to Tangla and then it extended to Balipara in 1932. After 1933 there was no extension of railway lines in Assam region till the partition of India. After independence due to creation of Pakistan the major portion of the Assam-Bengal Railway went over to the then East Pakistan (Bangladesh). Owing to this, there ceased to be any direct rail-link between Assam and the rest of India. As Assam is a frontier state and one of the richest natural regions of India, commercial, strategies and political considerations rendered the establishment of rail-link between Assam with the rest of India. So a direct link of Assam with the rest of India was constructed running through 19 km gap between Nepal and Bhutan in the north and Bangladesh in the south. This line of direct link with a length of 228 km (metre gauge) was begun in January, 1948 and opened several months ahead of schedule in January 1950.

After creation of railway zone, the Assam part of former Northeastern railway came into the zone of North-East Frontier Railways with headquarters at Maligaon (Guwahati). This zone came into existence on 15th January, 1958 by spreading a portion of Northeastern railway. The Northeast Frontier Railways include the northern part of West Bengal as well as the northeastern part of Bihar. The expansion and improvement of the existing railway lines including conversion of meter gauge to broad gauge have been taking place since the creation of the zone of Northeast Frontier Railway (1958). The Saraighat rail cum road bridge was constructed during 1958-1962 and then the north bank railway line from Balipara to Murkongselek (Dhemaji District) was extended and opened in 1966. A 310 km long broad gauge line was constructed from New Jalpaiguri to Jogighopa in 1965 and another broadguage line was completed from Pancharatna to Kamakhya on the south bank of the Brahmaputra river. In 1997 the broad gauge routes covered 960.76 km and the metregauge 1564.25 km accounting a total railway length of about 2525 km in North East India. The length of railways per 100 sq.km. in Assam, Tripura and Nagaland are 3 km, 0.12 km and 0.08 km respectively which is very low and the region is very poorly served by the railways.

Roadways

The advent of road transport in modern sense in North East India, as elsewhere in the country has developed during the British period. The Britishers with their rather different motive of reorienting the economy of this region brought a great change in pattern and trend of transport development. In 1866 the project of making a connected trunk road through the province of Assam had been started. By the end of 1873 about one-fourth of the road i.e. 154 km from Agia through Guwahati to Kalong river was completed. The road was begun with the design of a first class metalled road of 7.32 metres top width. Some old roads had however, been improved during this period. The principal lines of roads constructed by Britishers which provided direct route between important centers were the south trunk road from Goalpara to Saikhowaghat, Guwahati-Shillong Road, Amingaon-Hajo Road, North Guwahati-Barpeta Road, North Guwahati-Tezpur Road, Dimapur-Kohima-Imphal Road with its extension to Tamu (on Indo-Myanmar border) and Makum-Leshapani Road connecting Stilwell Road to China.

The Public Works Department was established as early as 1868, but roads were the concern of the Deputy Commissioner assisted by a committee. In 1882 such committies were replaced by Sub-divisional Local Boards which were entrusted with the maintenance of all roads excluding a few main lines within their jurisdiction. In 1890 provincial roads and ferries were taken over by the Public Works Department. The introduction of railways resulted in negligence for the development of road systems in the region. Under the Government of India act, 1919 road communication became purely a provincial subject and the government of India remained concerned with roads of strategic importance. A Road Board was constituted for Assam in 1926-27 and since then the construction of roads made some headway. During this period a separate board was constituted for the adminstration of the Tea Cess Fund for improvement of roads. Roads were classified into metalled, graveled and unsurfaced and adoption of mechanical means of construction was proposed. It may be noted that there was considerable increase in motor transport just after the World War I and public started demanding more and better roads. At the time of independence in 1947 the then Assam (which included Mizoram, Meghalaya and Nagaland) had only 6284 km of road, out of which only 1977 km were all weather black topped roads. The road development of this region has been very slow because of the difficult hilly geologically unstable terrain interspersed with a large number of river and tributaries.

All motor services in Assam and other states were privately run on purchase of licences from the governments till 1948. But such services provided by the private parties were very irregular and unsatisfactory. In order to improve travelling facilities the policy of nationalisation was introduced in Assam by 1948 under the Road Transport Nationalization Act, 1948. Gradually this policy of nationalization has been introduced in other states of the region by 1970's. Then the State Transport organization was converted into a corporation, named the Assam State Road Transport Corporation on August 31, 1971 and the same has been extended to other states of the region. Besides corporation buses there are privately owned public buses which ply between various important places of the region.

The Central Government is responsible for the development of and maintenance of National Highways under the National Highways Act, 1956. As per 2001 census the National Highways network of 57,737 km constitutes less than 2% of the total road network, but carries about 40% of the total road traffic. Recently the Parliament approved the National Highways (Amendment) Bill, 1995. This provides for private investment including foreign aid, in the building of national highways and their maintenance. Of the 57737 km of national in India, North-East India shares only 6513 km. The government of India tookup a programme of building national highways. Just after independence. These national highways serve as the principal arteries road network connecting important places including provincial capital cities of the region. The region includes the following national highways (N.H.). National Highway No. 31 runs from Siliguri to Jalukbari (Guwahati) and it is 1125 km long. It contains three branch lines namely 31A (92km) runs from Sivok to Gangtok, 31B (19 km) North Salmara to Jogighopa and 31C (235 km) runs from Golgali to Bijni. National highway no. 37 (680 km) runs from Pancharatna to Saikhoaghat and its branch, 37A (24 km) runs from Kunwaritol over the Kaliabhomora Bridge to Tezpur. National highway no. 36 (170 km) runs from Nagaon to Dimapur, NH No. 39 (436 km) runs from Numaligarh to Moreh (Indo Myanmar border). NH 38 (54 km) runs from Makum to Lekhapani and NH 40 (216 km) links Jorabat and Dawki. NH 44 (630 km) runs from Shillong to Agarta linking Jowai, Badarpur, Karimganj and Dharmanagar and NH 53 (320 km) runs from Badarpur to Imphal via Silchar NH 51 (149 km) runs from Krishnai to Dalu (Bangladesh border) linking Tura. NH 52 (580 km) runs from Baihata-Chariali to Pasighat connecting Mangaldai, Tezpur, North Lakhimpur and Jonai and its branch line 52 A (25 km) runs from Bandardewa Itanagar. Besides NH 99 Pathsala-Namlong (Bhutan) NH 61 Kohima-Jhanji, NH 62 Damra-Dalu, NH 150 Aizawl have also been declared as National Highways.

It may be mentioned that all the major Indian rivers had been bridged prior to independence. But the river Brahmaputra which divides the Assam valley into two parts remained an exception till the early 1960's and the lack of bridges across it creates a barrier in transportation between the north and south banks of the Assam valley. A road-cum-rail bridge between Pandu and Amingaon over the Brahmaputra constructed during 1958-62 and to this bridge, named Saraighat did succeed in removing one bottleneck of transport with the rest of the country. Since then two more bridges, the Kalia Bhomora, a road bridge near Tezpur and the Naranarayan Setu (rail-cum-road bridge) at Jogighopa have been constructed in 1987 and 1998 respectively. The fourth one at Bagibil near Dibrugarh is under construction.

Generally a large road programme has been undertaken by the state governments in their plans and the NEC is responsible for filling up the gaps regarding inter-state roads. A new category of road has also been undertaken by NEC which are roads of economic importance required for the exploration and exploitation of natural resources. Such roads are being constructed by the Border Road Organization that link the location of industrial and economic development of the region.

Airways

The entire North East India is isolated and strategically this region is very important. It has borders with four foreign countries such as Bhutan, People's Republic of China, Myanmar and Bangladesh. The region has been suffering for long for its weak transport system. The terrain conditions of the region impose restrictions on surface communication and so for national security and solidarity including commercial reasons. The North East India needs a well developed air transport system.

Air services were introduced in this region during the World War II when the Allied Forces built up some small airports at Kahikuchi (Guwahati), Mohanbari (Dibrugarh), Salanibari (Tezpur), Rawraiya (Jorhat), Lilabari (North Lakhimpur), Dimapur and Imphal. Guwahati is the main airport of the region providing links to other airports served by the Indian Airlines Corporation. Kahikuchi Airport has been shifted to Borjhar which is named as Lokapriya Gopinath Bordoloi Airport. The Airport Authority of India has constructed some more airports like Itanagar, Umroi (Shillong), Turival (Aizawl) etc. in the states of North East India Most of the airports are served by air transport services to Kolkata and Delhi.

13

Regional Development of North East India

It is already mentioned that barring Assam the other States of North East India are late comers to the process of economic development as they were created subsequent to the first decade of planning. Nagaland was granted full statehood in 1963 and then Manipur, Meghalaya and Tripura were created in 1972 and finally Arunachal Pradesh and Mizoram in 1987. In all the hill states and the hilly areas of Assam, Manipur and Tripura majority of the population is tribal, density of population is low, infrastructure is weak and production technology is also primitive and traditional. At that time some areas experienced political unrest and disturbances affecting the pace of economic development. Considering all these including geographical factors, the reorganisation of North-East India was undertaken. During the pre-plan period the entire region was restricted to the level of self sufficiency. So a regional planning body "North-Eastern Council" was constituted to look after the common econmic interest of different states of the region. This councl came ino existance on 1st August 1972 under NEC Act 1971 and was formally inaugurated by the Prime Minister on 7th November 1972. This advisory body is responsible to prepare plans and programmes on inter-state transport, power, communication and flood control etc. and utilises the agencies of the region's, state governments and central organisations to whom funds are advanced through the NEC. Recently, the NEC was upgraded from an advisory body to a statutory regional planning body to ensure speedy implementation of development plans and programmes of all the states including Sikkim of the region. A balanced development of the region, especially its vital infrastructure, such as power, roads, transport and telecommunication is to assume a prominent role in the economy of Southeast Asian countries. These countries including neighbouring Indian States can also derive benefit provided with critical infrastructure support and linkage.

Delineation of regions for Planning Purposes

The process of placing actions into a particular order to achieve an objective is called planning. Infact all areas of human activity have an element of planning within them. The planning of region's economy is necessary to increase the productive capacity and thereby raising the living standard and general well being of the people. Economic Planning is very important in the countries of the Third World where limited resources must be allocated efficiently to stimulate balanced development. So development of various regions of India including North-East India should be viewed as parts of a single process. The Indian planners should chalk out investment planning so that regional imbalance may be narrowed within a short period and a backward area like North-East India catch up with the national average.

The North-East India is a region endowed with rich natural resources, but economically backward with intra-regional disparities in levels of development. The states of the region share certain physical, social and cultural pattern including three types of fundamental backwardness, namely areas of tribal concentration, hill areas and chronically flood affected areas. Physiographically the region is not a homogeneous unit at all and about 60 per cent of it is mountainous, 13 per cent plateaus and 27 per cent plains.

The chapter examines these conditions for the delineation of regions for planning purposes and attempts to suggest a design for integrated economic development of North-East India as a whole, taking a resource development approach. For the purpose of a economic planning for resource development, political divisions or natural divisions may not be suitable because planning has to depend on the availability of adequate resources that can be developed into self sufficient economies. It is from this point of view, an attempt has been made here to redemarcate the North-East India into certain viable planning units and indicates the development potential unitwise.

Methodology : In order to demarcate regions for the purpose of planning, administrative or political units are not helpful because they have been created and changed, according to the political need or administrative convenience. The Brahmaputra valley, the Barak Plain, Meghalaya Plateau, Tertiary hills and basins are the natural regions of India's North-East. The delineation of such natural regions is based on the homogeneity of landscapes with their zonal and local character. Such regions are not helpful for planning purposes because they may not have sufficient resources to develop self-sufficient economies, viable for resource development for planning purposes. So delineation of planning regions at micro-level for North-East India is made by grouping of areas (not of states) having the comon river-basin. A river-basin or a drainage basin is bounded by a ridge line and forms and independent natural unit for surface hydrology. The planning Commission, Govt. of India has now adopted a new concept "drainage basin" as microplanning unit. There are six drainage basins in North-East India, namely the Brahmaputra basin in the north, the Chindwin in the east, the Barak in the Central part of the region, the Gomti in Tripura and Karnaphuli and Kaladan in Mizoram. There are diverse resources, such as soil, forest resources, mineral resources, hydel and thermal power potential and agricultural resources in such basins. Although the region as a whole falls under six drainage basins, it may only be divided into two major planning regions namely, the Brahmaputra basin and Barak basin including eastern hills and basins. Each is different from the other in its environmental conditions and resource potentials calling for intelligent planning for resource development at micro-level. In order to evaluate the resources for meeting the needs of the locality the region and the nation as whole; each region may be sub-divided into some micro-economic regions for planning purposes. Thus the Brahmaputra Basin can be subdivided into six micro planning regions. (Fig. 11)

(1) Arunachal Pradesh

(2) Upper North Bank Plain of the Brahmaputra Valley

(3) Lower North Bank Plain of the Brahmaputra Valley

(4) Upper South Bank Plain of the Brahmaputra Valley

(5) Central South Bank Plain and Hills and

(6) Lower South Bank Plain of the Brahmaputra Valley and the Northern part of the Meghalaya.

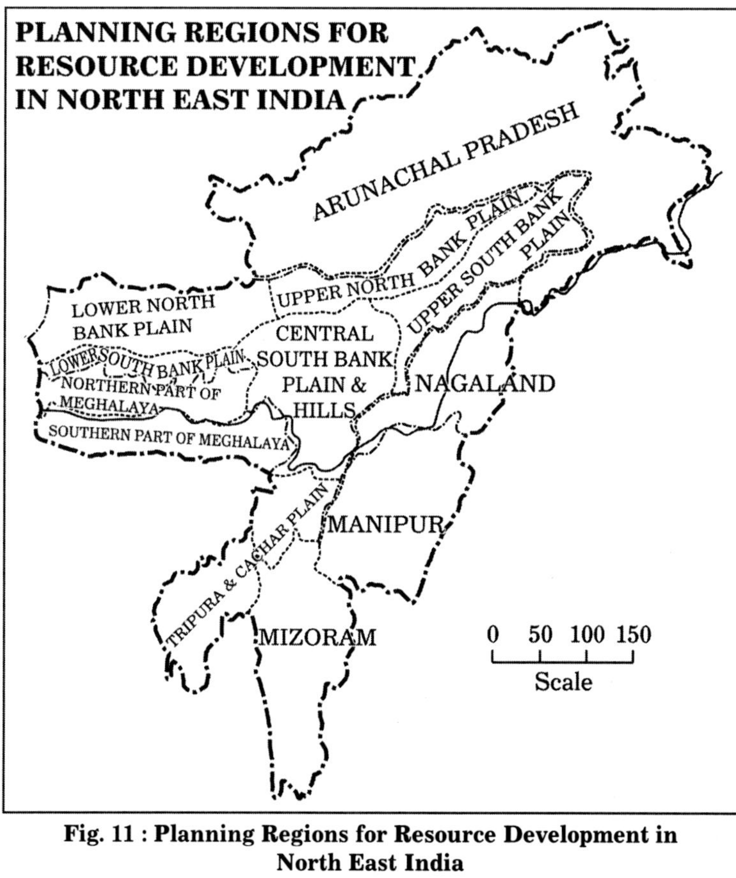

Fig. 11 : Planning Regions for Resource Development in North East India

Similarly the Barak plain and Eastern hills and Basins can be divided into three micro planning units. These are—

(1) Southern part of the Meghalaya state (south of the watershed)

(2) Cachar Plain and Tripura and

(3) Mizoram, Nagaland and Manipur

Such resource development regions are delineated on the basis of indices like natural resources, level and structure of economic development and agricultural potentialities. The existing administrative divisions, revenue divisions, natural regions and planning department zones etc. are not completely ignored.

Micro-Planning Regions

The above micro-planning units are delineated for the evaluation of resources of local, regional and national importance which will provide opportunities to the planner of the country to tackle various development programmes of the North-East India.

Arunachal Pradesh has not yet achieved much progress due to lack of infrastructural facilities, difficult terrain and formidable geopolitical obstacles. The accessibility is very low and so it does not bring spatial integration of resources. The state supports a population of 11 lakhs (2001) and the inhabitants are drawn from diverse ethnicity, speaking various languages and living at varied stages of socioeconomic and political development. Since cultivation is primitive in nature, the agricultural lands of the region do not produce enough crops, so the region needs planning for land development and for providing irrigation facilities. Proper care is to be taken so that in the name of agricultural development, ecological balance is not upset. The region has the potentiality of producing sufficient cereals, oil seeds, pulses, vegetables, potatoes and fruits like pine apples and other temperate and sub-tropical fruits. This planning unit has tremendous hydraulic potential and the C.P.W.D. has so far completed some Micro-Hydel Electric Schemes such as Tawang, Ziro, Kalat Kang, Taksing and Along Hydro-Electric Schemes etc. and some other schemes are in different stages of completion. The nodal centres for its development would be Bandardewa-Itanagar and Pachighat region.

The upper North Bank Plain of the Brahmaputra Valley (Sonitpur, Lakhimpur and Dhemaji district) is delineated by tea of national importance and rice and other food crops of regional importance. Important places like Tezpur, Jamuguri, Chatia, Biswanath-Chariali, Gohpur, North Lakhmipur, Dhemaji, etc. have developed on such agro economic base. Generally, agro oriented industries may be located in such growth centres so that they integrate the development process in their hinterlands. Tezpur would be future nodal center of national importance because it is already connected with Silghat by the Kalia Bhomora Bridge. The entire region has the potentiality for agricultural development and therefore the region needs modern inputs and innovative measures.

The lower North Bank Plain of the Brahmaputra valley (Darrang district, northern part of Kamrup district, Nalbari, Barpeta, Bongaigaon, Kokrajhar and northern part of Dhubri district) has the agrarian economy with jute production of national importance and food crops of regional importance. Flood hazard is a gigantic environmental problem in the riverine areas of this region. Greater production can only by obtained by increasing yields per hector which require considerable investments in flood control measures including capital equipment. The nodal centre of the region are Mangaldai, Rangia, Nalbari, Barpeta, Barpetaroad, Bongaigaon, Kokrajhar and Dhubri. In all the areas of the region, population is dense. special attention is to be paid to the nodal centres of economic growth with production impulses to their surrounding areas.

The upper South Bank plain of the Brahmaputra valley (Dibrugarh, Tinsukia, Sibsagar, Jorhat and Golaghat district) is delineated by production of oil and natural gas and tea crop of national importance, coal, timber, forest and agricultural products of regional importance. The distribution, quality, quantity and economic usefulness of all these resources are to be assessed for exploitation. The region shows potentiality of petro-chemical and tea industries of national importance based on its resources. Dibrugarh-Tinsukia-Diboi-Naharkatia can be called the economic core of the region. In future this economic core are can develop several processing industries and shows the production specialisation cycles, such as petroleum-gas cycle, wood chemical cycle and thermal power industry cycle.

The Central South Bank plain and Hills comprise the Karbi Along, North Cachar Hills, Nagaon and Marigaon districts. Here two physically seperated tracks are united to form one micro planning unit because the tracks exist close to each other and their economices are interrelated. The two hill districs (Karbi Aglong and North Cachar) of Assam have a self-sustained agrarian economy and existing and potential hydro-electric power resources. The varied relief features of these hills must first be evaluated in order to find out stable and non-usable areas. This can provide infrastuctural base to the planner, The Nagaon and Marigaon districts produce jute, tea and varieties of food crops. Thus the whole region has potentiality for developing agro based industries and hydel power etc. The prospective nodal centres are Silghat, Nagaon, Diphu, Hflong, Donkamukan and Marigaon.

The lower South Bank plain of the Brahmaputra valley (South Kamrup, Goalpara and southern part of Dhubri districts) and the northern part of Meghalaya (south of the watershed) is delineated by production of sillimanite, horticultural products, forest products and food products. The knowledge of these areas on the basis of such a regionalisaion can help in laying down a foundation for economic planning of this entire region consisting of hills and plains. The primary development need lies in introducing settled scientific cultivation in the hill areas and making agriculture more productive in the plains. For all these a comprehensive terrain evaluation is necessary. The whole region has the potentiality of developing industries based on forest and horticultural products and also water resources. The nodal points of the region are Gauhati-Mirza, Goalpara and Barnihat.

The southern part of the Meghalaya has varieties of resources. The region is very rich in coal, limestone, feldspars, glass sand and gypsum. The Tura-Rongrengiri region has the large reserve of unexploited coal and limestone. Similarly, the Shillong-Cherapunji has large reserve of coal, limestone, hydel-power resources, forests and fruits like oranges, pineapples, banana, pears and plums. Thus the whole region shows the potentiality of developing coal chemical, cement industries, newsprints, fruit preservation industries. But the difficult terrain with high gradients and extensive forests stand in the way of development of transport and communication which retard the economic development. The primary developmental need lies in the wholesale improvement of means of transport and communication in the right direction. The region also need some more urban and service centres capable of providing central and social services to support economic growth. The nodal centres for the region would be Tura, Shillong and Cherapunji.

The economy of Cacher Plain and Tripura is agrarian in character with tea, jute, forests and food crops of regional importance. The region has the potentiality of developing paper and pulp, hardboard and plywood industries, jute industries and fruit preservation industries. The prospective nodal centres may be Silchar, Badarpur, Karimganj, Hailakandi, Agartala, Dharmnagar and Udaipur.

The Nagaland, Manipur and Mizoram form one planning unit and this remote unit of India ranks among the least known parts of the country. The lack of cartographical data is ample proof of the difficulties of the terrain. This is a complex physiographical unit with a monsoon climate.

The altitudination variation is great within short distances and all these factors have led to the prevalence of varied natural vegetation and deep forests. The soils are thin on the uplands and hills. Generally, there are red soils and are poor in many aspects. The soil are relatively deep in the basins and lowlands. The agriculture is mostly crop farming for local consumption. Next to agriculture, forestry is the main land-use in the region. The highland areas of the region have the potentiality of rearing sheep for wool. In future this region may be developed for wood-chemical, hydro-power and industries based on food crops and forest products. The development of such industries based on its resources will demand for construction of more good roads.

Conclusion

It is observed that the pace of socioeconomic change has not been equal among the various groups in North-East India. Lack of growth of a strong economy, premodern technology of productive economy, slow urbanization etc. have contributed this state of affairs. So the development strategy of the entire region lies on the mutual understanding of different states. The economies of North-East India should be treated as a single economy with free interstate flow of commodities and the development strategy has to be based on the efficient utilisation of its vast unexploited resources as discussed above.

The knowledge of all the above problems, potentialities and prospects for regionalization can help in laying down a strong foundation for planning economic and social welfare for the people of North-East India. To collaborate in development to achieve mutual benefits, all the seven states of the region must work together to find an workable formula for sharing cost and benefits of the development of water, mineral, industrial and human resources. With systematic development of these resources, the region will become one of the strong economic areas in India.

The above study suggests only broadly generalized macro and micro-planning regions of North-East India possessing diverse type of resources. For greater precision in delineating the network of planning regions of North-East India some more details of the existing and potential resources including detailed social and economic accounts and their developmental possibilities are required and may prove more meaningful. So the NEC can play a great role in this direction. A detailed study can be done with the help of a team-work of economists, Statistians, geographers and other scientists as suggested in the study. Then a network of planning region for resource development may be formulated and implemented in the North Eastern region of India.

14

Geopolitical Problems of North East India

The study of the influence of geographical factors on political systems is generally known as geopolitics. It means country's politics as determined by its geographical position. The application of this geographic concept to politics was developed in Germany between the two world wars. Rudolf Kjellen developed the basic ideas of ***Geopolitik*** by using Ratzel's analogy of a state as an organism which required room to grow. Karl Houshofer drew his geopolitical ideas from Kjellen and stated that ***geoplitik*** is the art of using geographical knowledge to give support and direction to frame the policy of a state. Thus geopolitics investigates the state primarily in relation to its environments, its space and attempts to solve all problems resulting from spatial relationships.

Geostrategically, North East India is one of the most important and vulnerable regions in India and the very important geopolitical premise of the region is its strategic location. A region lying along the edge of a country is called borderland or frontier which provides defence and permits exchange to occur. Every border consists of three zones, two of which are the periphery of the adjoining states and the third a central zone, known as borderland where there is mingling of the two countries. Generally the strong and wise countries show close ties between the border zones and the core areas. India's land border is about 17,7000 km and of this length North East India shares approximately 5,200 km with China, Bhutan, Myanmar and Bangladesh. All the seven northeastern states are border states and thus Assam shares border with Bhutan, Arunachal Pradesh with China and Bhutan, Nagaland, Manipur and Mizoram with Myanmar,

Meghalaya and Tripura with Bangladesh. With its very long land border, North East India occupies an extremely strategic position. Its is connected with the main land of India by a narrow corridor of foothill land in North Bengal. The width of this corridor is about 33 km on the eastern side and 21 km on the western side and the link is subjected to occasional disruptions due to heavy rain and floods. Such terrestrial location of the region converts it into an isolated pocket and this is one of the most important causes for alienation of its population.

The terrain conditions of North East India like Tertiary mountains and hills, Archaean plateaus, river valley and mountain basins etc. make the region an isolated pocket. All such relief features including the river Brahmaputra and other rivers and dense monsoon forests have great bearings on the geopolitics of the region. Such rugged physical geography together with very poor transport and communication facilities favour a separatist tendency among the people. In fact, there is a long history of alienation between the people of plains and hill tribes in composite Assam.

The present Sino-Indian border is the product of Manchu Policy, Chinese Republican Policy and British Policy. This border in the Eastern sector is 1140 km long and it includes Bhutan foothills, Arunachal Pradesh, major parts of Darrang and Sonitpur district of Assam. The boundary line in this sector passes from the North-Eastern corner of Bhutan to the tri-junction of China, Myanmar and India and it covers 9.53 per cent of the total land boundary of India. This line was drawn up by Sir Henry McMahan and was agreed upon by the representatives of India and Tibet in 1914. But the agreement was not formally ratified by the government of China. McMahan was an enthusiatic believer in the buffer state concept and equated frontier with buffer. He also defined both as an area of neutral territory separating two important neighbours. In 1951 the Chinese occupied Tibet and thus India lost northern buffer protection. Between 1954 and 1962 India's northern border was continuously threatened and invaded this border area and claimed 5200 sq. km. border territory south of the McMahan line. Forests provide main source of income and agriculture is limited in this border region with rice as staple food.

The border area of Nagaland, Manipur and Mizoram with Myanmar is peaceful and non-controversial. In this border the boundary line passes through deeply forested hilly areas, with Mizo hills, Manipur and Naga hills on the Indian sides and the Chin hills, Kachin state etc. On the Myanmar side, this line was drawn by the British under the treaty of Yandaboo in 1826. Agriculture is practised on the shifting basis with rice as the main crop.

The border area of Meghalaya, Assam, Tripura and Mizoram is hilly. The length of the border is about 1500 km and covered with forests. Some hill slopes are used for the tea and rice cultivation. The entire borderlands of North East India is under developed and needs urgent attention of the government. Influx of illegal foreigners and smuggling across the border has been a common feature in many areas along the international border between Bangladesh and Assam and Meghalaya and between Myanmar and Manipur border. The isolated location of the region appears to be standing on the way of industrialization and urbanization.

The Political map of North East India has undergone many changes since independence. The region has witnessed may political events which affected the demographic structure as well as territorial boundaries of composite Assam. After partition of India, the Muslim majority district of Sylhet with the exception of four Thanas, namely Badarpur, Patharkandi, Karimganj and Ratabari had gone to the then East Pakistan following a referendum in the district. These four thanas were added to Cachar district. Thus at the time of independence Assam lost an area of about 18,969 sq. km. However, the princely states of Manipur and Tripura came to be members of the northeastern region of India. Then a treaty was made between the Government of

India and the Government of Bhutan on August 8, 1949 and accordingly a strip of a land measuring 82 sq. km. in an area known as Dewangiri had be retroceded to Bhutan to mark the friendship existing and continuing between the two countries. The third truncation took place when the Naga Hills district of Assam and the Tuensang area of NEFA were separated for the formation of Nagaland in 1957 in the wake of insurgency there. The new administrative unit was kept under the Ministry of External Affairs to be administered by the Governor of Assam. The Dimapur area of Assam was also merged into the state of Nagaland and it was elevated to a full state in 1963. After conceding Nagaland it was very difficult to keep the other hill areas of Assam from getting their respective states. The Garos and Khasis had been agitating for a hill state and so an autonomous state named as Meghalaya was formed with two districts namely, Garo hills and the United Khasi and Jayantia Hills of Assam on April, 1970. Prior to this, Government of India setup several commissions and committees including Pataskar Commissions (1964), Ashok Mehta Committee (1967) for resolving the issues related to grievances of hill people and their demand for autonomy. Series of discussions between the government and APHLC and other groups were held and eventually the whole North East India has been reorganized under the North Eastern Reorganisation Act of 1971. Meghalaya was granted full statehood along with Manipur and Tripura, Arunachal and Mizoram were made Union Territories. Insurgency also plagued Mizoram for two decades during 1966-86. The historic peace accord reached in June 1986 between the government of India and the insurgent outfit, Mizo National Front, brought peace to Mizoram and in February 1987 Mizoram and Arunachal Pradesh gained full statehood. This way Assam has been truncated several times and treated as it were, a guineapig for experimentation of small states with lingering apprehension for further fragmentation.

Both history and geography have contributed substantially to the emergence of a centripetal force among the traditional inhabitants of the region. It became a melting pot for different ethnolinguistic groups like Austro-Asiatic, Tibeto-Chinese, Aryan etc. and a type of Mongoloid culture has been created in the region. Even the Assamese and the traditional Bengali Speakers are distinguished by their Mongoloid bias. But due to the imposition of various political and economic forces compounded by linguistic and political gulf existing between different groups of people, the centripetal force has now become weakened in the policy of North East India. In fact, the present crisis of this region is due to the past isolation and long years of neglect and sudden exposure of relatively backward societies to the complexities of modern system imposed from the distant New Delhi, the capital city of India. During the British period communal politics were encouraged and the centrifugal forces continued to work to divide the country. The same politics and forces still continue to work in the region. So the political and socio-cultural assimilation of the various social groups has become impossible. The wrong policy of the government, along with geographical distance and differences have stood in the way of integration of the states of the region with the rest of the country. The indigenous population of the region have to face a new complex situation and fear of losing their identity, and political consciousness has been aroused recently among the different groups of people. Thus a king of geopolitical unrest is prevailing in the region.

The secessionist movement first started in the Naga Hill during the time of India's independence. A.Z. Phizo met Gandhiji in New Delhi on July 7, 1947 and asked for independence of the Nagas living in Naga Hills and its surrounding areas. Gandhiji was very sympathetic to the Nagas and told him that nobody would force the Nagas to join the Indian Union-Phizo interpreted Gandhiji's words as signifying his approval for Naga Hills as a part of India. Phizo started a movement to secure freedom for the Nagas. This movement became violent under the banner of Naga National Council with guerrilla warfare being launched with arms and ammunition procured from foreign sources. The movement continued for over two decades when an agreement between a section of the Naga rebels and Sri L.P. Singh, then Governor of Assam was signed at Shillong on November 1, 1975 suggesting that the Naga problem could be solved. The majority of Nagas accepted the Indian Constitution and a small section did not accept the Shillong accord and continued their violent movement under the banner of the National Socialist Council of Nagaland. A section of this group is now demanding a unified Naga State of Nagalim at the cost of neighbouring states of Arunachal Pradesh, Assam and Manipur.

Another secessionist movement started in Mizoram towards the end of sixties. Here also a section of Mizos led by Laldanga took terrorism in the Mizo Hills. This little known Hills district of Assam hit the head lines of news papers on March 1, 1966 when the militant Mizo National Front (MNF) led by its president Laldanga raised banner of revolt against the Government. The objective of MNF was a sovereign Mizoram comprising the Mizo Hills and the Mizo inhabited area of Myanmar, Bangladesh, Cachar and Manipur. The MNF and its leader, however realised after two decades of hostilities that an independent Mizoram was not a practical proposition So Laldanga signed an accord in 1988 with the central government within the framework of Indian constitution. With the signing of the peace accords, both by the Nagas and Mizos the insurgent movements believed to be collapsed. But the peace had not returned to this part of India.

Inspite of recorganization of the region, geo-political unrest is not over, the separatist aspirations of the United Liberation Front of Assam (ULFA), autonomy of Boroland, insurgency of Manipur by the Peoples Liberation Army (PLA) and interstate boundary disputes are still absorbing much of nations resources and time. It is to noted that post-independent India has by and large deviated from the path of non-violent demonstrations to achieve political objectives. It is believed that the militancy and insurgency in the region find support from neighbouring countries of India.

Serious tension developed both in Tripura and Assam due to heavy influx of immigrants from across the border since independence. This unabated influx of immigrants from neighbouring Bangladesh and distant Nepal has drastically changed the demographic profile of these two states and created poor economic conditions and scarcity of food grains. The Tripuris in Tripura also started violent movement under the banner of the Tripura National Volunteers (TNV). It is reported that a section of the Tripuri Tribals who have forged links with the Mizo hostiles are being imparted training in guerrilla warfare in Chittagang hills of Bangladesh. While the Tripuris have already been reduced to a minority in their own homeland, the Assamese harbour genuine fears that they would be completely swamped by the Bangladeshi nationals very soon. So the Assamese would like to correct this situation by removing the foreign nationals from the soils of Assam. All these created an unrest in Assam since 1979. It is mentioned that a militant organization called United Liberation Front of Assam (ULFA) has taken up arms to achieve its goal of independent Assam. The activities of this organization have added a new dimension to the political scene of this part of India. This militant organization is an offshoot of the six year old Assam movement on the foreigners issue and the organization was declared unlawful on November 27, 1990 along with the imposition of president's rule in Assam. The members of this organization did not participate in 1985 election. Rather they silently built up their organization at the grassroot level with a number of welfare activities like eradication of drink and drug habit, construction of school buildings, roads and financial assistance to the poor. It is also alleged that they have collected several crores of rupees from the business communities and tea planters. Development activities cannot take place in the region because of militancy, insurgency and terrorist acts of lawlessness. The army's continued presence can prove to be counter productive and the deployment of more army is not the answer. All human beings want peace. So the solution for this problem of the region is to create a new economic and political environment without taking recourse to the use of force. The existing constitution of India has also created a sense of alienation in the minds of people living in the peripheral areas of India. The aspiration of the people of the entire North Eastern region of India may be fulfilled by adopting some constitutional measures. The real *geopolitik* demands that all the states of the region must co-exist peacefully and honourably adopting the James Monroe Doctrine in political and economic sphere.

15

Assam

Assam possesses a very marked individuality and in the broad sense the state is transitional towards High Asia and Indo-China. It is situated in the North-east corner of India between 24°3'N and 28°N latitudes and 89°51'E and 96°1'E meridians of longitude. The state covers an area of 78,438 sq. km. i.e. 2.39 per cent of the total area of India and supports a population of 3.12 million (2011) accounting for 2.60 per cent of the total population of the nation. The state is surrounded by two foreign countries namely Bhutan and Bangladesh and seven Indian states like Arunachal Pradesh, Nagaland, Manipur, Mizoram, Tripura, Meghalaya and West Bengal.

Physiography

Assam consists of four physiographic divisions : The Assam on Brahmaputra valley is extension of the Indo-Gangetic trough, while the Karbi Anglong is essentially a part of the Meghalaya plateau which is an outlier of Peninsular India, North Cachar Hills belong to the Extra-Peninsular mountain and Barak plain is simply an extension of the Surma valley.

The Brahmaputra Valley : The Brahmaputra valley is a great ramp-valley from Dhubri to its blind end beyond Sadiya, extends about 720 kilometres with an average breadth of 96 kilometres. The general slope of the valley is extremely gentle, falling at an average rate of 12 centimetre per kilometer. Sadiya, situated at the head of the valley has an altitude of 135 metres above sea level, the altitude of Tezpur, situated in the central part is 78 metres and that of Dhubri located in the western most part of the valley is only 34 metres. But the northern margin of the valley is very precipitous with

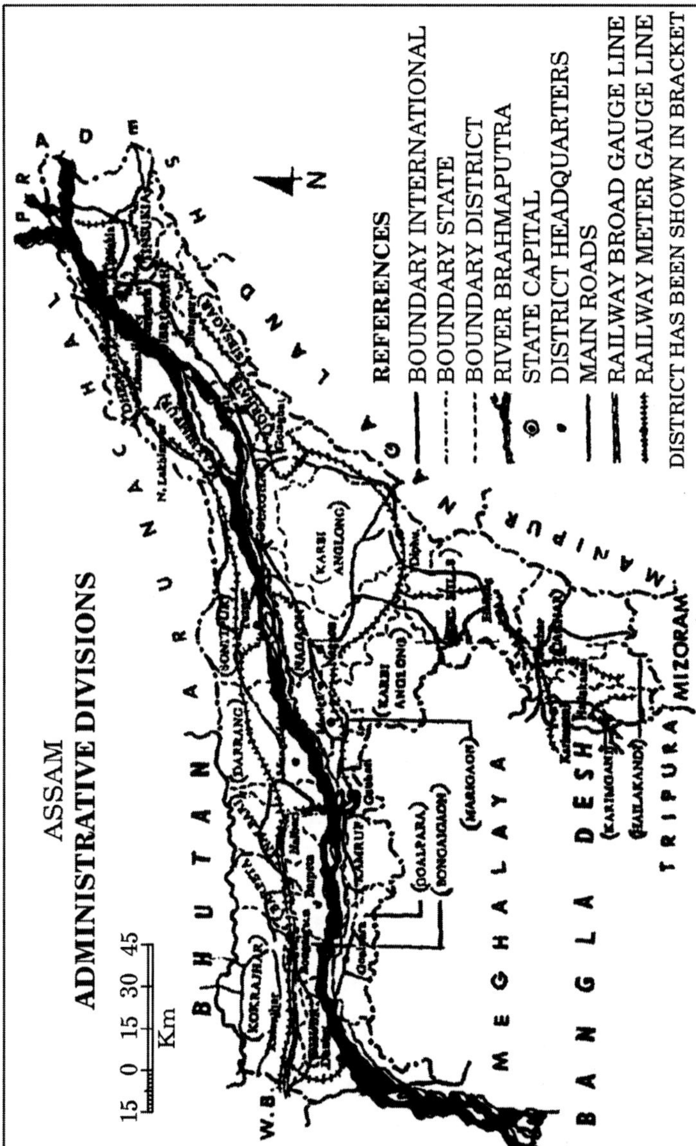

Fig. 12 : Assam : Administrative Divisions

Himalayas falling abruptly from a height of 500 metres to 150 metres and the boundary touches 150 metres contour line. The southern boundary of the valley is rather gentle except the eastern part bordering Tirap and Naga Hills. From both the northern and southern margins the valley plain gradually dropes down towards the river Brahmaputra. The Brahmaputra valley is also known as the Assam valley and it covers an area of 56194 square kilometers i.e. 72 per cent of the total area of the state of Assam.

The Brahmaputra divides the valley into two parts : The north bank plain and the south bank plain. In the margin of the north bank plain all along the foothills of the Himalaya there is a narrow zone of coarse alluvial debris known as Bhabar Belt. This belt is bordered southward by a narrow flat plain of semi-tarai character that support tall grasses. To the south of it and at about equal distances from the Brahmaputra river to the south and the hills of the Bhutan and Arunachal Himalayas to the north lies the strip of alluvial plain from east to west which is not only the most densely populated plain but also supports the rice fields. South of it there lies an active flood plain of the Brahmaputra with a series of swamps and beels.

The south bank plain of the valley is a bit different from that of the north bank plain. The plain is narrow and uneven in its outline. There is a series of terraces along the foothills of the Patkai and the Naga Hills. These terraces are replaced by a series of swamps and beels in the foothills of the Meghalaya plateau. The middle plain of the south bank lies to the north of the foothills terraces and swampy lands. This is the most densely settled plains with rice fields, vegetables and tea gardens. The flood plain which lies north to this belt is highly irregular. The monotony of the flood plains of the valley is broken by occasional hillocks and river levees on both the banks of the Brahmaputra. The river Brahmaputra is also highly braided due to its low gradient and as a result there are a large number of chors and riverain islands in the bed of the Brahmaputra.

The Karbi Plateau : The Karbi plateau covers the whole Karbi-Anglong district of Assam and structurally the area is a continuation of the Meghalaya plateau. The Karbi plateau is separated from the Meghalaya by the degradation of the river Kopili and its headstreams and from the Nagahills by the Dhansiri and its tributaries. The topography of the plateau is senile and the height of the central part is about 1400 metres. The plateau area slopes towards the north. The hills mostly follow south-west to northeast trend and their ridges are not sharp. The eastern part of this plateau region is made up of sedimentary rocks like limestone, sandstone, sale etc. of upper Mesozoic age. The core area of the plateau consists of Metamorphosed crystalline rocks of pre Cambrian origin.

North Cachar Hills : The North Cachar hills with rugged topography lie south of the Karbi plateau and cover the whole North Cachar Hills district of Assam. These tertiary Hills, known as Barail ranges are extension of the Barail ranges of Nagaland land. These ranges terminate at the river Kopili, to the west of which lie Precambrian ranges of the Meghalaya plateau. The average altitude of the region is about 1600 m and the Mahadeo peak (1953 m) is the highest point of the North Cachar Hills. The Barail range divides the district into two parts, the northern part falls under the Brahmaputra catchment basin and the southern part is under the Barak basin. The Barail ranges have been dissected by the Kapili and Dhansiri river systems.

The Barak Plain : This plain is surrounded by the hills on three sides and only the western side is open and joins with Bangladesh. The river Barak traverses this lowland from the east to the west. The northern part of the Barak plain is bounded by the Barail and the Jaintia Hills. The Bhuban Pahar lies on the southern side of the Barak river. The Rangti Pahar acts as the watershed between the rivers Dhaleswari and Sonai. The entire Barak plain is piedmont in nature and presents a mosaic of isolated low hillocks locally known as *tillas*. These *tillas* rise aloruptly from the alluvial ground of the plain. Besides the plain has swamps and beels created by the river Barak and its tributaries like Jiri, Modhura, Soani, Dhaleswari, Langai, Singla etc.

Drainage : The master-stream, Brahmaputra is one of the most astonishing rivers in the world. From the Tsangpo sources with its immense hairpin-shaped bend to the Meghna confluence it is about 28,800 km. long. As mentioned in earlier chapter, the river has a large number of tributaries and causes meanacing flood and thereby causes immense damage to Assam. But this river by depositing sediments has made the valley soil fertile, it helps in trades and commerce. So the state of Assam may be described as the gift of the river Brahmaputra. The other important river is the Barak of south Assam. Rising from the southern slopes of the mt. Iso on the Nagaland-Manipur border, it flows to Tipaimukh from where it takes a sharp u-turn to the north and forms the boundary between Assam and Manipur to the distance where its tributary Jiri river joins it. Then the Barak turns to the west and flows across the middle of the plain till it reaches Kondigram where the river bifurcates into two branches, namely the Surma in the north and Kushiyara in the south. The river receives numerous tributaries like Jiri, Jenam, Digli, Chiri, Sonai, Katakhal, Dhaleshwari, Singla, Langai, Modhura, Jatinga Larang, Balichara etc.

Climate : The climate of Assam shows some modification of the standard monsoonal type. The region receives high rainfall and that is why the hot season being shorter with low average temperature of about 28°C. Nearly 20 per cent of the total rainfall is received during the months of April and May from the nor-westers. The summer is very hot and humid. The period from June to September is of heaviest rainfall, June being the rainiest month of the year with an average temperature during this period is 37°C. Though on certain days of high rainfall, temperature falls down considerably, yet when clouds disappear temperature rises to a fairly high degree within a short time. During the period of the Retreating Southwest monsoon the low pressure system becomes weaker resulting gradual decrease in the southwest monsoon (June-September). About 60 per cent of the annual total rainfall occurs from the south-west monsoon and some amount of rainfall is also received in the post monsoon or retreating monsoon season (October-November). Rainfall is quite high, flood being more dangerous than drought. There is a rain-shadow zone comprising Hojai-Lumding area, parts of Karbi-Anglong district around Diphu and the area is surrounded by 150 cm isohyet. This area is in lee side of the Meghalaya plateau. The upper part of the Brahmaputra valley, greater parts of North Cachar Hills district including Barak plain receive more rainfall owing to Barail saddle. Rainfall is naturally higher on the foothills of Bhutan and Arunachal Pradesh. There is another of pocket of high rainfall (300 cm) at the extreme end of the Brahmaputra valley.

Foggy morning, sunny noon and clear night are the characteristic features of weather in the cold weather season (December-February). January is the coldest month in Assam with an average temperature of 13°C. But temperature diminishes towards the hilly region of Assam.

Natural Resources : The Natural resources of Assam are the assets and properties which are inherent to the landforms as described earlier. These resources are land and soil, water, minerals, forests, wild animals and all the resources need some efforts by the inhabitants to convert them into use.

Land and Soil Resources : The land in its spatial sense covers a large area apart from agricultural uses. It has other uses like buildings of villages, urban centers, roads and railways, port, airport, factories etc. and natures requirements like land for forests, drainage and hills. The total geographical area of Assam in 7852000 hectares and out of this 1522 hectares cover the two hills districts, namely Karbi-Anglong and North Chachar Hills. The total cropped area of the two plains is 3294000 hectares and those of two hill districts is 166,000 hectares. The plains of Assam are blessed with fertile alluvial soils which is extensively distributed throughout the

Brahmaputra valley and Barak plain. The soils of the Brahmaputra valley are less acidic and are classified into two types : new alluvium and old alluvium. Both the types were deposited by the Brahmaputra and its innumerable tributaries. The new alluvial soils are found in the active flood plains, charlands and the middle parts of the both banks of the valley. The old alluvium is particularly found along the interfluves of the tributaries from the foothill region to the middle part of the valley. The old alluvium is more acidic than the new alluvium and contains phosphoric acid. Therefore, this type of soil is suitable for the cultivation of tea. Besides, peaty or silty soils are found in the lowlying areas of the Brahmaputra valley and Barak plains. Such soils support rushes and sedges. Red loamy soils occur in the North Cachar Hills and foothills of Karbi Anglong and the foothills of South Kamrup, Goalpara, Dhubri district and also in the foothills of Barak Plain. Red loamy soils are suitable for cultivating fruit-trees, especially oranges, lemon, pineapple etc. Some laterite soils are also in the southwestern parts of Karbi Anglong. This soils is suitable for potato cultivation.

Water Resources : All organisms depend water and so it is a biological necessity. It is generally used as a source of power, an industrial ingredient, a medium of transports a waste removal, a purifying agent and a recreational asset. It is generally available both underground and overground. Assam is generously blessed by nature with huge sources of water and the state is under the catchment areas of two river basins. The Brahmaputra and the Barak including their innumerable tributaries are the assets of the whole state. These rivers and their associated alluvial soils provide the most productive agricultural lands and hence the area supports 26.64 million persons. The two main streams and some of their important tributaries provide channels of inland transportation. The water resource of the Brahmaputra river is the highest in the world. The river has drainage area of 580,000 sq. km. And its average discharge is estimated at 19,830 m^2 per second at its mouth. The Brahmaputra basin receives an average annual rainfall of 230 cm. The river carries an average annual flood discharge of 51,156 m^3 per second at Pandu near Guwahati. Besides, there is a considerable amount of ground water resource, in Assam and in most cases it is contaminated with high concentration of iron, dissolved acids, toxic substances etc. Supply of such quality water to various consumers like Public Health, agriculture and industry requires treatment for better uses.

Mineral Resources : Mineral resources are regarded as the backbone of economic and industrial development in country or region. The development of modern society is mostly due to ingenuity of men in making use of minerals of the earth. The Brahmaputra valley is endowed with mineral resources like crude oil, natural gas and coal. Crude oil is the most important mineral of the valley. It was discovered by the British rulers in 1825 and its commercial production began in 1899. Crude oil deposites are found in Naharkatia, Moran, Hugrijan, Rudrasagar, Galeky, Nazira and Teok. Total production of crude oil was 21.71 million tonnes in 2000-2001 and total reserve of crude is estimated to be 876.46 million tones. The crude oil has been processed in the refineries located at Digboi, Noonmati (Guwahati), Bongaigaon and Barauni. The major products of these refineries are Kerosene, high speed diesel, petrol, carbon, wax and neptha. Natural gas is also found alongwith oil and the total reserve of natural gas in Assam is estimated at 23,000 million cubit metres, the major users being Namrup Fertilizer plant and Namrup Gas Thermal Power Project. Besides, there are minor occurrences of oil and natural gas from Badarpur areas of the Barak plain.

Like oil coal was discovered first in Brahmaputra valley in 1825 and commercial exploitation of coal started just after connection of coal fields by railway lines in 1884. Workable coal seams occur in Nazira, Jaipur, Makum and Namchik and total reserve of coal in Makum and Namchik fields is estimated to be 1600 million tones of coal. In the hill districts fairly good quality coal (32.4% fixed carbon) occurs at Koilajar, Silvetta, Khunbaman and Lenglio. The total reserve of these coal fields is estimated at 220 million tones. Limestone occurs in a number of places like Kopili and Kharkhor river valleys, Garampani-Umrangshu area and Diphu-Bokajan area. These area contain about 210 million tones of good quality limestone. Various types of clay also occur in the alluvial tracts of the plains of Assam. Such clays are generally used in the manufacture of bricks, tiles, earthenwares and in oil and tube well drilling. Besides, base metal, beryl banded hematite, muscovite etc. are found in a number of places but these minerals are not economically explotable.

Forest Resources : Vegetation and forests and called "green gold". These resources contribute to the regional and national economy and also ameliorate the regional climate and maintain ecological balance. The forest is a community of living plants and these are expressions of interactions of climate and soil.

The climate of Assam shows slight modification of the normal monsoon type, the hot season being shorter than in other parts of India with low average temperature and high average rainfall and humidity. The average summer temperature lies between 30°C to 33°C while the winter temperature ranges 6°C to 13°C. The physiography, climate and inaccessibility have contributed to the richness of vegetation in Assam. The total geographical area of Assam is 7850005 hectares and the area under forest is 1930289 hectares. Dense forest is mainly found in Karbi-Anglong and North Cachar Hills.

The natural vegetation in Assam falls under six major types : broad evergreen type, sal forest, mixed deciduous, savannah, bamboo and cane and miscellaneous varieties. The most important evergreen species are sam (artocarpur chaplasha), Gandsarai (Cinnamoum glanduliferum) Tita champa (michelia champaea), Makai (Shorea assamica) Nahar (Masua ferrea), Khair (accacia catchu), Ajhar (lagestrameia vegknee), Jack fruit tree (artecarpur integrifalia), Sanaru (cassia fistula), Gomari (gmelina arborea), uriam (bischoffiajavanica) etc. These evergreen species are mostly found in the districts of upper

Brahmaputra valley, parts of Karbi-Anglong, North Cachar Hills and Barak plain where annual rainfall is more than 200 cm.

The most important forest in Assam is the Sal forests. Extensive area of Sal trees occur in Kokrajhar, Dhubri, Goalpara, Barpeta, Kamrup, Marigaon, Nagaon, Karbi-Anglong and Darrang districts. The Sal (shorea robusta) is a large gregarious tree and has very high commercial value owing to its long bole. The tree grows upto a height of 40 metres and girth 4-5 metres under favourable ecological conditions. It is generally used for construction of houses, railway sleepers, bridges, boat making, railway wagons, carts and carriages.

The mixed decidons types occurs generally in the lower Brahmaputra valley in areas between Sal forests and Savanah forest. These forests are also found in some parts of the upper Assam, Karbi-Anglong and North Cachar Hills. Such forests contain tall trees like Simul (Bombax malabaricum), Makai and Sida (Lager Stroencia). The Simul tree has a high economic value. Its timber is used for the match box and plywood industries, packing cases etc. The flowers of Simul is used for manufacture of cushions, pillows, quilts and life-belts and Simul seeds yield oil which is used for soap making.

The Savannah vegetation is found in the well drained highland areas all throughout Assam. The decidous forests are common in the central parts of Assam including the two hill districts. Bamboo (Bombua), Cane (Calamus Ciliaris), reeds and various species of grass occur in different parts of the plains and hills. Swamp vegetation with luxuriant growth of many species of graminaceae including reeds, thatch and water-hyacinth occur in flood plains. Medicinal plants like Sarpagandha (Rauwolfia Serpentina) Amlakhi (emblica officinals gaestr) etc. are also found in different forests of Assam. Besides a large number of orchids, agar etc. also occur in some forests of the state. Agaru or agar contains oily essence and so it is used to prepare a very valuable perfume.

All these forests provide habitats for various types of insects, birds, reptiles, herbivorous animals and their predators. The water features of Assam are rich in fishes, turtles, tortoises and amphibians. Most of the wildlife habitats are located in the reserved forests of Assam.

The scientific management of forest areas has been introduced in India in 1862 and accordingly in Assam also 269 sq. miles of forest were converted in Reserved Forests for Scientific Management. Now area under reserved forests in Assam is 1742194.96 hectares. In order to conserve forests and wild lives government declared some areas as wild life sanctuaries and some as national parks besides reserved forests. These parks and sanctuaries alongwith their area are shown below:

National Parks & Sanctuaries	Area in Sq. km
A. National Parks	
1. Kaziranga National Park	430
2. Manas National Park	500
3. Nameri National Park	200
4. Dibru-Saikhowa National Park	340
5. Orang National Park	79
B. Wildlife Sanctuaries	
1. Gibbon Wildlife Sanctuary	21
2. Garampani Wildlife Sanctuary	6
3. Lowkhowa Wildlife Sanctuary	70
4. Chakrasila Wildlife Sanctuary	46
5. Burachapati Wildlife Sanctuary	44
6. Barnadi Wildlife Sanctuary	26
7. Sonai-Rupa Wildlife Sanctuary	22
8. Pabitara Wildlife Sanctuary	39
9. Dipar Beel Bird Sanctuary	4
10. Panidihing Bird Sanctuary	34
11. Bordoibum Bilmukh Bird Sanctuary	11
12. Padumani Bherjan Borajan Wildlife Sanctuary	7
13. Namber Wildlife Sanctuary	37
14. Karbi-Anglong Wildlife Sanctuary	96
15. East Karbi Anglong Wildlife Sanctuary	212

Source : Statistical Hand Book, Assam 2001.

Kaziranga National Park : Kaziranga is Assam's living heritage and is located on the riverine plain of the Brahmaputra in Golaghat district. As early as 1905 Kaziranga Reserve Forest Act was enacted and in 1912 it became a Game Reserve and then in 1952 the name Game Reserve was changed to Wild Life Sanctuary. In 1974 this game Sanctuary was raised to National Park.

The existence of a species is dependent on many variable factors like climatic, edaphic, altitudinal, latitudinal variation etc. These factors govern the continuance or termination of a species and its propagation, growth rate and spread. It is said that one horned Rhino was found throughout the northern India. Then Rhino has been pushed to the unihabited Swamps and flood plains of Kaziranga and other flood prone areas of the Brahmaputra river. The riverine grasslands are the congenial habitats for the one horned Asiatic Rhino.

The 430 square kilometers grassland including wetlands and deciduous forests harbours about 1,600 one horned rhinos, 1,000 elephants, 1400 wild buffalos 90 tigers, 500 Swamps deer, 505 species of birds, 440 species of plants and 42 species of fishes. Besides, there are several other animals like leopards, sambar, wild boar, hog deer, bears, gaur, capped langurs, gibbons, hoolock Bengal florican, pelican, horn bill and several species of swamp bird's. Now this national park alongwith other protected areas have been under illegal occupation. About 8% of Kaziranga National Park is under encroachment. Poaching and annual floods are other problems of this oldest National Park of Assam.

Manas National Park : Manas National park is located on the bhabar-tarai region of the Bhutan Himalayan foothills in the Barpeta district. In 1928 the Manas Reserve Forest Act was adopted and then it was raised to the status of Game Sancturaries. In 1973, the then Prime Minister Late Indira Gandhi initiated the 'Project Tiger', a kind of global conservation programme with a view to protecting the tigers and its habitat in India. The first project tiger in Assam was opened at Manas Sanctuary in 1973. The Sanctuary area was treated as 'core area' of the 'Project Tiger' which stretches from the river Sonkosh on the west to the river Dhansiri on the east. Since 1975 tiger population has been increased reasonably. Besides tiger, there are swamp deer, sambor, hog deer, chital, gaur, wild buffaloes, wild boar, elephants, golden langur, common capped langur, pigmy hogs, porcupine, peacock and few rhinos.

The park area is an attracting spot for the visitors. The sparkling waters of the Manas sweep through the Bhutan ravines and spill into the plains of Assam forming three rivers namely the Manas, the Hakma and the Beni. All there rivers abound with fishes.

Nameri National Park : The nameri wildlife Sanctuary was upgraded to the status of a national park in 1998. This is located in the foothills of the Arunachal Himalayas of Sonitpur district. The important animals of this park are tiger, elephant, capped langur, Black Panther, Leopard, Sambar etc. The most important problem of this park is encrochment which is highest (11%) among the five national parks of Assam.

Dibru-Saikhowa National Park : The park area is formed by the two great rivers namely the Brahmaputra and the Lohit at the head of the Brahmaputra valley. The heavy siltation with continuous erosion and accretion by the above mentioned rivers including their tributaries have formed this habitat ideal for wildlife. The park area supports wet evergreen, semi evergreen and moist deciduous forests including tall grasses. The important wildlives of the park are the rarest white winged wood duck (Deohanh) and wild horse.

Orang National Park : Orang National Park is also known as Rajiv Gandhi National Park. It is located on the western side of the Jia Dhansiri river which is a north bank tributary to the Brahmaputra river. The parkland contains deciduous forests and grasses. This is the habitat of rhinoceros, wild buffalo, hog deer and several species of birds including migratory birds.

Thus Assam has many reserve forests, wildlife sanctuaries and some parks. These are the habitats of thousand of wildlives including animals, birds reptiles, fishes and other organisms. Rampant poaching and pilferage of forest products have been the causes of deferioration of habitat quality. Some of the man made forests with monoculture or mixed plantation of few commercial species are proved to be not a good habitat for wildlife. All these problems need to be solved for the protection of wildlives.

Human Resources : In the present day technologically advanced civilization quality of population is a far more important element of a state than population size, density or distribution. Now a days population of a country needs to be matched with resources and skill. The total number of population of a country has its own significance up to a certain point; but beyond that point, it is the quality of the people which matters most. Generally in an under developed country a large number of people are illiterate, half-red and diseased. That is why a certain density of population may create a seemingly unbelievable economic and political situation. But in a developed country having a very high level of education and technology including high standard of health and living, the same level of density of population can present a comfortable situation owing to some other avenues of employment that modern technology makes possible. The term quality of people means the social and political organization of a group of people, their cultural values, their economic efficiency, productivity and the level of their growth in science and technology and skills.

Of the several qualitative factors, the productivity or economic efficiency would account for the current of level of social and economic well being of the people of India including Assam, Food and medical facilities are important prerequisities for any people to be healthy workers. The healthy workers much possess necessary skill. Only technical and professional training would increase the productivity of a healthy worker manifold. Thus any country which wants to develop socio economically must take properly its resources including human resources.

In spite of its vast resources as described earlier Assam lags for behind in respect of rate of economic development. High rate of population including large scale infrastructural facilities, low level of resource utilization, subsistence economic base and multiple socio-political problems are some of the reasons of her economic backwardness. Assam is the most populous state in the North-East India with 2,66,38,407 persons as per 2001 census. This is 69.27 per cent of the total population of North-East India and 2.59 per cent of the total population of the country. On the basis of population size Assam ranks thirteenth among all the states of India as per 1991 and 2001 census. It ranks fourteenth among the states of India in terms of population density. A decline of 5.39 per cent and 2.52 per cent of decaded growth rate have been found in Assam and India respectively during inter-censal period of 1991-2001. In 2001 the total male population was 13,787,799 and female population was 12,250,608, accounting number of females per 1000 males were 932. The literacy rate in the state was found to be 64.17 per cent as against India's 65.38 per cent. About 88.06 per cent of the state's population lives in rural areas and the remaining 11.94 per cent in urban areas. The rate of population growth in Assam was as high as 581.35 per cent compared to 255 per cent of India during the last 100 years (1901-2001). The rate of growth for pre and post partition period is given below:

Period	Assam (in Percent)	India (in Percent)
1901-41	103.51	33.67
1951-91	179.17	134.38

These figures shows that the rate of population growth in Assam was consistently high compared to India as a whole. The natural growth rate of the population of Assam and India was more or less similar. The migration of people from other parts of India to tea gardens of Assam continued till 1931 from the early years of the 20th century. Then the movement had stopped thereafter. Similarly migrants from Nepal also contributed to the high growth of population in Assam. But the most important contribution to the unnatural growth of population of Assam was the large scale migration of poor Muslim peasants of East Bengal. The immigrants and their descendants who are the main cause of the rapid increase of population in Assam may be grouped into six categories: East Bengal Muslim peasants, East Bengal Hindu Refugees (post-partition refugees), Tea Garden Labourers, Nepalis, Rajasthani Traders and North Indian Wage Labour Immigrants.

The East Bengal Muslim Agricultural Immigrants are most illiterate, landless poor peasants and are seen to have occupied mainly the uncultivated Charlands of the Brahmaputra valley. After the partition in 1947, owing to discrimination against the religious minorities by the Muslim rulers in the then East Pakistan, which resulted in large scale migration of Bengali Hindus from that country of Assam. This group of immigrants mostly settled in urban and semi urban areas of the region. They are engaged in retail trade and unskilled jobs. The Nepali Hindus came to Assam during the British period as soldiers, policemen, sentries, graziers, farmers and wood cutters. The tea garden and ex-tea garden labourers which form another sizeable category of the immigrants and descendants of the aboriginal tribes who came to this region from Bihar, Orissa and Madhya Pradesh. Almost all the Rajasthani settlers of the state are from the business and trading community of Rajasthan. The entire business in wholesale trades in foodstuff and consumer goods including construction materials are handled by this immigrant group. The north Indian Wage Labourer immigrants are mainly engaged in laundry, scavenging, cobblering, construction works etc. and they are mostly settled in urban and semi-urban areas of Assam. During the war of liberation of Bangladesh in 1971 a total of 10,00,000 refugees took shelter in Assam alone. While many of them returned to their native place following the liberation of Bangladesh, about 1,00,000 of them are believed to have stayed in Assam. This has now been a never ending process and its effects have led to the change of demographic and settlement pattern of Assam. Thus the trans-border migration in to Assam remains unchecked and the population control, has, therefore become meaningless. The rapid growth of population due to natural increase and migration has affected the socio-economic and political life of the people of Assam. Fresh immigrant have created many socio-economic problems besides disturbing the original ethnic structure.

Religious Communities	**Total population of Assam**	**Percentage to total population**		**Growth rate during 1971-91**	
	1971	**1991**	**1971**	**1991**	**1971-91**
Muslims	3,592,124	6,373,204	24.56	28.43	77.42
Non-muslim	11,033,028	16,041,118	75.44	71.57	45.39
Total	**14,625,152**	**22,414,322**	**100**	**100**	**53.26**

The population of Assam grew at a rate of 19.93 per cent compared to the all India growth rate of 13.31 per cent in the decade 1941-51. In the next two decades ie. 1951-61 and 1961-71 the growth rate of Assam's population were 34.98 and 34-95 per cent compared to the growth rate of India 21.51 and 24.80 per cent respectively. This is the unnatural growth of population which must be due to influx of population from outside Assam. In 1981 census could not be conducted in Assam and the growth rate during the period of 1971-91 showed as 53.26 per cent and in 1991-2001 it was only 18.85 per cent. It has been observed that the flow of Hindu migrants of Assam from Bangladesh has considerably come down since 1971, that is after the Indira-Mujib Pact was signed. But the influx of Muslim population was higher compared to previous two decades which can be proved by the following census statement.

The decadal grow rate of Assam has abruptly come down to 18.85 percent against the growth rate of India (21.34 per cent) during 1991-2001. Such variation has been observed in the district of Nalbari (11.98 per cent) Bongaigaon (12.23 per cent), Dibrugarh (12.43 per cent) and Golaghat (14.21 per cent). Higher population growth (above national norm) has been observed in the districts of Dhubri (23.42), Goalpara (23.07), Kamrup (25.75), Nagaon (22.30), Karbi-Anglong (22.57), North Cachar Hills (23.47) and Karimganj (21.57). During this decade (1991-2001) the density of population of Assam has gone up to 340 as against 324 in India. Highest population density has been observed in the district of Nagaon (604), followed by Dhubri (584) and Kamrup (579) and the lowest is found in North Cachar Hills (38). The sex ratio has shown an improvement from 923 in 1991 to 932 in 2001. the highest sex ratio is observed in the district of Goalpara (955) and lowest in North Cachar Hills (883). Similarly the growth of literacy in Assam has also shown slight improvement from 52.89 per cent in 1991 to 64.28 per cent in 2001 with 71.93 per cent for male and 56.03 per cent for females. The highest literacy rate has been recorded in the district of Jorhat (82.76%) followed by Sibsagar (82.08%) and Kamrup (81.24) per cent while the lowest is seen in Dhubri district (49.86 per cent).

The overwhelming majority of population in Assam is rural scattered over 24,500 villages. The entire state is very poorly urbanized with a total urban population of 33,89,413 representing on 12.72 per cent of the total population of it against 27.78 per cent of the whole nation. This low degree of urbanization in Assam is due to the fact that the state has a subsistence agricultural economy. The only important industry in Assam is the tea industry. The tea gardens with their own markets in Kolkata and traders tend to prevent rather than help the formation of urban settlement. The other major industries are petroleum and petroleum products which are also colonial in nature. During the colonial rule the development process started in Assam with export oriented tea plantation, exploitation of forest resources and oil. Such activities have poor linkages with the other economy. The ownership and control of such industrial activities including trade and commerce are mostly in the hands of the migrants and as such investible surplus is siphoned out of Assam.

Prior to the advent of railways, the agricultural product of the plains of Assam which was often a surplus moved through the Brahmaputra and the Surma river systems. For the same reasons large number of villages and towns have clung to their banks since time immemorial, Dhubri, Guwahati, Tezpur, Jorhat, Sibsagar, Silchar are the old established towns of Assam. Recently in addition to this navigable river factor, roads and railways also play an important role in the location of urban centers in the plains of Assam. The British who came to Assam built some trading posts, military garrisons and cantonment in a number of places. Alongwith these other British services such as administrative functions, railway, medical, educational institutions, banks etc. were added to the gathering points and these places in due course were transformed into towns and potential urban centers. Old established towns like Guwahati, Sibsagar etc. were expanded in the process of accretion and development of bazaars. Most of the district and subdivisional headquarters established during the British period became urban centres. Similarly, the introduction of railway during this period led to the formation of urban centers like Rangia, Chaparmukh, Furkating, Simaluguri, Mariani, Lumding, Tinsukia etc.

In 1947 India became indpendent and since then due to gradual extension of motorable roads and means of modern transport and industrialization new market towns like Abhayapuri, Barpeta Road, Howli, Hojai, Mirja, Kharupatia, Nazira, Tihu, Tangla, Bihpuria, Dergaon, Moranhat etc. and mining towns like Duliajan, Namrup and Margherita and service-cum administrative town like Diphu, Haflong etc. grew up. Some existing towns like Guwahati (8,08,021), Silchar (1,42,393), Dibrugarh (1,22,523), Tinsukia (1,08,102), Nagaon (1,07,471), Jorhat (1,08,102) were also greatly expanded by swelling and infilling with additions of industrial estates, planned housing colonies and unplanned bastis. These are all cities with a population of over a lakh each Guwahati city attained this status in 1961 census which has a much more vigorous growth than all other towns owing mainly to the concentration of commercial, industrial and administrative functions of Assam in this city. It is followed by Silchar which is a service-cum trade and commercial centre. Tinsukia is also a trade and commerce-cum service centre. Such functions are seen in the cities of Nagaon and Jorhat. Functionally Guwahati and Dibrugah are rich because they have four important functions like service, trade and commerce, manufacturing and transport. The other towns of Assam are still in primary stage of development on account of their functional character, socio-economic condition and unscientific foundation of planning.

Agriculture : Assam is predominately an agrarian state. About 69 per cent of the total working force are being engaged directly or indirectly in agriculture and allied activities. According to Economic Survey of Assam, 2000-2001 the contribution of agricultural sector in Net State Domestic Product of Assam at constant 1993-94 prices was 34.79 per cent and at current prices 35.09 per cent in 2000-2001.

Although agriculture is the backbone of economy of Assam, the pace of development of this sector has not been up to the expectations. The factors responsible for the backwordness of agriculture in Assam are the pressure of population of land, lack of motivation inadequacy of non-farm services like provisions of finance and marketing, small and fragmented holding, pattern of land tenure, poor techniques of production and inadequate irrigation facilities.

The pressure of population on land has been so high that between 1970-71 and 1995-96 the average size of holdings in hectares declined from 1.47 to 1.24 despite slight expansion in acreage. So agricultural sector cannot be improved unless growth of rural population is checked and the pressure of population on agricultural land is reduced. A vast majority of cultivators of Assam are very poor and illiterate and it is very difficult to motivate them to adopt modern techniques of production. About 36.09 per cent of the total 26.64 million population of Assam are below poverty line. The poor farmers belong to this group and they have no means to improve their economic conditions.

The poor farmers do not get their proper price from their agricultural products and farming activities of Assam have suffered because of inadequacy of such non-farm services. The agricultural holdings in Assam are not only small but also they are fragmented. That is why modern means of scientific agriculture including improved implements, seeds etc. are very difficult to introduce in agricultural operation in Assam. A sizeable number of farmers are landless and the fate of the tenants still depend on the wish of the landowners. Such farmers are tradition bound and they have to depend an rainfall for farming activities. Only few of them can avail of the facilities of irrigation. So it is not possible to expect the poor farmer to increase agricultural productivity. Recently there has been a growing awareness among a section of farmers for the use of improved inputs like modern implements, seeds and fertilizers etc.

Major Crops and Their Distribution : Agricultural operations in Assam begin with the onset of monsoons and the two vitally important agricultural seasons are Kharif and Rabi. The Kharif crops are sown after the onset of the rains (June-July) and harvested in autumn. The important, Kharif crops are rice, maize, jute, sugarcane, pulses (arahar, blackgram, greengram), oilseeds (sesamum, castor, groundnut). The rabi crops are sown in autumn after the rains and the crops are harvested in late spring. The important rabi crops are rice, maize wheat, pulses (gram, blackgram, greengram, peas, lentil), oil seeds (rape and mustrd, linseed seasamum, soyabean, groundnut, and sunflower). Generally Kharif and rabi are not sown on the same ground. The Kharif crops are usually grown on the flood plains while the rabi crops are essentially the crops of river doabs and uplands.

Rice : Landforms, soils, climate including rainfall and temperature are very suitable for rice cultivation. Rice occupies about 70 per cent of the total gross cropped area of Assam and more than 90 per cent of the total area under food crops. Rice is grown in all the districts of Assam including the two hill districts – Karbi-Anglong and North Cachar. Area under rice is less in the hill district because of terrain conditions. It has been observed that there has been a gradual decline in the area coverage under Autumn rice in recent years owing to switching over the area under this crop to Summer rice which has higher productivity. The principal crop of Assam is winter rice. The area coverage under this crop is also registered a slight decrease to 17.77 lakh hectares in 2000-2001 from 17.94 lakh hectares in 1999-2000. The crop was affected by the flood during that year. The area under total rice cultivation was 26.46 lakh hectares in 2000-2001. Similarly the yield of total rice in Assam was 1531 kilograms per hectare during 2000-2001 as against 1927 kilograms for India for the same year. The area under high yielding variety of rice have been indicating a gradual increase over years and the newly introduced high yielding varieties are *rangit, bahadur, masare, lut, chilarai, IR-50, I-R-36* etc.

Maize : Maize is not seriously cultivated in Assam. It is generally grown in the jhum field of Karbi-Anglong and North Cachar Hills. In 2000-2001 Assam produced 12,000 tonnes of maize under 15,000 hectares of land.

Pulses : Some quantity of pulses are grown in every districts of Assam. These are grown as rabi crops which include gram, blackgram, greengram, peas and other pulses, Arahar, blackgram and greengram are also grown as Kharif crops in some areas. In 2000-2001 Assam produced 6800 tonnes of pulses (Total varieties) and the areas under these crops was 122000 hectares.

Wheat : Wheat is not a popular crop of Assam and it has been introduced only in recently. Wheat is grown as a rabi crop mainly in the districts of lower Assam. In 2000-2001, the area under wheat was 70,000 hectares and the yield rate of wheat recorded a decrease to 1,219 kilograms per hectare (2000-01) against that of 1,279 kilogram in 1999-2000.

Oilseeds : Assam is not self-sufficient for cooking oil. Seasamum, castor, soyabean, groundnut are the main Kharif oil-seeds and rape, mustard, linseed, sesamum, soyabean, groundnut, sunflower are grown as rabi crops Mustard and rape are grown on the flood plains of the Barak and Brahmaputra valley. Sunflower and soyabean have been recently introduced in Assam and these two oil crops are cultivated mainly in Karbi-Anglong, Marigaon and Barpeta districts. The area under different oilseeds in 2000-01 was 316000 hectares and total production was 1,73,000 tonnes in 2000-2001.

Jute : Jute is regarded as the golden fibre because it supports the jute textile industry in India. It grows well in the flood plains of the Brahmaputra and Barak rivers. Its production has increased to 6.68 lakh bales in 2000-2001 from 6.58 lakh bales in 1999-2000.

Mesta : Mesta is a dominating fibre crop of Darrang and Sontipur districts of Assam. The production of it recorded increase to 0.26 lakh bales in 2000-2001 against that of 0.25 lakh bales in 1999-2000.

Cotton : Cotton is not an important fibre plant of Assam. Karbi Anglong and North Cachar Hills have some favourable condition for growing cotton plant. About 1900 hectares of land are devoted to cotton cultivation in Assam.

Sugarcane : The physical conditions of Assam are quite suitable for sugarcane cultivation. It is an important cash crop of Assam and its production has come down to 9.88 lakh tones in 2000-2001 from 11.55 lakh tones in 1999-2000.

Tea : Tea grows well in deep, fertile well-drained moist soils with warm climate. Assam is the leading producer of tea and tea gardens are confined to the Brahmaputra valley and Barak plain. About 30 lakh people belonging to the tea Tribes community live in over one thousand tea gardens scattered all over Assam. Tea plantation and processing is the major industry of Assam. The state had 2,30,978 hectares of land under tea in 1998 and the average yield per hectare was 1995 kilogram.

Rubber : The physical conditions of Assam are suitable for plantation. So plantation of rubber was introduced recently and about 9,900 hectares of land area is devoted to rubber cultivation.

Coffee : The environment conditions are suitable for coffee cultivation in Assam and about 1438 hectares of land is under coffee cultivation. Besides, potatoes, tobacco, areca nut are also grown in Assam. Animal husbandry and fishing are now important occupations.

Industry : Industry is the principal component of the secondary sector and its main function is to provide work for the growing population, to satisfy the demand for manufactured goods and to raise the standard of living by the per capita income of the state. It is responsible for converting raw materials into finished products which is turn encourage the development of tertiary sector like servicing, marketing and transport. It may be observed that industry migrated from households to spacious workshops and mills and factories which, in turn, developed into towns and cities. The transfer of persons engaged in primary sector to secondary and tertiary sectors are usually visualized as social changes brought about by industrialization.

The industrial side of the economy of Assam was very much neglected. So manufacturing industries have not been made any headway even after independence. This is mostly due to factors like its isolated location, poor linkage and infrastructure, lack of adequate power and capital, absence of efficient and skilled labour and market etc. Of the existing industries tea manufacturing, oil refining, fertilizer industry are important.

Tea industry has been discussed earlier. It is one of the important earners of foreign exchange and thus tea industry helps. Indian economy by making the largest contribution in India's trade. It is also a source of revenue. Besides tea industry has given rise to many subsidiary industries. For example the plywood factories of Assam are engaged mostly in the making of chests for packing manufactured teas. Thus tea industry has given rise to timbering and saw milling.

Petroleum refining including petrochemicals is another major industry of Assam. Oil was first discovered in Digboi area in Assam during the colonial period and a refinery was made at Digboi for the refining of oil obtained from its wells. Since modern industry is run by power-operated machines, three more refineries were set up in Assam namely Noonmati, Bongaigaon and Numaligarh. All these refineries produce about 2.5 million tones of petroleum, diesel, kerosene, furnace oil, coke, liquified petroleum gas, methanol, carbon black, aviation turbine fuel etc.

A major fertilizer plant has been set up by the Fertilizer Corporation of India by using natural gas in 1950s. The plant produces about 1,00,000 tonnes of ammonium sulphate, 80,000 tonnes of urea, 70,000 tonnes of sulphuric acid including by products. Some minor fertilizer plants have been set up at Chandrapur, Bonda, Khanapara (in and around Guwahati) Choukathy (Bongaigaon) and at Mehenga (Nazira). The source materials of these plants are oil and natural gas.

According to new Industrial Policy, 1997, the Govt. of Assam seeks to maximize utilization of locally available resources and focus on the development of industrial sectors like food processing, handloom and textiles and rural non-farm sectors.

Besides there are some growth centers in Assam for promotion and development of small scale industrial units and tiny industrial units. The thrust areas for such growth centres are tea processing machinery, chemical, plastic, rubber, engineering, handloom, handicraft, fruit and food processing, electronic, ceramic, paper fabricants, drug and pharmaceutical, cold storage plants and other minor industries. A total number of 2256 small scale industrial units and 2363 handicraft units went into commercial production creating additional employment of 8460 and 5366 respectively in 2000-2001. Similarly under 20 point programme 1239 of small scale industrial units and 747 handicraft units started production upto the end of September, 2001. An Export

Promotion Industrial Park is under construction with all the required infrastructural facilities at Amingaon.

There are about 116 Khadi Production Centres including sub-khadi production centres is rural areas of Assam. The production of Cotton Khadi, Endi, Muga and Pat and Moslin Khadi are made in these centres. The local spinners and weavers work in such centres and earn their wages as per rules of Khadi and Village Industries Commisision, Government of India. There are 28 Departmental Training-cum-Production Centres and 73 Development-cum-Demonstration Centres in rural areas of Assam. The Assam Khadi and Village Industries Board has been implementing several village industrial activities through these centres. This Board has a marketing wings with 59 Khadi Gramodyog Bhanders. These are located at various places of Assam and also one at Kolkata.

Transport and Communication : It has been mentioned that owing to its geographical isolation, transport has been a major bottleneck for the economic development of Assam. Assam may be called the gateway to the other six states of North East India and as such the improvement of transport and communication facilities should be the first consideration in all planning and development programmes of Assam. The existing infrastructures and facilities of transport and communication are weak. However, Assam is served by all the modern means of transport like roads, railways, waterways and airways.

The Karbi Plateau and North Cachar Hills occupy a large part of Assam and heavy rainfall has led to the growth of natural vegetation in many areas including the hilly parts. There are two important river systems with their too many tributaries and the plains of Assam have been formed by silt deposited river flood. All these are the main reasons for poor development of roads and railways in Assam.

At the time of independence, India's legacy from the colonial phase included a kind of transportation panoply of imperialism i.e. the major ports, the related 'steel frame' of broad-gauge railways, feeder lines of metre and narrow gauge, road net-work included trunk roads, important feeder roads, totaling under 1,61,000 km of surface road, beyond which were the dirt roads and the village tracks (Indian & Pakistan by Spate and Learmonth, 1972). In Assam also there were 320 km of gravelled road, 6400 km dirt roads suitable for bullock carts and 5680 km of village tracks in 1903-04. The Brahmaputra valley is divided into two parts by the east-west flowing Brahmaputra river. So two trunk roads one along the north bank and the other along the south bank were constructed during the British period. At that time road system of Barak plain was linked with Sylhet district.

From the First Five Year Plan onwards, the Governments have constantly given a high priority to the developments of transport network. The three bridges at Saraighat, Kaliabhomora and Pancharatna across the mighty river Brahmaputra have greatly facilitated surface communication system in Assam.

The major roads including National Highways connect district and sub-divisional headquarters of Assam. Some of these important roads run beyond the state boundary to connect important places including capitals of other states of North East India. Generally the important places of the state are linked by the P.W.D. roads, rural service centres and villages are connected by the district roads and Panchayat roads. There were 33,343 kilometres of road under Public Works Department in Assam including 2044 kilometres under National Highways in 1998-99 as against 33,064 kilometres in 1997-98. The proportion of surface roads to the total roads in Assam was about 26 per cent as against 46 per cent in the entire country. The state has only 1.41 kilometres of road per 1000 persons as against 2.77 kilometres for India.

The important means of communication for the movement of goods and passengers traffic is road transport. The transport facilities in Assam are mainly provided by Assam State Road Transport Corporation (ASRTC), a state

Government undertaking and private transport operators. The Assam State Road Transport Corporation is generally concerned with the movement of passenger traffic on the nationalized routes while the other organization operate intra-state and inter state movement of both goods and passenger traffic. The total route length covered by the Assam state road transport corporation was 8130 kilometres in 1998-99 and the fleet strength comprised of 469 buses, 14 trucks, 28 cars and 4 tankers. Besides, a large volume of traffic is handles by private operators. The number of motor vehicles on roads in Assam was 4.01 lakh in 1999-2000. Recently the government of Assam has started construction work to setup an Inter-State Bus Terminal at Garchuk (Guwahati) to facilitate inter-state transportation of passengers.

A very few feeder lines of metre and narrow gauge railways have been introduced in Assam as early as 1882 connecting the tea, coal and oil producing areas with the river ports of upper Assam. Then the state was linked with other parts of India by the eastern Bengal railways. A major part of existing railways has been developed during the British period. After independence the Assam link was completed connecting Fakiragram with Siliguri. In 2000-2001 the total length of railway route was about 2516 kilometres of which 1186 kilometres under Broad Gauge and 1330 kilometres under metre gauge. The length of railway route constitutes only 3.8 per cent in the total railway route length of India.

During the British Period inland transport by country boats was important in Assam supplemented by steamboats and steel barges. The Britishers used both the rivers Brahmaputra and Surma including Barak river. There are numerous tributaries of the Brahmaputra and the Barak which are navigable by country boats. The Brahmaputra is a national waterways. There are two public sector organizations, namely the State Directorate of Inland Water Transport and Central Inland Water Transport Corporation are operating water transport services between Guwahati and Kolkata for movement of goods.

The total length of navigable waterways in Assam is about 4100 km which is 22 per cent of the total navigable water ways in India. The department of Inland Water Transport operates 74 ferry services of which 50 ferry services are in the Brahmaputra valley and 24 are in Barak plains. This water transport department also operate its commercial cargo service from Pandu to Narayanganj, Siraganj and Khulna (Bangladesh) and from Guwahati to Kolkata via Bangladesh.

The important urban centres of Assam like Guwahati (Lokapriya Gopinath Bordoloi Airport), Tezpur (Salonibari), Jorhat (Rowriah), Dibrugarh (Mohanbari), Lakhimpur (Lilabari) and Silchar (Kumbhirgram) are connected by Air with Kolkata, New Delhi and other places of India. Thus Assam is regularly served by Indian Airlines, Sahara, Jet Airways etc. The recent development of Guwahati airport, establishment of Customs clearance, export-import banking and other infrastructural facilities would definitely go a long way in economic development of the region and its neighbouring countries.

16

Arunachal Pradesh

Arunachal Pradesh is the largest state of North East India on the basis of area. It occupies an area of 83,743 square kilometers with a population of 10,91,117 according to 2001 census which is scattered over 12 towns, and 3649 villages. The state is situated between 26°28'N and 29°30'E latitudes and between 91°30'E and 97°30'E longitude. It shares a total of 1,630 km of international boundary with neighouring countries like Bhutan in the west, Tibetan part of China in the north and northeast and Myanmar in the east. The border states of Arunachal Pradesh are Nagaland and Assam are in the southeast and south respectively. The Mc Mahan line defined the international boundary between British India and Tibet in 1914. At that time the agreement had not been formally ratified by the Chinese Government. In 2011 the total population of the state increased to 1382611.

There are widely scattered archaeological remains at various part of Arunachal Pradesh which bear testimony to its rich cultural heritage. This state finds mention in the literatures of Kalika Purana and Mahabharta. Sages and Rishis were more familiar with this Himalayan state than other people in ancient times. It was here that sage Parashuram washed away his sin in Brahamakunda or Parasuramkunda near Tezu. A big Mela is held every year at the Kunda site during Makar-Sankranti in mid-January and lakhs of devotees make pilgrimage to this spot. Besides Sage Vyasa meditated, Lord Krishna married his consort Rukmini and King Bhishmaka founded his kingdom in the Arunachal Himalayas.

The hill slopes of the Arunachal Himalayas have been inhabited by many culturally rich tribal groups. Monpas and

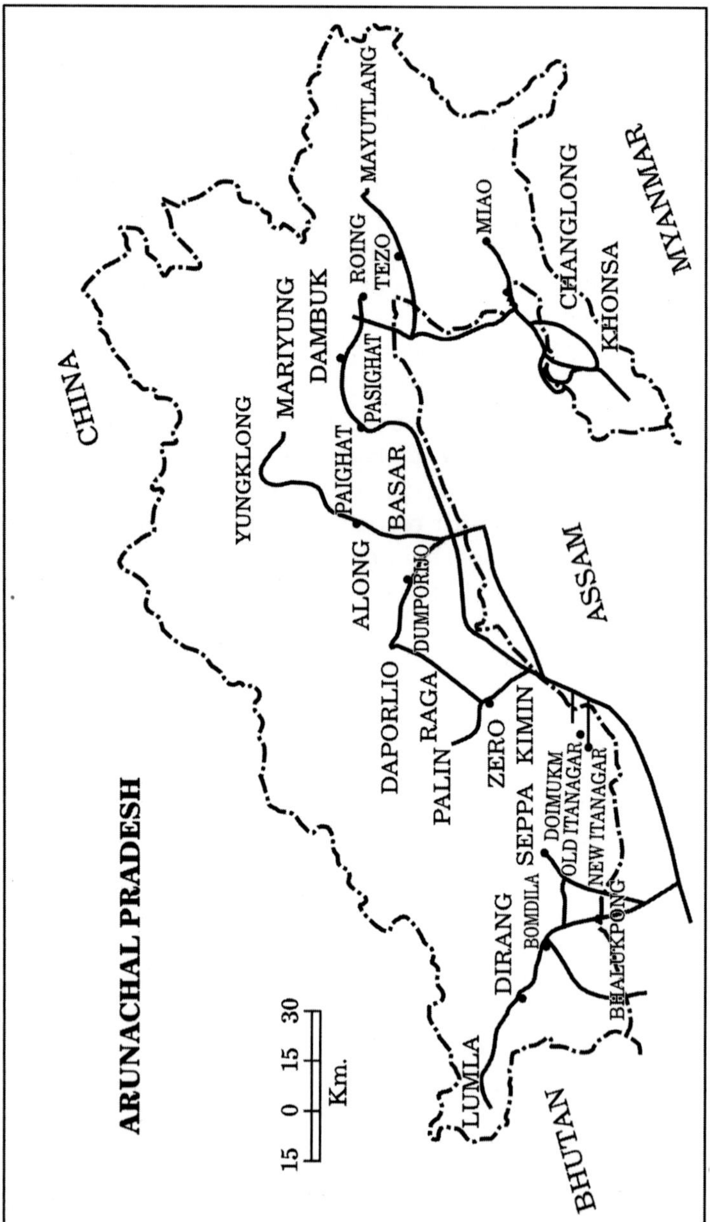

Fig. 13 : Arunachal Pradesh

Sherdukpens of Tawang and West Kameng districts (followers of lamaistic tradition of Mahayana Budhism) Adis, Akas, Apatanis, Bangnis, Nishis, Mishmis, Mijis, Thongsas (followers of Donyi-Polo and Abo-Tani), Noctes and Wanchos in the Tirap district. Each of these groups had a district territorial base and they uses to maintain cordial relations with the Assamese people living in the Brahmaputra plains. During the British period the present Arunachal Pradesh was loosely knit with the administration of Assam. Then the Inner Line Regulations have been introduced in 1875. In 1914 the tribal areas were separated, from the then districts of Darrang and Lakhimpur of the province of Assam to form North Eastern Frontier Tract. This tract come under the Govt. of India order of 1936 (Excluded and partially excluded areas). After independence the tract became an integral part of India which was administrated by the Ministry of External Affairs with the Governor of Assam acting as agent to the president of India. In 1954 this frontier tract was redesignated as the North Eastern Frontier Agency (NEFA). The NEFA became a Union Territory and aquired the name of Arunachal Pradesh. Then statehood was conferred on Arunachal Pradesh on 20th February 1987.

Physical Features : Arunachal is a mountainous state and the entire territory of this Eastern Himalayan state forms a complex system of mountain ridges with varying elevations ranging from 50m in the foothills and gradually ascending to about 7000m. The configuration of the land surface is traversed throughout by a number of rivers and their tributaries. The major structural feature of the higher part of the state is the main boundary thrust. The Siwalik belt of the state is delineated against the pre-Siwalik formations to the north by the Main Boundary Thrust. Again a system of frontal faults separate it from the Brahmaputra alluvium in the south. The land gradually rises towards the north from the foothills of Assam and eventually penetrates into the high mountain ranges of the Arunachal Himalayas. Nearly 64 per cent of the area of the state is above 1200m, 16.43 per cent between 600m and 1200m, 10.70 per cent between 300m and

600m, 7.20 per cent between 150m and 300m and 1.67 per cent is below 150m. The important peaks of the region are Namcha Barwa (7,756m), Gyale Peri (7151m), Kangto (7,090m) etc. The Arunachal Himalaya may be divided into seven major lithotectonic belts which are Siwalik belt, Gondwana belt, Dedza-Menga belt, Bomdila belt, Se La belt, Tuting-Tidding belt and Mishmi belt.

Drainage : The entire state is drained by the rivers of the Brahmaputra system. Some of these rivers are snow-fed. The westernpart of the state is dominated by the rivers like Bhorelli, the Bichom, Tengapani and the Dikrang. The important rivers of the Eastern part are the Subansiri, Kamla, Khru, Sipi, Palin Ponur, Poma, Popum par, Siang, Dibang, Lohit etz.

Soil : The limited river valleys in Arunachal Pradesh contain alluvial and diluvial soils. Red soils are found on all the hill slopes and hill tops except in higher altitudes. Generally mountain soils mixed with glacio-fluvial deposits occur above 4500m. In most cases soils have distinct characteristics and contents of schists, sales and conglomerates. The acidity of the soils ranges from medium to high which is due to high rainfall. The humus layer of the newly cleared forests are normally washed away by rains exposing rocky surface.

Climate : The climate of Arunachal Pradesh is dominated by the eastern Himalayas with their topographic variations. So climatic conditions vary with short distances and distinct contrast in temperature and rainfall conditions occur on the high mountain ridges, foothills and sheltered valleys. The southern and south central parts of the state have humid sub-tropical climate and sub-alpine and alpine climate predominates in the northern part. The summer season is short and moderate and average temperature of this season is about 38°C. The winter in Arunachal Pradesh is quite cold. During this season temperature ranges 0°C to 2°C in the southern part, but in the northern part it falls below the freezing point. Most of the areas having over 1500m experience snow fall and alternate rainfall. The valley areas of the Subansiri, the Dihang and the Lohit receive very high rainfall ranging from 350 cm to 400 cm. In other areas of the state, rainfall varies from 90 cm to 200 cm.

Natural Resources : The natural vegetation of Arunachal Pradesh varies greatly with the climate and attitude of the state. It ranges from a rain forest belt at the foothills and low lying areas in the eastern part to the tropical and sub-tropical vegetation upto the height of about 2134 metres. These vegetations are distinguished by valuable trees of great size, climbers, bushes alpine meadow etc. They can be classified into five broad types : tropical, sub tropical, pine, temperate and alpine forests. In the degraded forests varities of bamboos and other grasses are of common occurrence. Besides, there are more than 200 different species of orchids and many of them have commercial value. The richness of life forms in these forests presents a panorama of biological diversity with over 5000 plants, about 85 terrestrial mammals, about 500 birds, a large number of butterflies, insects and reptiles.

A large number of tribal population is found to live in the forests. They use a wide variety of forest resources for sustenance and livelihood. To encourage peoples participation in the management of forestry related activities several schemes have been introduced by the Govt. of Arunachal Pradesh. Such schemes are 'Apna Van'. Aided Natural Regeneration, Minimum Need Programme, Minor Forest Produce, Area Oriented Fuel Wood and Foddar Project etc.

Population : As per 2001 census the population of Arunachal Pradesh was 10,91,117. Which increased to 14 lakh in 2011. They are distributed in 12 towns and 3,649 villages. The state traditionally a sparsely populated area because of its rugged terrain condition and the density of population as per 2001 census was 13 persons per sq. km. and 17 per sq. km. in 2011. But the population of the state has grown by 26.21 per cent in 2001 as against decadal growth rate of 21.34 per cent at the national level. In 2001 the sex ratio of Arunachal Pradesh was at 901 females to 1000 males which was lower than the national average of 933. The number of literates was 4,87,796 in 2001 and the total literacy of the state rose to 54.74 per cent from 41.59 percent in 1991. Dominance of small villages and low rural density of population is the general rule of the state. The rural people are mostly dependent on forest and the horticultural resources. Therefore the villages need larger area and space and spacing of the villages in the state is about 6.6 km. Dispersed settlements are more common and semi-compact villages are mostly found in the foothills. Of the 3649 villages, about 3000 villages are very small having less than 200 persons. Similarly the urban settlements are only 12 and they are widely spaced.

Agriculture : Development works of the last 33 years has brought about vast changes in the field of agriculture and allied activities. The traditional method of jhuming is gradually giving way to modern methods of production using improved varieties of seeds, artificial supply of water and other inputs. About 22,000 hectares of land have now been developed for permanent cultivation. In the newly developed areas of the state topioca, maize, paddy, millet, ginger, peas, turmeric, cotton etc. are being produced.

Jhum cultivation is still the most common agricultural practice in Arunachal Pradesh. An area of about 700 sq. km. is under shifting cultivation annually which supports nearly 54,000 families. Maize, Paddy, ginger, potato, tobacco, millet, bean etc. are grown on jhum fields. The jhum practice has various adverse effect on ecology and silting problems in the plains because millions of tonnes of soil is eroded and washed down through rain water depleting the nutrient status of the soil of high lands every year. In order to check such erosion it is essential to cover jhum fields by horticultural crops of economic importance so that rural people may get employment and generate income through such activities.

Industries : The states immense water power potential have now been harnessed for hydel generation. The first micro-hydel project in West Kameng district had been commissioned in 1972 and started supplying power to the district head quarters i.e. Bomdila. Besides, some more projects were commissioned or under execution or awaiting for approval. Besides water resources, oil, coal, limestone and dolomite are also found in several areas in the state. But inspite of such resources, the pace of industrialization in the state is very slow and poor. Various factors like topographical, infrastructural, financial, lack of entrepreneurship are standing as barriers to industrialization of the state.

The people of Arunachal Pradesh have a tradition of artistic craftsmanship. Practically every tribal family is a self sufficient unit for making domestic articles like weaving cloth, baskets, wooden utensils, bows arrows, traps, sleeping benches, knife etc. Modern industry of Arunachal Pradesh is a recent phenomena. A small cement plant at Tezu, Citronella distillation plant and light roofing sheet factory at Pasighat, food processing unit at Along, TV and Walkman stereo assembling unit at Itanagar etc. are important public sector undertakings of the state. The government of Arunachal Pradesh has established 13 industrial estates in different central places for providing infrastructural facilities. Thus industrial activities of the state is very limited.

Tourism : The business of providing accommodation with amenities for people who are travelling through or visiting a locality for pleasure is known as tourism. In some countries of the world tourism is the main industry with many people being employed by the hotels, entertainment centres, tourist spots etc. A great deal of valuable foreign currency is earned from tourism by countries having such industry.

Arunachal Pradesh is not a linguistic state but it is ethnic state inhabited by colourful tribal people of diverse culture and lifestyle. The tribes have their own unique culture and traditions. Nature have provided them with a deep sense of beauty, which finds delightful expression in their songs, dances and crafts. There exists enormous scope for adventure and nature tourism like tracks for challenging trek, river rafting, angling etc. in the state. The most interesting and challenging trek in Bomdila-Tawang area is around Tawang Chu which starts from Jong, the bus-head in between Sela and Tawang. The trek-route passes from Jong to Mago through a wonderful jungle studded with magnificient waterfalls. Other important trek-rounds are Bomdila-Daimara-via-Ramlingam and Chakku. Bomdila-Seppa, along-Mechuka, Daporijo-Taksing, Pasighat-Tuting, Pasighat-Mariang, Daporijo-Along, Itanagar-Ziro-Daporijo-Pasighat and Margherita-Mian-Namdapha etc. Besides. River rafting may be tried along Kameng (Seppa-Bhalupung) Subansiri (Taliha-north of Daporijo), Siang, Dibang (Anini-Assam border)[1]. Other important places of tourist's attractions are Buddhist monastery at Tawang, Malinithan, Parasuram Kunda, Namdapha National Park, Gerisen Peak etc. In a major policy change in 1992, the Union Home Ministry agreed to allow foreign tourists to visit this state to trek, raft, angling on select nature trails. The state has a bright prospect of tourists industry.

Transport and Communication : The means of transport and communication system both at inter and intra-regional levels are poorly developed in Arunachal Pradesh. This is mainly due to its geographical location including remoteness, difficult terrain conditions, dense dendritic pattern of drainage, dense forests and very sparsely populated state of the country. These are factors which retarded the efforts towards the state's economic development including the means of transport and communication. Recently in view of administrative re-organisation including creation of new sub-divisional and district headquarters and strategic importance of the state more attention has been paid both by the state and central administration to the speedy development of transport and communication. The state department of Forest, Public Work Department and Rural Work Department concentrated their efforts on the development of transport and communications. It may be mentioned that the North

1. News Report, "Arunachal Pradesh Celebrating 19 Years of Statehood", *The Assam Tribune,* 20 February, 2005.

Eastern Council and the Border Road Organisations helped this state by expertise and resources in strenghthening the transport infrastructure of the region.

Thus the development of transport network has been spectacular. Prior to 1947, this Himalayan region was dominated by bridle path, Porter's track and there were only two roads. One of these was a war time strategic highway, the Stillwell road to Myanmar which served no appreciable rural population and the other, an approach road to the plains of Pasighat area, but was wiped out during the 1950 earthquake. Now there are about 11,300 km surface and unsurface roads as well as over 4000 km of bridle paths and porter's tracks.

It may be noted that the physical configuration of Arunachal Pradesh is not favourable for the construction of east to west roads in its area. All the towns, central places, district and sub-divisional head quarters of this state have to be linked with the towns of the Brahmaputra valley by some north-south roads. Some of the important roads are Gahpur-Itanagar, Tezpur-Bomdila-Tawang, North Lakhimpur -Kimin-Ziro-Daparijo, Likabali-Along, Pasighat-Along, Kakapathar-Namsai-Tezu, Margherita-Ledo-Changlang, Naharkatia-Joypur-Khonsa, Sadiya-Tezu etc. All these roads make horizontal linkages in the state. Generally Bus Services are being run by local co-operative societies. These societies also operate goods-cum-passenger services particularly on routes like Tawang-Bomdila-Tezpur, Pasighat-Dibrugarh etc.

Arunachal Pradesh has only 1.26 km of meter gauge railway which forms a part of Balipara-Bhalukpong meter gauge section. It may be mentioned that surveys for new railway lines including terminal points are in various stages of completion.

Arunachal Pradesh has about 18.50 km long ropeways which have helped the administration and transportation of personels. Since the state has very limited road linkage, some civil aviation schemes are under consideration. Some air strips have already been constructed at Daporijo, Ziro, Pasighat and Tezu and from there Vayudoot sevices are operated. Helicopter services are available in certain important places of Arunachal Pradesh. An airport at Itanagar, the capital of Arunachal will be constructed soon. Because of strategic and commercial reasons this frontier mountainous state needs efficient and strong air links with other important places of India.

17

Meghalaya

The political map of Assam has undergone many changes since independence. A major truncation took place when the Naga Hills district including Dimapur area of Assam and the Tuensang are of NEFA were separated for the formation of Nagaland in 1957 in the awake of insurgency there. It was elevated to full state in 1963. After conceding Nagaland it was very difficult to keep the other hill areas of Assam from getting their respective states. The Garos, Khasis and Jaintias had been agitating for a hill state with utmost restraint, discipline and peaceful means. So an autonomous state named as Meghalaya was formed with the two hill districts namely Garo Hills and United Khasi and Jayantia Hills of Assam on April 2, 1970. The Government of Assam tried best to avoid granting full fledged statedhood to these two hill districts within Assam as Shillong being capital of Assam for over a century. Besides there had been a large number of non-tribal population mainly in Shillong city area. But under the North-Eastern Recorganisation Act of 1971, Meghalaya was granted full statehood on 21 January 1972. This is one of the smallest states of India and lies between 25°5'N and 26°6'N latitude and 89°47'E and 92°47'E longitude. It has an area of 22,429 sq.km with a population of 23,06,069 (2001). The state in bounded by Bangladesh on the south and about one fourth of western border and the rest in bounded by Assam. In 2011 the population of the state increased to about 30 lakh with density 132 per sq. km.

The geomorphology of this area was first studied by Professor S.P. Chatterjee in detail in 1932. Then he published his findings under the name and style as Le Plateau the Meghalaya in 1936, Paris. Earlier the area was known as

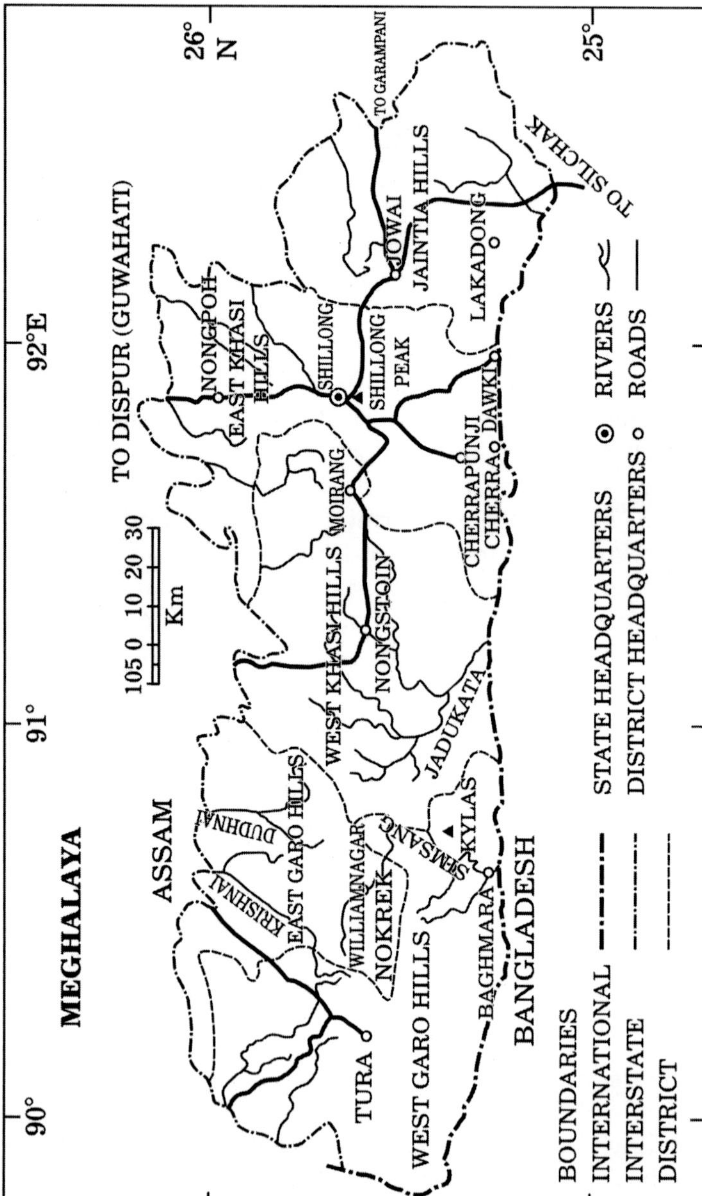

Fig. 14 : Meghalaya

Shillong Plateau. During the period of his fieldwork Professor Chatterjee observed execessive cloud cover greater part of the plateu and therefore he named the Shillong Plateau as Meghalaya (Megh-means cloud and alaya-abode). This name appeared in the Gazetteer of India, 1965 and the Home Ministry, Govt. of India adopted it to name the newly created state formed by Garo Hills and United Khasi and Jaintia Hills as Meghalaya state.

Physical features : Geologically the whole Meghalaya including the Karbi Anglong district of Assam is a detached part of the peninsalar India. It is separated by the Malda gap which resulted of river erosion of the Ganga and the Brahmaputra. Thus the landscape evolution of the plateau is closely linked with the Indian peninsula and its landform story consist of different types of erosion, sedimentation, folding, intrusion, movements of land and sea emissions. The core of the plateau is an ancient mass of gneiss, schists and granite which have been exposed in the north but hidden in the south beneath Createceous and Tertiary deposits and a Masozoic trap known as Sylhet trap. The whole plateau was under sub-arial erosion form the Cambrian to the Jurasic period. It contains within its face the marks of peneplaination which ranges from precambrian to recent and sub-recent periods. The peneplain are at varying attitudes of 1860-1920 in around Shillong, Latkor peaks 1440-1500m and 1410m in Umkhrah valley.

The Meghalaya is characterised by great diversities in physical features. The northern side of the plateau is highly dissected and of irregular terrain while its southern side is steep with regular slope. Its northern boundary is not well defined due to presence of discontinuous low hills. The plateau may be divided into three parts : Garo Hills or Western Meghalaya, Khasi Hills or Central Meghalaya and Jaintia Hills or Eastern Meghalaya.

The Garo Hills or Western Meghalaya is a highly dissected area with an average height of 900m from the mean sea level. This part of the plateau is separated form the Central part by the Maheshkhola-Adabari ranges. The important ranges of Garo Hills are the Tura range, Kylas range Arbela range etc. The Tura range runs form Siju to Tura and Nokrek (1529m) is its highest peak. The whole region is cris-crossed by a number of streams like Simsang, Krishnai, Dudhnoi etc.

The central part of the Meghalaya plateau is called Khasi Hills which lie to the east of the Garo Hills. The general height of this part of the plateau is about 1066m-1400m. Towards the South of Shillong city there runs an east-west range known as Shillong range. This is the highest range of the plateau with its highest peak known as Shillong peak (1961m). To the west of Shillong city in the Diengiei range which rises to the height of 1823 metres. Infact the Central Meghalaya plateau descends through a number of steps towards north to meet the Brahmaputra valley. The southern face of the central plateau is the steepest part of the entire region. The central upland descends by nearly 150-200m towards south on a number of steps and structural platforms which are built of gently dipping sandstons and limestones of cretaceaus age. These structural platforms are divided by deep valleys. The pressure of such structural features has given rise to number of waterfalls including the Mawsmai waterfall near Cherrapunji. There are numerous features like pot-holes, limestone caves, underground tunnels, stalactites and stalagmites etc. in the limestone topography of the region.

The Jaintia Hills is the eastern part of the Meghalaya plateau which forms a contiguous part of the Khasi Hills consisting of northern undulating hills, Jowai upland and the southern escarpment. There are more flat lands in the Jaintia Hills than that of the Khasi Hills. The general height of this part of the Meghalaya is in between 1250m and 1750m. The Jowai upland acts as a watershed between the Brahmaputra valley and the Surma valley. The middle part of the Jaintia Hills is mainly constituted by the rocks of the pre-cambrian age. The pre-tertiary and Tertiary rocks occur above these rocks which form the basement for younger formation. The Jaintia series of rocks predominantly composed of sandstones with clay, coal seams and fossiliferous limestones. These are all tertiary formations and belong to the shelf facies, The Jaintia series can be geologically sub-divided into three stages, namely Kopili stage, Sylhet limestone stage and Theria stage, The Jaintia Hills is formed of various types of rocks with varging lithological characters. Different agents of denudation like rainfall, rivers and temperature conditions have played an important role on the rock types in moulding the landforms of the area. The Jaintia Hills is bounded in the east by the Kopili river and the north eastern part is highly dissected by the headstreams of the Kopili river. So this section of the Jaintia Hills is associated with several embayments while the southern side contains a good number of structural and erosional platforms.

Climate : The climate of Meghalaya differs from the plains of North East India mainly due to its elevation. At the foothillsof the plateau the climate is humid and warm The central upland experiences very cold night during the winter where temperature goes down to 1.7°C. The temperature never rises above 26°C in any part of the year. The 18°C isotherm of mean daily minimum temperature, encloses the area around Shillong which is located on 1500m mean elevation from sea level. This is the coldest area of Meghalaya in summer. In winter the mean daily minimum temperature isotherm of 4°C covers this area (Shillong region) indicating to the coldest part of the entire state of Meghalaya. In winter the mean daily temperature is high in the areas western Meghalaya. These areas are covered by 12°C.

There is a great variation of rainfall in the plateau from south to north due to a rain shadow effect on the areas lying to the north. For example, Cherrapunji which is located on the high ridge has a rainfall over 1200 cm, while Shillong being located 50 km to the north of it gets only 230 cm. In fact a large part of Garo, Khasi and Jaintia hills of the state is enclosed by the isohyet of 300 cm which may be called as high rainfall area of Meghalaya. The average minimum rainfall is 251 cm and maximum is 367 at Jowai and this station does not experience any rainshadow effect.

On the basis of prevailing weather conditions, four seasons in a year are normally recognised for the state as a whole. They are : cold season-December to end of February, warm season-March to May, rainy season-June to September and cool season-October to November, Occurrence of clouds is a common weather phenomenon in the state. Generally the moisture laden winds and cyclonic disturbances bring clouds to the plateau. It is also observed that the density and frequency of cloud cover have been declined in recent years perhaps due to deforestation and other anthropogenetic causes. Consequently the weather is becoming warmer during summer in Meghalaya.

Drainage : Meghalaya is drained by a number of small rivers and they are controlled by its topography and rainfall. The central upland of the Khasi and Jaintia hills form the watershed from which one group of rivers flow towards the Brahmaputra valley in the north and the other to the Bangladesh plain in the south. The Khri, Digaru and Umiam etc. are the group of headstreams is responsible for the formation of embayments on the Assam-Meghalaya borderlands. The rivers of the southern group like Kynchiang, Wmical, Mymgot etc. form some deep valleys on the faulted structure before flowing to the Bangladesh plain. The rainfall is also high in the Garo hills and this hills is criss-crossed by numerous streams like Simsang, Bhogai, Nitai, Bandra, Sanda, Kalu, Krishnai, Ringgi, Didak, Didram and Dudhnhai etc. Of these Krishnai, Kalu and Simsang are navigable in their lower reaches.

Soil : The major parts of the Meghalaya consists of red loamy soil, red yellow soil and laterite soil. These soils are usually acidic, rich in organic matter and nitrogen but deficient in phosphate and potash. Such soils are good for cultivation of fruits, potatoes arecanut, betelvine and hill rice in the hill slopes and terraces. Because of high rainfall the top soils in the upland area is very thin and in some places rocks like granite, slate, limestones, sandstone, coal etc. lie bare in patches. Thus the effect of topography alongwith the conditions of climate and natural vegetation is reflected in the soil characteristic of Meghalaya. There are four major types of soils in the state and they are : Red loamy soils, laterite soils, red and yellow soils and alluvial soils. Red loamy soils are derived from the weathering of igneous and metamorphic rocks like granite, gneiss, diorite etc. Such soils are loamy but deficient in nitrogen, phosphoric acid, humus and lime and these are suitable for cultivation of fruit trees, oranges, potatoes and also rice. Red loamy soils occur in the central uplands of Garo, Khasi and Jaintia Hills. Laterite soils are produced by weathering of rocks occurring near the surface. These contains the hydrated oxides of iron and aluminium and on exposure such soils become hard. These soils are not suitable for growing crops particularly at higher level. Laterites occur on the Cherrapunji region of Khasi hills. The red and yellow soils contain ferric oxides are fine textured. They occur in a belt in the southern part of Meghalaya. These soils are suitable for growing rice, potato and fruits. Alluvial soils are found in the foot hill of Meghalaya. These soils contain clay, nitrogen and highly acidic in character. Wide varieties of crops like rice, bananas, tabacco grow well in such soils.

Natural Vegetation : Depending on rainfall, topography and edaphic conditions, the Meghalaya is clad with varieties of vegetations ranging from tropical, sub-tropical and temperate vegetations. As per Forest Report of India, 1997, the actual forest cover of Meghalaya was 15,657 sq. km. accounting 69.8 percent of the total area of the state. The total area of recorded forest was 9496 sq. km. or 42.34 percent. Of this recorded forest area, 8503 sq. km. was under the Autonomous District Councils and private ownership and the other 993 sq. km. was 'reserve forest' protected by the government of Meghalaya.

Generally tropical vegetation is found within the elevation of 1200m. This group consist of evergreen, semi evergreen, decidous, sub-tropical pine and grasslands. The evergreen and semievergreen forests consists of many broad leafed trees including few deciduous trees, shrubs with scattered bamboos, timber trees like shorea robusta, shorea assamica, vatica lanceofolia, tetrameles nudiflora, mesuaferea etc. All these vegetation predominate the hill slopes of the lower part of Meghalaya. Plants like banana, araceae, maramtaceae herbs grow on the valley bottoms and water plants like monochoria, ottelia, vallisneria and salvinia etc. are found in broad sluggish streams. The hill tops with shallow subsoils support grasses and herbs like gentians, swertia, osbeckia and lamiacea herbs. Temperate vegetation like pinus insularis, elaeocarpus, manglietia spp. etc. are predominant in the upland area of the state. Besides, there are sacred groves in the state and they occur at an attitude of 1800m and above. The dominating plants of such groves rhododen dron arborea, and guercus sapp., Broad leafed trees like Cinnamomum, bucklandia, carpinus schima etc. are also found in different sacred groves of the state. The sacred groves are the relic floras of this state and are very dense with distinct stratification.

There is a change of forest cover due to the practice of jhum cultivation and unscientific felling of trees in recent years in Meghalaya. In the coal mining areas are now devoid of trees and scrubs. The unscientific mining of coal in different parts of the state has caused deforestation besides other problems of soil erosion, water and air pollution and general environmental degradation.

The forest resources of Meghalaya may generate a lot of economic and employment opportunities if these are wisely utilised. The forests in the state are rich in timber species, bamboos, aeromatic and medicinal plants, tan and dye species, sport goods species, orchids, wild food plants etc. Some important timber species are gamelina arborea, duabonga grandiflora, adina cardifolia, shorea robusta, tectona grandis, pinus kesiya, mesuaferea etc. There are 14 genera bamboos including 36 species which suitable for construction purposes. Several aeromatic and medicinal plants like cryptocarya andersonii, canarium resiniforum, litsea citrata, rauwalfia spp, holarhena antidysenterica, ginseng, aesculus assamica and many others have been identified. Meghalaya rich in plant species having the potentiality to produce tans and dyes and important species are casia fistula, accacia mollisima, terminalia bellerica, laenia coromardelica, myrica esculanteck. Sports goods species include juglan regia, toonacilliata, michelia champaca, gmelina arborea etc. There are about 98 genera including 352 species of beautiful and coloured orchids in Meghalaya. Most of these plants can be used for industrial and commercial purposes.

Population : The Khasis, the Jaintias and the Garos are the indigenous people of Meghalaya. According to historians the ancient Khasis and Jaintias were immigrants some where from the Cambodian region and from the banks of the Mekong river. They came into ancient Assam via Patkai range and finally occupied the Khasi and Jaintia hills. The Jaintias seem to have been an Aryanization of the original Austric word synteng which developed into Jaintia, Generally the Jaintias are called Syntengs or Pnars. The Khasis proper are known as Khynriams or Nonghims. The important sub-tribes of Khasis are war people, Amwi, war synteng, the Bhoi people etc. The Garos are the inhabitants of Garo hills and they belong to Tibeto-Burman group. Besides, Karbies, Tiwas, Hadems, Kholtangs, Khelmas, Kukis and nontribals like Nepali graziers are inhabiting in different part of Meghalaya. Shillong is the capital city of Meghalaya and so it is cosmopolitan in character with mixed population.

As per 2001 census the population of Meghalaya was 23,06,069 of which 11,67,840 were males and 11,38,229 females. The proportion of female per 1000 males was 975 as against 932 for Assam as a whole and 933 for the entire country. Thus, the proportion of female population in Meghalaya is higher than the country as a whole. In 2001 the population of the state constituted 0.22 percent to the total population of India.

Similarly the total urban population was 4,52,612 accounting 19.63 percent of the total population and the population density of the state was 103 persons per sq. km.

In 1901 the population of Meghalaya was 3,40,524 and grew to 23,06,069 showing increase of 19,65,545 persons in 10 decades i.e. 2001. It is observed that the population of Meghalaya has been increasing since 1901 with fluctuation in growth rate in different decades.

It is to be noted that in all the census decades from 1901 to 2001, Meghalaya experienced higher growth rates than the country as whole. When India experienced a decrease of population by 0.31 percent Meghalaya experienced an increase of 7.21 population in 1921. After independence there was a constant increase in growth rate (1951-1991) and in 2001 growth rate was 29.94. But sex ratio has been declined since 1901 to 1961 and after 1961 it has shown slight improvement. The density of population in Meghalaya has been constantly increased from 15 per sq. km. to 103 per sq. km. in 2001. The literacy rate in Meghalaya had increased to 63.31 percent (2001) from 49.10 percent (1991). The male population had a higher rate of literacy (66.14%) than female (60.41%). The state is predominantly inhabited by rural people and only 19.63 percent of the total population lived in urban areas in 2001.

Table - 17.1
Growth of Population (1901-2001)

Year	Total	Male	Female	Growth Rate	Sex Ratio	Density
1901	3,40,524	1,67,256	1,73,268	–	1,036	15
1911	39,405	1,95,706	1,98,299	15.72	1,013	18
1921	4,22,403	2,11,216	2,11,387	07.21	1,000	19
1931	4,80,837	2,43,993	2,36,844	18.83	971	21
1941	5,55,820	2,82,666	2,73,154	15.59	966	25
1951	6,05,674	3,10,706	2,94,968	8.97	949	27
1961	7,69,380	3,97,288	3,72,092	27.03	937	34
1971	10,11,699	5,20,967	4,90,732	31.50	942	45

1981	13,35,819	6,83,710	6,52,109	32.04	954	60
1991	17,74,778	9,07,687	8,67,091	32.86	955	79
2001	23,06,069	11,67,840	11,38,229	29.94	975	103
2011	29,64,007	–	–	27.82	986	132

Source : Calculated from Census of India.

Meghalaya is a hilly state and so the distribution of population is generally governed by topography, availability of water, mineral resources and accessibility to areas. Densily populated areas are mainly found in Shillong region, in and around Jowai, Cherrapunji, Dawki, the northern, western and southern borderland of Garo hills. Usually the rural settlements of Meghalaya are very small. But there are some large villages around Shillong and their inhabitants find markets for their agricultural product. Mining settlements are observed in Cherrapunji region. Sparsely populated areas are mostly seen in the northern and south-western parts of Khasi hills, large areas of Jaintia hills and interior parts of Garo hills.

Shillong, Tura and Jowai are the major urban centres of Meghalaya. Shillong grew as the regional centre of governance, capital of erstwhile Assam and now most urbanized and capital city of the state of Meghalaya. In 1878 the population of Shillong was only 2147 which increased to 38,192 in 1941. But after independence the town attracted more people and in 1961 recorded 1,02,398 persons. The growth of population has still been increasing and in 1991 it become 2,23,366 and in 2001 it increased to 2,67,811 persons. It is interesting to note that the increase of population in the sub-urban areas of the city is more than that the central part. While the growth of population in Shillong Municipality is 0.88 percent only. The decidal growth of population is 23.50 pecent in Mawlai, 26.99 in Nongthymai, 61.58 in Pythorumkhrah, 11.82 percent in Shillong cantonment, 85.82 percent in Madanrting and 100 percent is Nongmyson. These urbainsed areas are all included is Shillong urban agglomeration Shillong is a multifunctional urban centre with administration, commerce and education as major function.

The city spreads northward from the Shillong range to the Umshing river and then it extends towards east. Recently ribbon growth has been taking place to the north along the Guwahati-Shillong road, to the south-east on the Jowai road and to south-west Cherra road.

Tura is the headquarter of the West Garo hills district. It is a medium sized town of over 50,000 population with functions like administration, trade and commerce and transport services.

Jowai is located on the Shillong-Silchar road and is the only urban centre of Jaintia hills. It is the head-quarters of the Jaintia hills district and has potential for development as a marketing centre.

Cherrapunjee, Nongpoh, Nongstoin, Williamnagar, Baghmara etc. have been growing as central places and potential urban centres of Meghalaya. It may be mentioned that Cherrapunjee is the oldest urban centre and the seat of administration during the British period. The growth of this township is very slow but it has enormous tourist potential with beautiful landscape including a network of waterfalls.

Agriculture : Meghalaya predominantly rural and its topography is hilly. More than 80 percent of the people live in rural areas and agriculture constitutes the main occupation of these people. The rural land in Meghalaya including some forest lands except the government owned forests and other holdings, is either community-owned or privately owned. Such lands (community or privately owned) are subject to annual cultivation under the age-old primive method of shifting cultivation or slash and burn method. The average annual operational area under shifting cultivation is estimated to be 1 to 1.5 hectares per family. It is observed that growing pressure of population requires expansion of agricultural land either by diminishing forest areas or by reducing the length of fallow periods. Both the phenomena are seen in Meghalaya. The fallow periods have now been reduced from 10 years to 3 to 4 years in most of the jhum areas of Meghalaya. Similarly forest cover of Meghalaya has been changed from 15,875 sq. km. (1991) to 15,657 sq. km. (1997). Of the 22,48,900 hectares of geographical area of Meghalaya, only 2,23,370 hectares are total croppd area ie. about 9 percent of the total geographical area is available for cultivation. It is to be mentioned that only 13 percent of the total cultivated land is used to produce more than one crop. Recently Indian Council of Agricultural Research Unit at Shillong recommended at three tier landuse model for the hill regions of North East India. Accordingly the upper 1/3rd of slope be allotted for the development for forestry, the middle part of the slope be used for plantation and horticultural crops and lower 1/3rd of slope be used for terraced cultivation. This landuse model not inconformity with scio-cultural structure of tribal communities which are closely woven into and central age-old traditional method of agriculture. Hence this proposal was not-accepted by the hill cultivators. The shifting cultivation is identified as one of the biggest problems to be tackled in Meghalaya. Crops of Meghalaya are : food crops, commercial crops, plantation and horticultural crops and other crops. Rice is generally grown on hill slopes and valley bottoms. About 1,18,000 tonnes of rice are production annually under 1,14,000 hectares of land. Wheat has been introduced recently in the plain areas of Garo hills. Now it is cultivated in west Khasi hills district. The total area devoted to wheat cultivation is about 4600 hectares and annual production is about 5,900 tonnes. Maize is grown in about 8 percent of the total cropped area of Meghalaya and annual production of the crop is about 12,000 tonnes. Pulses like gram, tur and others are grown in some areas of Meghalaya. But these are not important crops of the state. Potatoes, Oilseeds, Cotton, Jute and Mesta are important commercial crops of Meghalaya. The ecological conditions are quite favourable for the production of horticultural crops like orange, pineapple, banana, lichi, guava, mango and jack fruits etc. 'Khasi Mandarin' oranges are very famous.

Suitable climate and grazing facilities are available for rearing of animals alongwith cultivating plots of agricultural lands. Of the animals reared in Meghalaya cattle, buffalo, sheep, goat, pig are important. Dairy farming is also important activity in Meghalaya. There is an urban milk supply scheme at Shillong. A milk chilling plant was set up at Nayabunglow, about 20 km north of Shillong which supplies about 5000 litres of everyday. Similarly a dairy extension centre is at Jowai which produces butter, ghee, cream etc.

Industry : Meghalaya is fairly rich in hydel, thermal and also in nuclear energy resources. Due to sufficient rainfall, hilly topography and swift flowing stream, the generation of hydel power has made a signification progress. It is perhaps the only power surplus state in the eastern part of India. Meghalaya is also rich in coal, wood and uranium but these are not significantly used for the generation of power. Some infrastructural facilities like electricity, transportation, level land and natural resources are required for all round development of a state. Apart from transportation other facilities are available in Meghalaya, but this state still continues to remain one of the industrially backward states of India.

A majority of population in Meghalaya lives in villages and its economy based on agriculture, collection of minor forest product and weaving. The orientation of rural settlements to produce whatever is needed for local consumption which results in lack of internal markets. There was no need for local people to go any other alternative economy earlier. But in recent years population has been increased which created pressure on agricultural lands and all possible efforts are now being made for the industrialisation of the state by the government.

Meghalaya produces large quanties of cement and limestone and on the basis of these two minerals, a few cement manufacturing companies like Mawla Cherra Cements Ltd. in Cherrapunji, Jaintia Cements (P) Ltd. in Shillong under private and government sectors have been developed and started production. A plywood factory has been setup at Byrnihat on the Shillong-Guwahati road to utilise timber resources of Meghalaya. A medium category factory has been established at Mawshamok in the southern part of the Khasi hills to produce essential oils and chemicals. Besides, cane and bamboo work, blacksmithy, sericulture and weaving are important industries of Meghalaya. Some industrial estates have been established at Byrnihat, Shillong and Mendipathar in Garo hills. Recently Government of Meghalaya has launched some special schemes for the local people to give more emphasis on self employment for the unemployed youths. There is also scope for development tourist industry in Meghalaya. Umjiam lake, Waterfalls at Mawsmai etc. are some of the important tourist spots.

Means of Transport and Communication : Meghalaya is land of hills, mountain ranges, gorges and steep valleys and high rainfalls which prevent construction of roads and railway. Railways are absent and water ways and airways are very insignificant. Two important National Highways of the state are : The National Highway No. 40 i.e. Jorabat-Shillong-Tamabil road and National Highway No. 44 which runs from Shillong to Agartala via Jowai and Badarpur. These two National Highways may be regarded as the backbone of the entire road network of Meghalaya. The important places of Garo hills like Tura, Phulbari are linked with the National Highway No. 37 in Goalpara district of Assam. The total road length of the state 8,400 km. which is not adequate for a state having more 2 million population.

Only the rivers of Garo hills like Krishnai, Kalu and Simsang are navigable in their lower parts.

18

Manipur

Manipur is a picturesque state in the extreme northeastern border of India. It is bounded by Nagaland in the north, Mizoram in the south, upper Myanmar in the east and Cachar district of Assam in the West. It lies between 23°51'N and 25°41'N latitudes and 93°2'E and 94°47'E longitude. The East India Company opened trade with Manipur through Sylhet in the early part of the 19th century. It came under British rule as a princely state in 1891. In 1949 Manipur was merged in the Indian Union and became a part 'C' state, under the administration of a Chief Commissioner from 26.01.50. An Advisory form of Government was introduced in 1950-51. Later in 1957, this was replaced by a Territorial Council. In 1963, a Legislative Act of 1963 and then the status of the Administrator was raised from the Chief Commissioner to the Lieutenant Governor. Finally, under the North Eastern Recorganisation Act of 1971, Manipur became a full-fledged state from January 21, 1972. The shape of Manipur is rectangular with Manipur or Imphal basin in the centre. It is a landlock state with only two important roads : Imphal-Kohima-Dimapur Road (NH 39) and Imphal-Cachar Road (NH 53) connecting the adjoining states of Assam and Nagaland. As per 2001 census the population of Manipur was 23,88,634 of which 18,18,224 live in villages and 5,70,410 in 33 urban centres. The density of population per square kilometre was only 107. In 2011 the Population of Manipur increased to 27,21,756 with density 122 per sq. km.

Physical Features : The state of Manipur is encircled by hills with an oval-shaped fertile basin in the centre. These hills are parts of the Himalayan system. It may be mentioned that the Great Himalaya represents the original axis of uplift of

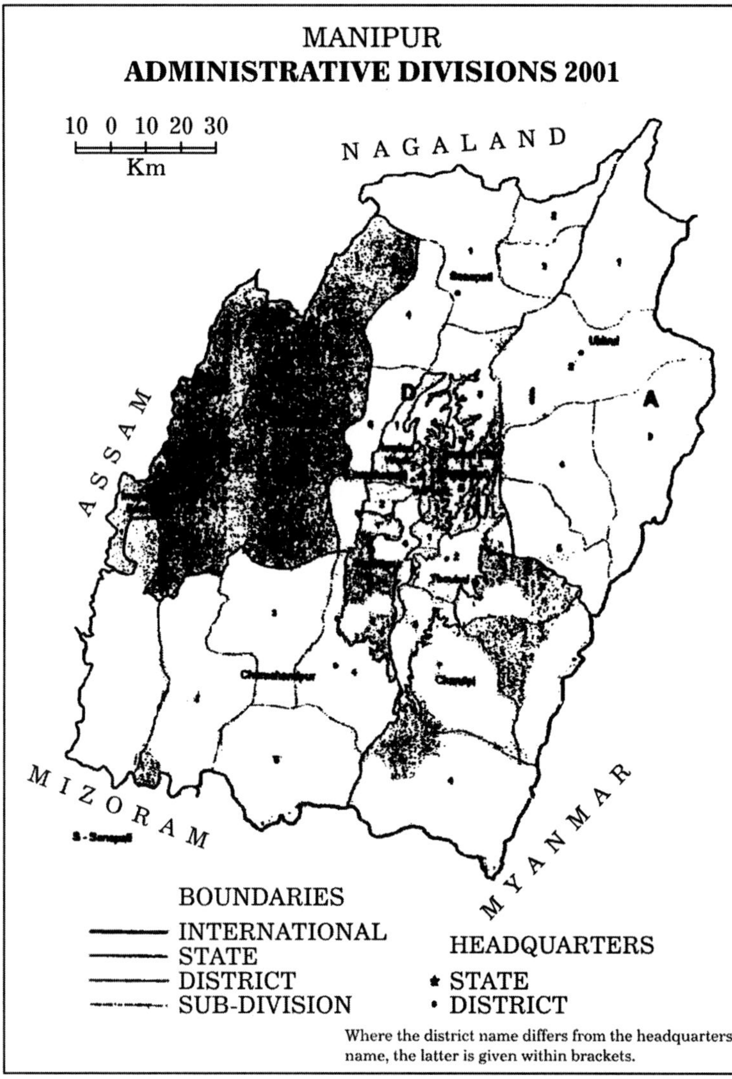

Fig. 15 : Manipur : Administrative Divisions 2001

the Tethys geosyncline, bending shaply southwards at each and into the Baluchistan and Assam-Arakan Ranges. The Assam-Arakan Ranges belong to north-eastern syntaxis of the Himalayas. The high hills of Manipur, Naga hills, Mizo hills, Chin hills are parts of the Assam-Arakan Ranges which are the southward extension of the Patkai-Himalayn ranges of the north. All the hills of Manipur are made up of sedimentary rocks and the central basin is composed of lacustrine deposits clays, muds, sands, loams etc. On the basis of physical set up, Manipur can be divided into two major parts : Central plain and hills.

The most striking topographic feature of Manipur is the Central plain or Imphal plain or Manipur basin. The area of this basin is 1843 sq. km. which is only 8.25 percent of the total area of Manipur. The plain slopes from north to south and its lowest part is Sugnu with an elevation of 746m above mean sea level. It is believed that this lacustrine plain was the site of an ancient mountain lake which was subsequently filled up with sediments and the remnant of that is the present Loktak lake. It covers an area of 96 sq. km. The central basin presents a flatland topography formed by the alluvial deposits during the tertiary period. Besides, there are a number of occasional hillocks like Pisun, Chinga, Chingalen, Kamuching, Waithou Langathel etc. which rise above the general level of the plain.

The major part of the state i.e. 91.75 percent of total land is occupied by the hills covering an area of 20,571 sq.km. The general elevation of the hilly region is about 900m to 3000m above the mean sea level. The region consists of a series of young folded parallel ranges extending from the Naga hills in the north and the Mizo and Chin hills in the south. These are broadly divided into two groups : The Manipur Eastern Hills and the Manipur Western Hills. The Manipur Eastern Hills run along the frontier of India-Myanmar for about 200 km. and form a compact and continuous belt. They are about 50 km. wide in the northern part and 30 km. in the southern part. This group of hills represent the ranges of Mapithal, Chingai, Mulai and Saramati, Khyayangbung (2833m), Siroy (2568m) and Kachaobung (2498m) are important peaks of this hilly region. The western part of Manipur is occupied by the hills like Yangpugilong, Daimikilong, Uning Thou, Koubru, Khoupum, Nurgba, Kala Naga etc. The hills are highly dissected by headstreams of the Barak river and the topography of the Western Hills is very much rugged. The important peaks are Tenipu (2994m), Leikot (2831m), Koubrue (2652m) etc. A small plain covering an area of 250 sq. km. is seen on the west of the Manipur Western Hills along the western margin of the state. It is mainly formed by the erosional and subsequent depositional activities of the Jiri river, the main tributary of the Barak river.

Drainage : The entire state of Manipur is drained by three important river system: Barak system, Manipur system and Chindwin system. The Barak is the longest river and it originates from the hill complex of the Nagaland-Manipur border near Japro peak of Nagaland. The river Barak runs westward for some distance forming the boundary of Nagaland and Manipur. Then it turns southward and flows through Manipur to reach Tipaimukh at the south-western corner of the state. It also forms the boundary of Manipur and Mizoram and then Manipur and Cachar district of Assam. At Jirimukh the Barak is joined by the river Jiri and from this point it turn towards west and flows through the Cachar and Sylhet plains as the river Surma, Irang, Makru, Tuivai and Jiri are its principal tributaries which form the Barak river system. The Imphal river flows the eastern half of Manipur including the central basin. The tributaries of Imphal are Iril, Thoubal, Nambul, Khuga and Sekmai form the Manipur river system. Some of these tributaries fall into the Loktak lake. The Imphal river flows on the eastern side of Loktak lake towards Myanmar to join the river Chindwin. The river yu is an important tributary of the Chindwin river. These three system of rivers and associated lakes including Loktak form water resourses of the state.

Climate : Manipur experiences sub-tropical mansoon climate with hot and wet summers and cold and dry winters. The greater part of Manipur falls under Koppen's cwg climate: The seasonal variability of weather including its characteristics are felt in the state due to the impact of terrain diversity, altitudinal variation, forest cover, water bodies including Loktak and its associated lakes.

Apart from topographic variations of temperature the mean annual temperature in the state decreases from west to east. For example, Jiribam in the Jiri river basin has a temperature of 23.6°C, Imphal in central plain records 20.4°C and Ukhrul in northeastern hills registers mean annual temperature of 18.20°C. Similarly 287.1 cm of average annual rainfall is recorded in the Jiri river basin, 108.5 cm to 143.4 cm in the Central basin as against 125.9 cm to 246.1 cm in the Manipur hills. Thus Jiribam is the hottest place of the state. Similarly Ukhrul and Tamenglong hill districts are the wetest parts of Manipur.

Traditionally there are six season in Manipur like Assam which are closely related to local weather conditions. The seasons are grisma (summer), barsa (rainy season), sarat (autumn), hemanta (pre winter), Sheetkal (winter) and basanta (spring). But the Indian Meteorological Department recognises four season namely northeast monsoon season (December-March), south-west monsoon season (June-September), transitional hot weather (April-May) and the transitional period of retreating southwest monsoon (October-November).

Northeast Monsoon Season : It is the cold season of Manipur and cover the period from December to February. The season starts by a decrease in temperature by about 5°C but January is the coldest month in which the mean daily maximum is well below 20°C and the mean daily minimum below 5°C. December is the driest month and rainfall is lowest during this season. Morning fogs are common in this season. Weather is generally fine and sometimes fine weather is disturbed by western disturbances and cause light winter rain which is useful for winter crops.

Pre-monsoon or Hot dry season : In Manipur hot and dry season starts from the later half of march and lasts till the end of May. The arrival of this season is usually marked by a sudden increase in temperature, disappearing fogs and occasional thunder showers and thunder storms. The frequency of rain increase towards the end of the season.

Hot and Wet or Rainy Season : This is the longest season of the year covering the period from June to September. The rainy season is associated with high temperature, heavy rainfall, widespread cloudiness, high humidity and week variable surface winds. The south-west monsoon provides heavy rainfall throughout the state and natural calamities like floods, high run-off and landslide occur during this season of the year.

Retreating monsoon or post monsoon Season : The month of October and November is a transitional period between the rainy season and the cold season. The rain bearing monsoon winds become weak and so rainfall gradually decreases but temperature increases. The season is characterised by short duration of morning fogs, cool pleasant nights bright sunny days. Fine weather is some times disturbed by occasional cyclonic stroms.

Soils : About 70 percent of the total area of Manipur is covered with fleshy sediments of Tertiary period. The northeastern part of the state, particularly Ukhrul region was formed by the rocks of upper cretaceoas period. Shale with minor mudstone, siltstone, sandstone of Desang series are confined to the hill districs of Manipur, namely Ukhrul, Chandel and Senapati district, Barail formations include areanaccens sandstone, clays and shales occur in the western part of Manipur alongwith Surya and Tipam series of sediments. The alluviums of the Central basin are of recent origin which were formed within the last 10,000 years. The geological structure as outlined above is mainly responsible for the formation of residual soils in the Manipur hills. The other type is the alluvial or transported soils of the Central plain which was brought by running water from elsewhere.

The greater part of Manipur is covered by hill soils or residual soils. The hill soils may be laterised and non laterised. The laterised soils are formed under conditions of high rainfall with a well marked dry season. These soils are coarse in texture, red in colour and rich in phosphate and nitrogen. They generally occur in the hillslopes of Western Hills.

The non-laterised red soils cover an area of about 17,800 sq. km. in the hilly area of Manipur. They may be ferruginous red soil or ferruginous red gravelly soils. The major part of Western Hills is covered by the ferruginous red soils. The other groups-ferruginous red gravelly soils are found in Eastern hills of Manipur. They are characterized by yellow and red in colour, and shallow in depth.

Transported soils are mainly confined in the Central basin of Manipur. The soils of the basin are composed of sands, clays, silts, and sedimends of fluvio-lacustrine origin Alluvial soils and riverine soils also occur at both sides of river banks like Jiri, Thoubal, Imphal etc. Such soils contains nitrogen, phosphorous, high acidity and abundant organic matter.

Natural Vegetation : Manipur is rich in her natural vegetation. Topography, climate and soils of Manipur have provided favourable ecological conditions for luxuriant growth of plant communities. A plant community predominantly of trees and other associated organisms of large area is called forest. The forest areas of Manipur are mainly confined to its hilly areas. The major part of the Central basin are used for human settlement and agriculture. The total area covered by forests is 15,154.95 sq. km which is 67.76 percent of the total geographical area of Manipur. The forests of Manipur can be classified into five broad categories. Tropical wet evergreen, Sub-tropical pine, Tropical dry deciduous and montane wet temperate forest.

Trophical wet evergreen forests occur in the Barak drainage basin in Tamenglong and Churachandpur districts. These forests contain several species of bamboos and canes. Tropical moist semi-evergreen type is confined in a narrow belt of Assam-Manipur border where rainfall exceeds 200 cm. The important species of this forest are bamboos, cane, cinnamon, agar, jarul, ironwood etc. Sub-tropical pine forests are mostly found in elevated area like north-eastern part of Ukhrul, south eastern part of Tamenglong and some parts of Chandel and Churachandpur districts. Pine, Khasia pine, Oak, chestnut including several varieties of orchids are found in these forest. Tropical dry deciduous forest generally occur along the Manipur-Myanmar border. Teak, Kangin, Khen and several other timber species are found to grow in these forests, Scattered patches of temperate trees (mostly pines) are found to occur along the foot hill areas and also the riversides in the hilly areas of the state.

Population : Nearly two-thirds of the population of Manipur are concentrated in a fertile area of 1843 sq. km. encircled by mountains. The whole human geography of Manipur is connected with this small central plain of Manipur. The majority of population of this area are the Meiteis, while the rest comprises about 29 tribes belonging mostly to Naga and Kuki groups and they are distributed in the surrounding hills. A sizeable percent of the population belongs to scheduled tribes, namely Hmars, the Paites, the Vaipheis, the Gangtes, the thadous, the Kabuis, the Kachas and about two percent belong to scheduled castes like the Lois Yaithibis.

As per 2001 Census the total population of Manipur was 23,88,634 persons of which 18,18,224 lived in rural areas and 5,70,410 in the Urban Centres. Due to some political troubles and the Anglo-Manipur war of 1891, no census was taken 1900. But census records of 1901 are available. High growth of population is the most significant demographic feature of North East India including the state of Manipur. During the last hundred year i.e. between 1901 and 2001, the population grew by about 8 times. In 1901, the total population of Manipur was 2,84,465 persons and in 1941 (before independence) it became 5,12,065 person which increased to 5,77,635 person in 1951 (after independence) and then in 1971, the total population became 10,72,735 persons and finally it increased to 23,88,634. It may be observed that there was no serious decrease population in any decade during the last 100 years except a small decadal variation during 1911-21 i.e. 10.92 percent, while the population of the country decreased by 0.30 percent. During this period the country was serously affected by epidemics, famine and other natural calamities. At the time Manipur was not seriously hit by such calamities.

After Independence high growth of population has been observed in every decade (see table - 18.1). This is mainly due to migration from other parts of India, Bangladesh and Nepal and decline in death rate with the improvement of medical facilities.

Table - 18.1

Year	Population of Manipur	Decedal Variation in P.C.
1901	2,84,465	21.71
1911	3,46,222	21.71
1921	3,84,016	10.92
1931	4,45,606	16.04
1941	5,12,069	14.92
1951	5,77,635	12.80
1961	7,80,037	35.04
1971	10,72,753	37.53
1981	14,20,953	32.46
1991	18,37,149	29.29
2001	23,88,634	30.02
2011	27,21,756	18.65

Sources : Census of India.

It is stated earleir that 91.75 percent of the state of Manipur is covered by hilly areas. Such areas being agriculturally less productive, cannot support dense population and distribution of population in hilly areas in sparce. Higher concentration of population is seen in the small fertile plain in the central part of Manipur. This tiny plain is only 8.25 percent of the state area but it contains 62.70 percent of the total population of Manipur. The Manipur hills support about 35.45 percent of the state population and the Jiri basin on the Assam-Manipur border contains 1.85 percent of population of Manipur. Thus the distribution of population in Manipur is uneven having large concentrations of population in the plain districts like Imphal East, Imphal West, Thoubal and Bishnupur and very sparse and scattered in the hill districts like Senapati, Churachandpur, Ukhrul, Chandel and Tamenglong. In 2001 the population density of the state was 107 per sq. km. But it differs from 25 persons per sq. km. in Tamenglong district to 847 per sq. km. in Imphal West district. The density of population in the hill districts is quite low ranging between 25 per sq. km. and 50 per sq. km. except Senapati district where density of population was high (116 per sq. km.)

The relative scarcity of women has been a demographic feature of India's population throughout the Census history of India. In 1901 there were 972 females per 1000 males and it decreased gradually to 933 in 2001. But in Manipur the sex-ratio has been found to be higher i.e. 978 (2001) than the national norm. In 2001 Imphal west and Bishnupur district in the central basin recorded the highest sex ratio-1007 and 1003 respectively.

In Manipur one in every three citizens is a tribal and there are 29 scheduled tribes of Manipur. Most of them belong to Naga-Kuki origin and are mostly concentrated in the hill districts, Aimol, Anal, Angami, Chiru, Chothe, Gangte, Lamgang, Mizo, Maram, Maring, Mao, Monsang, Moyon, Paite, Sema, Simte, Salhte, Thadou, Tangkhul, Vaiphei and zou are the important tribes of the highlands of Manipur.

Besides there are a few groups of people belong to scheduled castes which include Lois, Yaithibi, Dhobi, Muchi, Namasudra, Putni, and Sutradhar. They constitute about 2 percent of state's total population.

In 2001 the percentage of literacy in the state was quite high ie. 68.87 percent. In 1901 the literacy rate in Manipur was only 0.9% and during the last 100 years the state has achieved considerably in the field of education.

As per 2001 census 76.12 percent of total population lived in rurals areas and the rest 23.88 percent in 33 urban centres. In 1961 there was only one town with a total of 67,717 urban population or 8.68 percent of the population of the state as urban population. It grew to 33 urban centres with a total urban population of 5,70,410 in 2001. Of the 5.7 lakh urban population about 70 percent is concentrated in Imphal alone and the rest in the smaller towns like Bishenpur, Moirang, Ukhrul, Mao, Churachandpur etc. Imphal, the capital of Manipur is one of the largest cities of North East India. It is the centre of cultural, commercial and industrial activities with two war cemeteries maintained by the Commonwealth war Graves Commission.

Agriculture : Agriculture is the mainstay of the majority of the people of Manipur. About 76 percent of its population live in rural areas and nearly 70 percent of them depend on agriculture for their livelihood. It is estimated that over two-third of the main workers in Manipur are engaged in agriculture as cultivator and agricultural labourers. Although agriculture plays a significant role in the economic structure of the state, it is poorly developed and of subsistence type.

Agricultural areas are mostly found in the central basin, Jiri river plain, valley floor in the hills and on the hill slopes of the ranges. Forests covers about 68 percent or 15,15,000 hectares of the area of the Manipur. The area not available for agriculture constitutes 22.8 percent of the total area or 5,09,000 hectares. Net sown area covers 1,79,000 hectares or 8 percent of the total area of the state and of these area sown more than once is 9,000 hectares or 0.4 percent. Land under miscellaneous trees including fruit trees and groves is about one percent or 24,000 hectares.

Agriculture depends mainly on timely monsoon rain. In years of drought, agriculture suffers and prices of agricultural products soar high and for all these common people suffer. Three types of agricultural practices are prevalent in Manipur: Shifting or Jhuming is seen in the hills, terraces are mainly found on the hill slopes and some tiny valleys and settled farming is practised on the plains of central basin. The crops can be classified into four categories: (1) Food crops like rice, maize, pulses and wheat. (2) Cash crops- oilseeds, cotton, tobacco, jute (3) Horticultural crops-banana, papaya, pineapple, orange etc. (4) Other crops - sugarcane, chillies, patato, onion, betel leaf etc. Rice is the most dominating crop of Manipur. It occupies 98.17 percent of the cropped land of

Manipur basin and 92.13 percent of the total cultivated area of the whole state. Recently double cropping has been practised with the help of modern mechanization and irrigation facilities At present 54,100 hectares of land are under irrigation in 2000-01. The total area under rice was 156,960 hectares with annual production of 381,690 tonnes. Maize in the second important crop of Manipur and it is mostly grown in the jhum fields as well as in the dry fields of the plains. In 2000-01 the total area under maize crop was 4670 hectares and total production was nearly 10,900 tonnes. Sugarcane is grown on a limited scale throughout the central plain. A Khandasri Sugar mill has been established at Khangabok which encouraged farmers to grow more sugar. Cotton in grown is the hill areas on jhum fields. Wheat is relatively a new crop and it was introduced recently by Nepali farmers Pulses including peas and soyabean and oilseeds are grown in different areas throughout the state tabacco is cultivated mainly in plains of Manipur. Patato, cabbage, cauliflower, tomato, onion, ginger, garlic, chilli, turmeric are grown in many areas on the jhum fields as well as on the plains. Recently tea cultivation has been introduced on the hillslopes of Western Manipur. Similarly coffee and fruit cultivations like pineapple, orange, pear, lemon etc. are taken up in the hilly areas of Manipur.

Besides animal husbandry and dairy farming have been made remarkable progress in the rural areas of Manipur. The main beneficiaries such programmes are the small and mariginal farmers. There were about 28,46,700 animal population and 64,18,600 poultry in 1995. Of the animals kept in the state, cattle, buffaloes, sheep, pigs are important and milk, ghee, butter, curd, eggs, meat, hides etc. are usually obtaind from these animals. There are several sources of fishes like rivers, beels, Loktak lake and large numbers of marshes are available in Manipur. All kinds and sizes of fishes are caught but production of fishes in the state is not adequate to meet the local needs. To meet the local needs scientific fisheries may be set up in different areas of Manipur.

Industry : Industrially Manipur is listed as one of the most backward states of India. The state is for behind the other states because of deficiency of infrastructure, consisting of power, transport and communication including skilled labour. During the first three five year Plans, perhaps no effort was made to set up a base for industrial development in Manipur. However, during the fourth Five year plan attempts had been made to develop transport and communication, power and investigation of states industrial resources. As a result of such attempts a number of industrial schemes have been taken up and some of them already executed.

The mineral resources of Manipur is not properly surveyed. In recent years the Geological Survey of India and the Sate Department of Geology and Mining have been investigating the mineral reserves of the state. Accordingly some minerals like limestone, copper, lignite, nickel, chromite, cabalt, asbestos are reported to occur in the districts of Ukhrul, Churachandpur and Chandel. As there is no coal and petroleum, the only sources of power is water. There had been a great improvement in the power position of the state with the commissioning of Loktak Hydro Electric Project in 1984.

It may be mentioned that Manipur made a modest beginning with the establishment of the Khandsari sugar mill at Khangobok, Paper (insulated) mill at Karong, paper (bamboo based) mill at Chandighat, spinning mill at Loitang Khunou, Cement Project at Ukhrul and Industrial Estate at Takyel. Beside, a number of small-scale industries like carpentry, black smithy, pottery, bamboo and cane works have been developed in Manipur. Handloom, sericulture and handicrafts are also very important in Manipur. Handloom industry has occupied an important place in the life and culture of the People of Manipur. This is one of the oldest industries of Manipur and has been playing a major role in the economy of Manipur. It is reported that Manipur is the sixth state of the country having more then 2 lakh looms with 2 lakh part time employees. Most of them are women and they are skilled workers. The handloom products are very much artistic and durable which made their product very popular. Some of the important handloom products are bed cover, pillow cover, scarfs, screen and curtains, table covers, growns, saries, dhotis and these find good market throughout the country. Silk reeling, spinning and weaving are also carried on by women in their homes. Sericulture is not as important as handloom. Jewellery, wood carving pottery, doll making, ivory works are important handicrafts of Manipur.

Transport and Communication : Under developed means of transport and communication are mainly responsible for retarding economic progress of Manipur. The state has practically no railways except Silchar-Jiribam railway. Thus modes of transport facilities available in the state are roads, airways and inland water ways. Only important plain is the central basin and as such it has better transport facilities than the surrounding hills. Large areas of difficult terrain is yet inaccessible. The only link between Manipur and the rest India is the Imphal-Dimapur road, ie. National Highway No. 39. This National Highway connects Imphal with Dimapur, The railhead of Nagaland and the road may be called the lifeline of Manipur. The National Highway No. 53 connects Imphal with Jirighat. The road passes through dense forest and difficult terrain of Tamenglong district. The length of these two highways is about 434 km. The state highways connects the district headquarters with the capital city of Imphal, and the district roads connect block and subdivisional headquarters with district headquarters. The total length of these highways was 1,623 km in 1998. The important state highways are the Tiddin road, Imphal-Sugnu road, Imphal-Ukhrul road, Imphal-Tamenglong road, Imphal-Kangchup road etc. Among the major district road Kangpokpi-Tamei, Tamei-Tamenglong, Bishnupur-Nungba, Moirang-Kumbi are important. Besides, there are inter-village roads which connect the villages with the nearest district roads. The total length of inter village roads 3563 km in 2000. Motor transport in the state is partly nationlised and Manipur State Transport Corporation is the biggest public carrier. Besides, there are few co-operative societies which run their buses and trucks in several routes.

The Indian Airlines Coporation operates daily air service form Kolkata to Imphal via Silchar and Delhi Imphal via Guwahati and Bagdogra. Recently one Vayudoot Service has been introduced between Kolkata, Imphal and Dimapur. It may be noted that road transport in Manipur suffers from landslides during the rainy season. At that time air transport is the only alternative which links Manipur with the other parts of the country. Thus roads and airways are the chief means of transport and communication in Manipur.

Inland waterways are practically insignificant like railways. In early days inland water transport in the river, lakes and marshes of Manipur plains was an important means of transport. With the development of various categories of roads, this inland water transport becomes insignificant and limited in Manipur. However, in Loktak lake and in the lower reaches of Barak streams including Jiri river small country boats are used to transport man and materials from one place to another.

Post Office, Telegraph, Telephone, Radio and Television are the important means of communication in Manipur. The growth of telecommunication service in the state is remarkable since 1961. A medium and short wave radio station and one television transmitting centre have been setup at Porompat, Imphal. There were 693 Post office, 48 P & T Officer, 1007 Public call offices, and 25494 teleconnection in the year 1999-2000.

19

Mizoram

Mizoram, the land of Mizos lies sandwiched between Myanmar on the east and Bangladesh and Tripura on the west its southern tip touching the Chittagong Hill tracts in Bangladesh. In the north Mizoram has common boundary with the Cachar district of Assam and Churachandpur district of Manipur. The state has a common border with Bangladesh over a length of 250 kilometres and with Myanmar, 410 kilometres which consititute 70 percent of the total boundary length of the state. Mizoram is located between 21°25'N to 24°39'N latitudes and 92°16'E to 93°39'E longitudes. Under the British administration, it was known as Lushai hills district of Assam. The name was changed to Mizo Hills district in 1954. It was carved out of Assam as a Union Territory of Mizoram on 21st January 1972 and then it became a full fledgd state of India on 20-2-1987. As per 2011 census the total population of Mizoram was 1091014.

The Mizos belong to Mongoloid stock and are believed to have migrated into Mizo Hills between 17th and 18th century from upper Myanmar. During the pre-British period Mizo hills was its pre-state society. At the early part of British administration, the Mizos raided British territories and the British army occupied their territory in the last quarter of the 19th century. Then the entire Mizo territory was formed into the Lushai Hills District and made a part of Assam in 1898. Insurgency plagued Mizoram for two decades from 1966-1986. The historic Peace Accord was signed between the Government of India and the Mizo National Front on june 30, 1986 which brought peace to the territory and in February 1987, Mizoram attained statehood.

MIZORAM
ADMINISTRATIVE DIVISIONS 2001

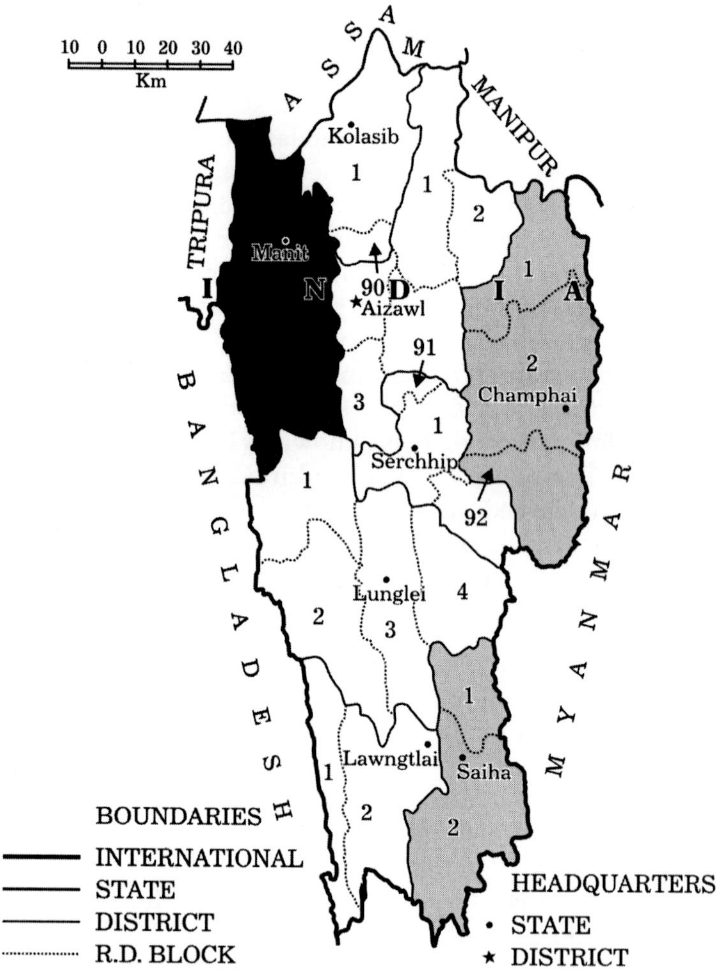

1. Parts of R.D. Block (90) and (91) of Aizawl district fall in Kolasib and Serchhip district respectively.
2. Part of R.D. Block (92) of Serchhip district falls in Champhai district.

Fig. 16 : Mizoram : Administrative Divisions 2001

Physical Features : Mizoram is a hilly state and the highest point is 2165 metres above sea level on the Blue Mountain. The hill ranges run from north to south direction and in between such parallel ranges of hills there are narrow valleys and deep gorges. The average height of this mountainous state is 900 metres above sea level. The major structural trend is almost north-south direction and is parallel to the regional tectonic lineaments. The folds of the ranges are characterised by compressed anticliness alternating with broad, gently depressed synclines.

The topography of Mizoram is young and immature. The oldest rocks of the region are the Barails overlain unconformally by the Surma group. The Bhuban formation of this group is very well developed. This formation is subdivided into three sub-groups. The lower Bhubans are predominantly arenaceous; middle Bhubans are predominantly arenaceous with interlaminations of pelagic shales and muds and upper Bhuban are also arenaceous. Overlying it is the Bokabil formations of feldspathic sandstone and shale.

The general landforms of Mizoram are moulded by the process of running water and topographically the whole state may be subdivided into two parts: eastern part and western part. The relief of the eastern part is quite higher and the slope are more steeper than in the western part. The average height of the ranges along the indo-Mynmar border is 2000m above the sea level. The western part of Mizoram consists of ridges and valley type features. The average height of these ridges is about 1000 m and the highest point is not exceeding 1600 m. The relief of this part is rather low.

Drainage : It is mentioned that the ranges of Mizoram run from north to south and the intervening areas are occupied by the long main streams. In fact, the rivers adjust themselves to the structure of the landforms. The landforms including their geology are quite favourable for the development of trellis pattern of drainage. The main streams develop along the soft rock strata, parallel with the strike and the short streams follow the slopes of the hills. Such long and short streams are quite numerous in Mizoram. These are mostly ephemeral in nature depending on monsoon rains. Most of the rivers originate from the central part of the area and flow towards north or south. The rivers like Tlawng or Dhaleswari and Turial or Sonai flow towards north and finally join the Barak river in Cachar district of Assam. The river Karnaphuli flows toward north initially and then turns towards west to enter Bangladesh where it has been tapped to generate hydel power. The river Kaladan is the south flowing river of Mizoram. The valleys of such rivers are narrow and deep and their erosional activities are more than the depositional works. The rivers are mostly developed in softer formations. The erosional and depositional activities of some important rivers have succeded in formations of small plain areas in the south-western part of Mizoram.

Climate : The greater part of Mizoram enjoys a humid sub-tropical monsoon climate and the narrow belt of the Indo-Myanmar border has a cold, humid, high altitude climate. The average annual temperature in the areas having sub-tropical monsoon climate is between 10°C to 20°C. During summer the temperature is sufficiently hot (18°C-25°C) and winter is cool, longer and drier. The temperature is usually low in the Indo-Myanmar border lowest below 0°C in winter and highest is not exceeding 20°C during the summer. The entire Mizo hills falls under the direct influence of southwest monsoon and receives sufficient amount of rainfall. The average annual rainfall for the whole Mizo hills is 250 cm. The summer season is quite wet and July and August are the rainiest months. Winter season is quite dry. Soil erosion and landslides are the common phenomena during the rainy season in Mizoram.

Soil : The landforms of Mizoram are hilly and of sedimentary origin. Due to weathering of the surface rocks, The summits and slopes of the hill ranges are left with only a thin layer soil that formed by local weathering. These are residual soils and are mostly found at lower altitudes over the hills and mountains. The colour of such soils is red because of the oxidation of the iron content present in it. The red soils of the central part are usually loamy and so it is known as red loamy soil. The greater part of Mizoram is occupied by red and yellow soils which are fired textured. Alluvial or transported soils are found in small plains and valley bottom of the state.

Natural Vegetation : The total geographical area of Mizoram is 20,987 sq. km. and of this 18,775 sq. km is under forest cover (1997). Due to wide variation in topographical, climatic and edaphic conditions, several forest types ranging from tropical evergreen to sub-tropical types are found in Mizoram.

Teak, garjan, champa, several varieties of bamboo bushes and grasses grow in abundance in the forest of Mizoram. Forests constitute more than 89 percent of the total geographical area of Mizoram. A large portion of forest area (524 sq. km.) is under the category of the unclassed forest. Such forests are either owned by the communities, village durbars and individual families. Reserved forests include 905 sq. km. and protected forest 1647 sq. km. The area of forest in Mizoram has been declining since 1991. In 1991 the total forest area was 18,583 sq. km. and in 1997 it became 18,775 and during the period 1991-97 forest cover in Mizoram had reduced by 78 sq.km. The decrease of forest land in Mizoram is mainly due to conversion of forest land to agricultural land, overgrazing, shifting cultivation, indiscriminate felling of trees for timber need etc.

These forests including tropical climate create favourable habitat for wild lives. Elephants, leopards, tigers, bears, wild dogs, deer, wild pigs, gaur, goral, serow, various species of primates, raptiles and birds are found in the forests of Mizoram. In recent years many of these animals and birds were killed and their number had reduced.

Population : As per 2001 census the total population of Mizoram was 8,91,058 of which 4,59,783 were males and 4,31,275 females. The density of population was 42 per square kilometre. The density decreases from north to south and also from west to east because of dificult terrain conditions. In Mizoram there were 938 females per 1000 males in 2001. Mizoram had a high degree of literacy ie. 88.49 percent which was the second highest in the country. It may be mentioned that the Mizos came under the influence of a missionary society called "The Arthington Aborigines Mission" in 1894. Many Mizos were converted to Christianity and Missionaries helped them to achieve a high literacy.

The growth of population in Mizoram has almost been consistently higher than the all India rate since 1951. The decadal growth rate of population for the last five decades in Mizoram is give below :

1961-71	1971-81	1981-91	1991-2001	2001-2011
24.9	48.6	38.98	29.18	22.78

In the decades 1971-81 and 1981-91 the change has been very significant 48.6 percent and 39 percent as against the national growth rate of 25 percent and 23.5 percent respectively. The higher rate of urbanisation was experienced by the smaller states in North East India. This is not linked to broad based economic progress but to administrative and other factors like political movement and migration. Mizoram with an urban population of 4,41,040 (2001) or 49.50 percent has a greater degree of urbanisation than the national norm. Aizawl, the capital of Mizoram is one of the largest cities of North East India. Among the urban centres, Aizawl city with more than two lakh population seems to have borne the chief stress of population pressure. In the decades of 1960s and 1970s the population of Aizawl had gone up by about 123 and 135 percent respectively. On the other hand the growth of rural population is not that high. In the 1981-91 decade the growth rate of rural population was much lower than those of the earlier decades. It may be mentioned that one in every 20 persons in Mizoram was engaged in government jobs which were available in some urban centres including Aizawl. The growth of urban populatin in Aizawl has been phenomenal resulting in congestion. The hilly terrain does not allow easy widening of roads which are narrow and create trafic jams. So a plan was formulated to build up an additional town complex near Aizawl to relieve the congestion and maintaining an urban enviroment of this enchanted city. The project is yet to be implemented as planned. The other urban centres of Mizoram and Champhai, Kolasib, Lawngtlai, Lunglei, Manit, Saiha and Serchhip. All these centres are district headquarters and the importance of these towns are due to their administrative and commercial function. There are about 700 villages in Mizoram. The villages are mostly small and isolated. Only in certain pockets of Mizoram villages are large. Such villages in Mizoram grow along the roads like a service centre or an administrative centres, giving rise to nucleated pattern of rural settlement.

Agriculture : Agriculture may be called the only occupation for the people of Mizoram. In the post statehood period, Mizoram along with other hill states of North East India, had been declared 'a special category state'. It receives adeguate subsidy in the form of grants-in-aid to cover its excess non developmental expenditure on revenue account over revenue income. There was much pressure on land due to increase of population and the pressure drive the agricultural population of Mizoram towards extensive cultivation. In 1980 the area for rice cultivation in Mizoram was 29,000 hectares which increased to 48,500 hectares in 1987-88. But the yield per hectare was marginally increased. This implies that there was hardly any improvement in the technique and method of cultivation or other input. Very little had been put to double or multiple cropping. Besides, there has not been any substantial reduction in the traditional or jhuming cultivation. Of the 65,000 hectares net cropped area, only 3000 hectares are double or multiple cropped area. Rice is mostly grown on the Jhum field and in recent year terraced farming is being tried. In some areas farmers have been made to settle in group centre and terraced farming has been introduced in every group centre. Improved seeds of paddy, modern implements, fertilizers and other inputs have been provided to the farmers by the government.

Besides rice, other important crops of Mizoram are maize, wheat, mustard, sesame, potatoes, pumpkins, beans, cucumbers, brinjals, chillies, pulses and tobacco. Some new schemes have been introduced in Mizoram to grow sugarcane, rubber, tea and other horticultural crops.

Industries : It may be mentioned that the entire Mizoram is a Notified Backward Area and the state has no major industry. But there are some unorganised traditional village and small industries like Khadi and village industries, handloom, sericulture, handicrafts and coir. Besides, providing some income to the poor agricultural labourers and artisans these traditional industries preserve craftmanship and art heritage.

Mizos are talented crafts-persons. The government of Mizoram declared a new policy– The Industrial Policy of Mizoram, 1989 for an allround development and gainful employment to the local people and also to create self employment opportunities in the industries and allied sectors. Various types of supports including institutional, organisational, marketing, infrastructural, manpower training, initation to attract prospective entrepreneurs will be extending accordingly.

In 1982, the Mizoram Khadi and Village Industries Board was established various schemes operated by this Board are carpentry works, blacksmithy, soap making, bakery, sugarcane crushing, spinning and weaving. Similarly the Sericulture Training Institute has been set up at Zemabawk to extend technical and other facilities to the farmers co-operative and rural development department for the improvement sericulture industry in the state. In 1989, the Mizoram Food and Allied Industries Corporation Limited was set up in order to promote and improve food processing and preservation industry. The corporation has been looking after food preservation factory at Vairengte, ginger oil and Oleoresin plant at Sairang. The Cement Corporation of India has setup a cement clinker grinding unit at Kolasib.

There are at present 2,447 small scale units, 29

government sericulture farms and 909 private sericulture farms. The department of Industries, Govt. of Mizoram had established a number of Estates at Aizawl, Zuangtui, Lunglei and Saiha for the promotion of village and small industries.

Transport and Communication : The landforms of Mizoram is characterised by steep slopes, difficult terrain, parallel hill ranges with deep valleys running from north to south. The means of transport like waterways and railways are absent and roads and airways are insignificantly developed. It is also very difficult to construct roads across the state in the east-west direction because of terrain conditions. The Border Road Development Organisation and the State Public Works Department are the main agencies for the development of road transport in Mizoram.

There are three type of road in Mizoram: National highway, State highway and district road. The National highway No. 54, connect Silchar with Tuipang, in the southern corner of Mizoram through Kolasib, Aizawl and Lunglei. This road has now been extended from Lunglei to Theriaghat and Demagiri as National highway 54 A. The National highway No. 54 B connects Venus-Sedel with Saiha. The roads under state highway are all weathered metalled roads. Some important roads of this type are Seling-Champhai, Seling-Tipaimukh, Sairang-Tuipuibari, Lunglei-Tlabung, Serchhip-Thenzawl, Kawnpui-Serkhan-Aizawl via Durtlong road. The unmetalled roads are district roads which include Kanhmun-Kawrtethawveng, Khawzawl-East Lungdar, Aizawl-Lunglei-via Thanzawl road, W. Phaileng-Tlabung via Marpara road. Besides there are a number of Jeepable roads.

Because of terrain conditions, construction of roads in Mizoram is a difficult task. The existing roads are with a number of obstacles like blind curves, steep gradients and landslides. The ranges of Mizoram are of sedimentary formation and so landslides on road are common phenomena. It is also observed that about 70 percent of the existing road network alignment is in north-south direction and the 25 percent runs east-west direction. The road density in Mizoram is very poor. The total length of roads in Mizoram in 1990 was 4850 and road length per 100 sq. km was 22.99.

Air transport in Mizoram is also not developed. A smaller airport was constructed at Tuirival near Aizawl. But it is yet to be connected with the important air-ports of North East India. For example, there is no regular air service from Guwahati to Aizawl. Recently a large size Air-port has been constructed at Lengpui, 40 km away from Aizawl. This geographically isolated frontier states needs more airports for strategic and economic reasons.

20

Nagaland

Situated between 25°6'N to 27°4'N and 93°20'E to 95°15'E, Nagaland occupies a strategic position in the geopolitical setting of India. It is bounded on the north by Arunachal Pradesh and on the south by Manipur, on the east by Myanmar and west by Assam. This state occupies an area of 16,579 sq. km with a population of 19,88,636. There are many tribes and sub-tribes like Angamis, Zeliangs, Rengmas, Kukis, Semas, Aos, Lothas, Phom etc. among the Nagas. In 2011 the total population of Nagaland increased to about 20 lakh.

The Naga Hills district of Assam and the former Tuensang frontier division of NEFA were separated for the formation of Nagaland in 1957 in the wake of in surgency there. This new administrative unit was kept under the Ministry of External Affair to be administered by the Governor of Assam. The Dimapur area of Assam was also merged into the state of Nagaland. Finally it was elevated to a full state on first December 1963.

Physical features : Nagaland is a hilly terrain which consists of a series of awe-inspiring hill ranges separated by deep narrow valleys. The eastern part of the state is occupied by the Naga range which is the extension of the Patkai range. It forms the watershed between India and Myanmar. The mountain peak, Saramati with 3,826m is located on this-high range. This range has been cut by the Tizu river which flows towards the east to merge the Chindwin river of Myanmar. On the west of this Naga range there are other ranges running from north to south. A part of the Barail range enters into Nagaland from south-west to attain a height of 2995 m at the Japuo peak, near Kohima. At this point the Barail range is met with an extension of Arakan Yoma and from here the main range runs in a north, north-easterly direction. The general effect on the morphology of the main range is that of a gigantic 'L' in the reverse position the junction of the two arms forming an obtuse angle with minor ridges branching off on either side towards the east and west. The general slopes of the main range are moderate to steep. The ranges in the south have steeper slopes and gentle slopes occur in Mokokchung area. The topographical features of Nagaland are characterized by rugged terrain and the serrated ridges are separated from one another by narrow valley with torrential streams running from north to south.

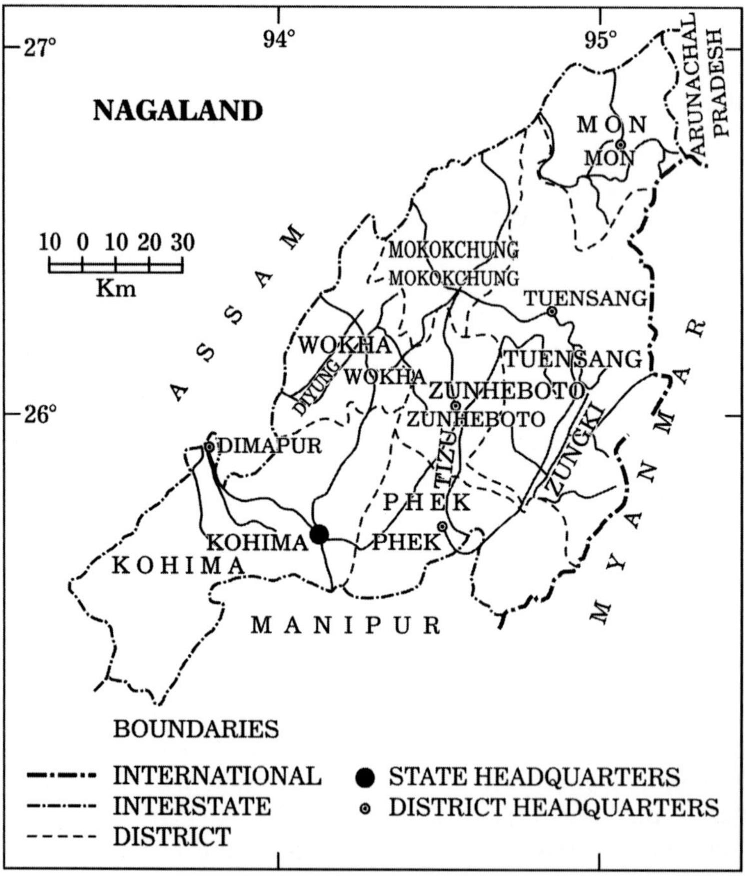

Fig. 17 : Nagaland

There is a series of complex overthrust with an imbricate pattern, extend along northeast to southwest on the northern part of the Naga-Patkai range. The outermost boundary of the thrust belt is known as Naga thrust and the innermost boundary of the belt is represented by the Disang thrust. The thrust system has affected the folded Tertiary sediments of both Assam and Nagaland. Another series of thrusts, namely the Nimi, Zephu and Tizu-Zunki thrusts run parallel to each other in Tueusang district. The Zepuhu thrust extends south-southwest to the Indo-Myanmar border. The Patkai Kohima Synclinoria enter into Manipur.

Drainage : There are three river systems which are engaged in draining Nagaland. These are the tributaries of the river Brahmaputra in the northwest sub-tributaries of the Barak in the south and the sub-tributaries of the Chindwin river in the east. Among the tributaries of the Brahmaputra Disang, Dikhu, Jhanzi, and Disai are draining Nagaland. The Disang is the largest river in Nagaland and it is navigable for a few kilometres within state before it enters the Brahmaputra valley. The river Tizu with its tributary the Lamier drains the south eastern part of Nagaland and then joins the Chindwin river, the main tributary of the Irrawaddy river of Myanmar. Some very small streams drain the southern part of Nagaland and then meet the Barak river. These three different systems of rivers are draining on the folded structure of Nagaland have developed the trallised pattern of drainage. Besides, there is a beautiful lake called 'Lacham' to the east of Meluri.

Climate : The climate of Nagaland is humid sub-tropical monsoon type with altitudinal variations. The summer temperature ranges between 18°C to 25°C. While in winter it does not fall below 0.4°C. The average annual temperature is between 10°-20°C. Nagaland is situated in between the Brahmaputra valley and the highland of Myanmar. Because of its situation in relation to the Brahmaputra plain the northwestern part of Nagaland receives more rainfall than the southeastern high ranges. The isohyet of 200 cm cover an wider area in southern Nagaland. The rainfall is very heavy along the foothill region, boardering Sibsagar, Jorhat and Golaghat districts. The average annual rainfall at some important place like Wokha, Chonghyimsen, Tuli, Tamlu etc. is over 250 cm. The rainfall decreases southeastward, away from the foothills. The average annual rainfall of Kohima (1561m) is 200 cm. But the amount of rainfall increases towards the east and northeast due to increasing height. Thus rainfall at Wokha is 290 cm and at Mokochung is 275 cm and at Tuensang is 305 cm.

The year of Nagaland can be sub-divided into four characteristic season on the basis of rainfall, temperature, fogs and thunder storms. These are winter (December to February), Pre-monsoon (March to April), Monsoon (May to September) and retreating monsoon (October to November) Nagaland has a very low temperature in winter. The hills of the state experience a minimum temperature of 4°C the winter in Nagaland is dry, cold, clear and sunny sky with morning fog. Rainfall occurs occasionally. The important characteristics of pre-monsoon season in Nagaland are sufficiently increasing temperature, disappearance of fog and occurrence of thunder-showers. The monsoon season prevails on Nagaland during the months of May, June, July, August and September. The season is characterised by heavy rainfall, high temperature and high relative humidity and the road transport suffers from landslide. The temperature begins to decrease from the later part of September, the number of rainy days decreases during the months of October and November. The weather is bracing. This is a very short season but the most pleasant one of the whole year. Haze and mist appear especially in the morning and evening because of slight fall of temperature.

Natural Vegetation : Apart from temperature, rainfall and soil conditions, altitudinal factor plays an important part in the distribution and nature of vegetation in Nagaland. The hill ranges of Nagaland are covered with luxuriant growth evergreen forests mixed with shrubs herbs and climbers.

There is a vertical zoning of vegetation in Nagaland. In the southeastern part of the state forests are mostly coniferous with oak and pine trees. The hills below 1200 metres are covered by wet monsoon and evergreen forests with important species like nahar, hollock, hollong, gamari, pama, sam, uriam, makari sal and bamboos. Due to pressure of population the forest resources of Nagaland have suffered from reckless fellings and burning for shifting cultivation. Where these forests have been cleared, high grasses, reeds, scrub jungle spring up is great profusion. In 1989 there were 14,339 sq. km. of forest cover which has been changed to 14,221 sq. km. in 1997. The forest of Nagaland are good habitats for wild animals like elephants, bisons, tigers, wild boar, wild buffaloes, leopards, sloth bears, sambhars, foxes, monkeys, Himalayan hornbills and other species of birds.

Soils : By and large the soils of Nagaland are thin, fine grained red soils which contain some organic and nitrogenous materials. But these soils are poor in iron oxide, phosphorous, potash and lime. Some laterite soils are also seen along the border of Sibsagar, Jorhat and Golaghat districts of Assam. The soils of the river valleys, valley bottoms and lowland with gentle slopes are clayey alluvium rich in organic matters. These soils have high moisture retaining capacity. In the areas of heavy rainfall and high ranges with steep slopes, the materials are washed away from the hill slopes and are deposited in the valleys and along the foothills. The red soils of Nagaland are suitable for growing rice, maize, millet and fruits. Cotton, wheat, pulses, potato, citrus fruits can also be grown under irrigation.

Population : There are 357 constitutional communities in North East India as recorded in the "People of India" by K.S. Singh, 1992. In Nagaland there are as many as 25 tribes and 18 sub-tribes while an equal number of tribes and sub-tribes live across the adjoing areas of Assam, Arunachal Pradesh, Manipur and Myanmar. All these tribes and sub-tribes have their own dialects and sub-dialects. These are varying from village to village within a single sub-tribe. It may be mentioned that each village of Nagaland is an epitome of the ancient Greek city states with own definite population, area and administration. So Nagaland may be regarded as a conglomeration of village republics. The major obstacles of Naga solidarity may be diversity Naga dialects and village republics. Pidgim Assamese, known as Nagamese is the inter-tribal language of communities.

The Konyaks (1.4 lakh) of Tuensang district are one of the numerically largest tribe. The another largest tribe is the Aos (1.7 lakh) who occupy the area between the rivers Disang and Dikhu. They are highly educated among the Nagas and contribute a large number of political leaders. The Semas (1.6 lakh) are the second largest tribe and a substantial number of semas in the state are recruited to the Indian armed forces. The other important tribes are the Anagamis, the changes, the Chakesangs, the Lothas, the Rengmas, the Phoms, the Sangtams, the Yimchungers and the Zeilangs. Each tribe has a distinctive character in social cultural and economic aspects because their habitations are sited at inhospitable terrain with minimum physical and cultural interaction.

As per 2001 census, the total population of Nagaland was 19,88,636 of which 10,41,686 were males and 9,46,950 were females. Thus number of females per 1000 males was 909 and density of population per sq. km was only 120 persons. The first census was taken in Naga hills when population was 96,637 and this number increased to 1,02,402 in 1901. In 1951 (The first census to be held in post independence period), the population of Nagas became more than doubled their total number stood at 2,12,975. in 1971 the same increased to 5,16,449 persons which revealed a decennia 1 percentage variation of 39.88 percent during 1961-1971. In the last census (2001), the total population of Nagaland rose to 19,88,636 person accounting growth rate of 64.41 percent during the period 1991-2001. In 2011 the total population rose to 6980602 with decadal growth rate of 0.47 during 2001-11.

According to 2001 census 82.26 percent of the population

of Nagaland lived in rural areas and the other 17.74 percent in urban areas. In 1981 there were 7,74,930 persons in Nagaland and of this 6,54,696 were in the rural areas and 1,20,234 were in the urban area and the percentage of urban population was only 15.52 percent. The urban population are mostly concentrated in the towns like Kohima, Dimapur and Mokokchung. Kohima is the capital and largest town of Nagaland. The government of India setup the Central University at Kohima in 1994. It is directly controlled by the Ministry of Human Resource Development and UGC. Kohima and Dimapur are the important tourist centres. Tourist attractions include war cemetery at Kohima and historic ruins of Kachari Kingdom at Dimapur.

As per 2001 cencus the percentage of literacy was 67 percent of which 71.77 percent males and 61.92 percent femlaes. In the early part of the 20th century the Christian Missionaries set up some primary Mission's schools which became instrumental in spreading education in Nagaland. Though their main purpose was to spread the teaching of Chritianity among the animist Nagas. The task could not fulfilled till the Nagas were educated. After independence, a number of schools were set up in the villages and upgraded the primary schools to the level of secondary schools and higher secondary schools. The financial aid provided by the government enable every Naga child to obtain education at their door.

Agriculture : Agriculture involves majority of the population in Nagaland. The absence of plain fertile lands make agriculture very difficult and very limited. Almost 90 percent of the agricultural area is privately owned. About one-third of the total land is cultivable. There are three types of agricultural practices in Nagaland: Jhum cultivation, terrace cultivation and permanent cultivation. Most of the hill tribes of North East India including Nagas practise a primitive type of cultivation known as jhuming. The farmers clear the jungles in the hill slopes with some primitive implements and in cleared area, they sow the seeds of rice, maize, millets, chillies and vegetable. The jhum fields give good return for the first two year and then exhaust the fertility of the jhum fields. The field allowed to remain fallow for 6 to 10 years. About 80 percent of the farm land is under jhum cultivation in Mokokchung and Tuensang district. This type is mostly practised by the Semas, Aos and the Lothas. The average size of jhum plot is about 0.6 hectares.

The Angami Nagas adopted wet farming under terrace cultivation. Generally they build up terraced field with stones which form the outer boundary of the fields. Terraces are constructed on gentle fields and skilfully graduated so that the excess water over flows from one step to another. The concentration of population in the Angami inhabited areas are relatively more and so this area does not admit the practice of jhuming. The main implements for this type are also hoe and dao. Rice, millet, maize, pulses, potato and sugarcane are raised. Rice occupies 60 percent of the total area under food crops. Fruits like orange, pineapple, banana, papaya etc. are grown on hill slopes. The land under permanent cultivation is very limited to small river valley and valley bottoms of the hills. The total cropped area in Nagaland is about 1,82,900 hectares but the yield of food grain is low i.e. 1252 kg per hectare.

The meat is one of the main items of food of the Nagas and cows, pigs and goats dominate in the life of the rural people. With a view to improve animal husbandry. A cow breeding centre has been set up at Januki; a national bison research centre has been established at Parua and a dairy processing plant has been setup at Dimapur.

Industries : The mineral resources of Nagaland is immense but unexplored yet. Amont the minerals coal, limestone, oil and nickel bearing magenetite are important. Coal in association with barils occurs in Mon, Wokha, Mokokchung and Tuensung districts Limestone is found in the metamorphic and ophiolite belts of eastern Nagaland. Nical-cobalt bearing magnetitie and nickeliferous chromite occur in Tuensang. Oil occurrences have also been reported along the Assam-Nagaland border. So there is a scopes for industrial development in Nagaland and at present the state is far behind many states of India.

Barring Assam, Nagaland and the North-eastern states are all nacent with under-developed economices. The developed activities in the 40 year has been focused on the provisions of infrastructure and basic amenities which were non-existent when Nagaland was created. The government of Nagaland failed to create any industrial base so far for the above reasons. Recently the government introduced some schemes for industrial development which are positively accepted by the people. The state has achieved remarkable progress in small and medium industries. There are 30 industrial units and more than 300 small-scale industries. The state has a small Khandsari sugar mill at Dimapur, a pulp and paper mill at Tuli and a small fruit canning centre at Chanki. Besides, wood work, pottery, bee keeping, sericulture, candle making are important industries of the state. Among the industrial products Naga shawls, bags, ties etc. are of unique design and colour. Some more industries may be set up in Nagaland. Development plans for industry may be formulated along with the development of agricultural activities, power, transport and mining. Development of industries cannot be made in isolation in an underdeveloped state like Nagaland. There is enough scope for small-scale and medium-scale industries is Nagaland.

Transport and Communication : Like any other hill state, Nagaland has poor network of transport. The state has only 8 km of railway route from Dimapur to Naginimara.

The road system of Nagaland is poorly developed. The main road of the state is the National Highway No. 39 which runs from Numaligarh to Kohima via Dimapur and then Mao to Imphal. The other roads of the state are: Amguri-Mokokchung-Tuensang-Mon road, Simalugiri-Naginimara road, Kohima-Phek road, Furkating-Wokha road. Recently some new roads have been constructed in Nagaland. One such road connects Mokokchung with Kohima via Zunheboto and the other run linking Wokha and Phek with Kohima. The Nagaland State Transport buses ply along the important roads. Thus these roads have been serving as the life-line of Nagaland. The Border Road Organisation, Govt. of India also constructed a road from Mariani across Disai valley linking Mokokchung and Tuensang via Chanki Road and railway communication is very difficult in this mountainous state. Now the government of Nagaland is trying hard to extend and improve transport system so as to make the economic development of the state of Nagaland. The total road length of Nagaland is about 13,750 km which account only 11 km road per 1000 population.

Air service is also available in Nagaland and a new airport was opened at Dimpur. This is reserved by Vayudoot services.

21

Tripura

Tripura is one of the border states of North East India and it is almost surrounded by Bangladesh except the northeastern part which is bounded by Assam and Mizoram. The state lies between 22°55'N and 24°32'N latitudes and 91°21'E longitudes. It has an area of 10,492 sq. km with a population of 31,91,168 (2005). Which increased to 36,71,032 in 2011.

Tripura was ruled by the Maharajas for about 1,300 year before its accession to India on October 15, 1949. It was a 'relic' of once a powerful kingdom, a part of 'Kirat Bhumi' often mentioned in the Ramayana and Mahabharata. It may be mentioned that India was respectably attached by the foreign aggressors since time immemorial but no one dared to invade physiographically inaccessible North East India including Tripura, Most of the parts of North East India were out of jurisdiction of British India during the British period. The princely states of this region came into friendly pact with Imperial government and then the British government did not show any interest to widen its direct supremacy in the princely states of the region. Tripura was integrated into the Republic of India on October 15, 1949. With the reorganisation of the states on September 1, 1956. Tripura made a Union territory and then it was declared a state of India on January 21, 1972.

Physical Features : Nearly 60 percent of the total land of Tripura is hilly, while the remaining 40 percent constitutes plain lands. The geological history of Tripura is not very old. The rock formations of the state range from Lower Tertiary to recent. These are represented by the Surma, Tipam, Dupitilas and recent formation. The Surma group is overlain

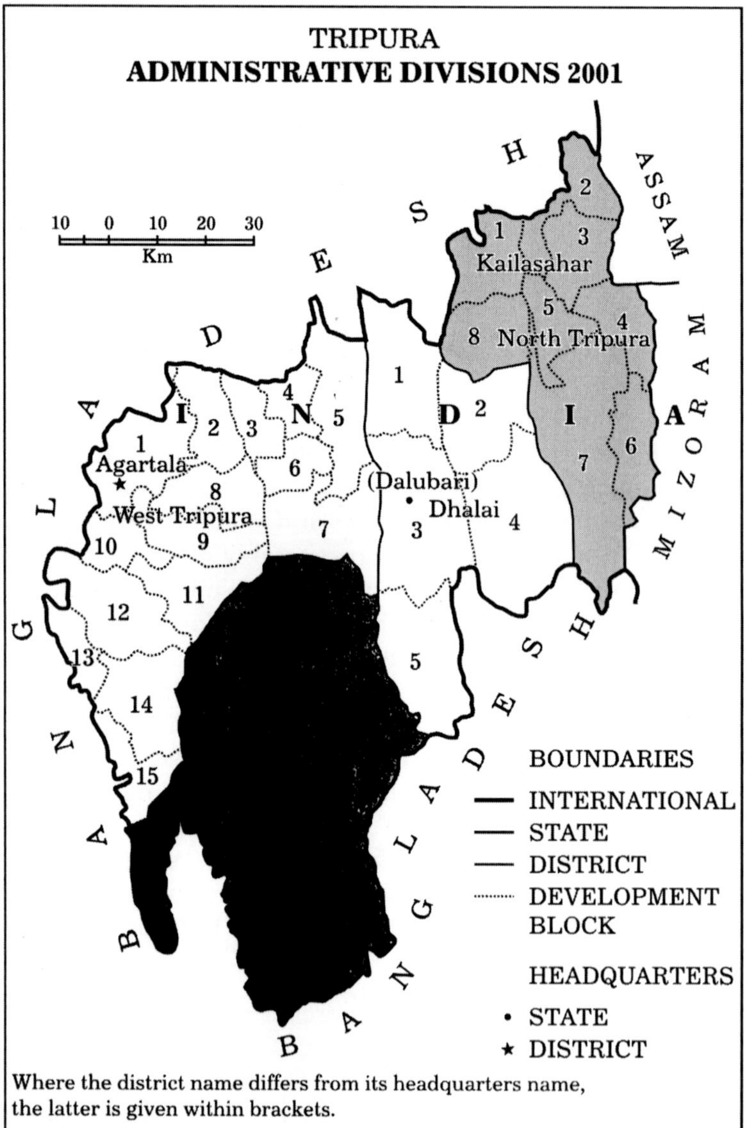

Fig. 18 : Tripura : Administrative Divisions 2001

by the Tipams and then by the Dupitilas and recent formation. The Tipam sandstone subgroup is again sub-divided into Lower Manu Bazar formations and the upper Champanagar formation. The lower Manu Bazar formations consist of medium sub-arkosic sandstone, sandyshale, silt and mudstone while the upper Champanagar formation is composed of massive coarse sub-arkosic sandstone with silicified fossil wood. The Surma group has two formation–Bokabil and Bhuban and the rocks are shale, siltstone, mudstone and conglomerate. Recent formation consits of younger alluvium with clay, sand, silt and gravel.

Like Mizoram, the major structural trend is almost north-south direction, parallel to the regional tectonic lineaments in Tripura. Generally the folds are characterised by compressed anticlines alternating with broad, very gently depressed synclines. There are six principal hill ranges increasing in height runs north and south with an average interval of about 19 kilometres. These hills are the Jampui, the Baramura-Deotamura, the Atharamura, the Langtarai, Sakhan Tlang etc. There are some disconnected open and low ridges like Gazalia-Mamumbhazna anticline, Sonamura anticline and Agartala dome towards the west of Baramura-Deotamura hill range. Besides, some minor geomorphic features like spurs, valleys and gorges.

The relief of Tripura is immature. The whole are dissected by number of long and broad valleys like the Agartala,-Udaipur, -Sabrum Khowai-Telimura, Amarpur-Silachar; Ambasa-Candachara, Kailashahar-Kumarghat, Dharma-nagar-Panisagar etc. The western section of the state is plain and it is dotted with isolated hillocks. Thus the physiographic variation is seem from the eastern to the western part of Tripura and the highest point being recorded at Jampui (992 m). The plain region of western Tripura is called Tripura plain and it is built up by the aggradational and degradational activities of the hill streams like Manu, Khowai, Titas, Gumti, Muhari and Fenny. This plain merges with the detaic plain of Bangladesh. The area of the plain is about 3500 sq. km and it a piedmont plain.

Drainage : Tripura is drained by several rivers like Kowal, Dolai, Manu, Jiri, Langal, Gomti, Fenny and their sources lie on the hill ranges as mentioned above of their rivers. The Gomti is important and near its source is a water fall known as Dampur. The river Khowai, Dolai, Manu Jiri and Langai runs towards north, while the river Gomti flows towards the west. The other rivers, namely the Fenny and Muhari flow towards the southwest of the state.

Climate : The climate of Tripura is under the influence of south-west monsoon, for which no extreme climatic conditions prevails. The state has a humid hot monsoon climate. The temperature in Tripura is generally high and the average maximum temperature is 35°C and average minimum 10.5°C. The hottest months of the year are July and August. The rain bearing monsoon winds reach Tripura towards the middle of May and continues up to the end of September. The state receives an annual rainfall of 230 cm mainly from the south-west monsoon winds. Generally storms and thunder showers are common during the premonsoon period. The south-west monsoon winds are replaced by light unsteady winds during the post monsoon season. The cold season is characterised by low temperature and dry weather. This reason includes November, December and January. The minimum temperature in this season is hardly going down to 10°C.

Natural Vegetation : Landforms, climate and other ecological conditions have provided favourable conditions for luxuriant growth of various types of natural vegetation. The monsoon forests form the natural cover over the areas of Tripura with an moderate rainfall of 80 cm to 200 cm. The moist forest form a small strip on the windward side of the highland of Tripura. Besides, there are marshy vegetation and riperian vegetation.

Out of the total geographical area of 10486 sq. km of the state 6,292 sq. km or 60 percent is covered with recorded forest. But the actual forest cover is 5,546 sq. km or 52.90 percent of the total geographical area. According to Forest

Survey of India Assam and Tripura showed more recorded forest areas than the actual forest cover. This may due to be large scale encroachment of illegal diversion of forest areas for non-forestry uses like shifting cultivation and rehabilitation of refugees from the then East Pakistan.

On the basis of legal status and ownership pattern the forests of Tripura can be classified into three categories:

(1)	Reserved forest (RF)	-	3588 sq. km
(2)	Proposed reserved forest (PRF)	-	509 sq. km
(3)	Unclassified state forest including clan/private forest	-	2195 sq. km
			Total: 6292 sq. km

The government of Tripura introduced several schemes like afforestation, fuel wood plantation, development of forest roads, rehabilitation of degraded forests, plantation of trees for industrial and commercial uses and conservation of forest resources including wild lives in recent years. The forest cover in North East India has shown consistently decreasing trend between 1991-97 except Tripura. In 1991 the forest cover of the state was 5535 sq. km which changed to 5538 sq. km in 1995 and became 5546 sq. km in 1997 showing a gain of 11 sq. km. This may due to the introduction of afforestation scheme. In recent years teak, sal, gamari, champa, bamboo etc. were planted by the forest department of Tripura.

These forest are the habitats of many wild animals including elephant, tigers, monkeys, bears, deer, porcupine wild dogs and reptiles. In order to conserve the forest resources the government of Tripura declared some important forests as reserve forest, and some wild life sanctuaries. There are two such wild life sanctuaries in Tripura, namely Trishna Wild Life Sanctuary and Sipahijala Sanctuary, Trishna wild life sanctuary has an area of 198 km^2. This sanctuary consists of rare varieties of plants and Indian Gaur. The area of Sipahijala Sanctuary is about 195 of km. There are several varieties of animals and birds including some rare one.

Population : As per 2001 census the total population of Tripura was 31,91,168. The original inhabitants of Tripura were the tribals. The demographic scenario of this state has been completely changed due to partition of the country. The influx of Bengali Hindus from the then East Pakistan to Tripura outnumbered the original inhabitants. These migrants have taken over increasing charge of the administration, trade and commerce and cultural life of Tripura. The native Tripuri tribals with their traditional economy and archaic ways of living have had a subordinate place throughout in their own homeland. During the pre-independent period the tribals were divided into as many as 18 groups and sub-groups. They had similar ethnological characters and identical cultural and social trails. The major tribes of Tripura are Tripuri, the Hill Tipperahs, the Chakwmas, the Mugs, the Kukis, the Chims, the Lushais and Reangrs. The Tripuri and Reangrs comprise the earliest inhabitants of Tripura. The Tripuries fall junder the Boro group of Indo-Mongoloids and they follow a religion in the form of Hindu ideolatory.

The population complex of Tripura is different from that of any tribal state of the region. Because the tribals of Tripura were outnumbered by the Bengal Hindu immigrants from the neighbouring Bangladesh at the time of partition of India. So Tripura was not listed as a tribal state in the constitution of India, although its original inhabitants were the Tripuries and other tribals.

The population of Tripura from 1901 to 2011 is shown below:

Population of the Tripura (1901-2011)

(1000 persons)

Census year	Population	Census year	Population
1901	173	1961	1142
1911	230	1971	1556
1921	304	1981	2053
1931	382	1991	2757
1941	513	2001	3191
1951	639	2011	3671

Since 1901 onwards, the population of Tripura increased gradually (1901-41). But from 1951 onward the rate of increase was higher. The high rate of increase is primarily due to the influx of the immigrants from inside and outside of India. The increase of population during the last five decades is tremendous and this rise of population figure in the state is attributed to both natural increase and immigration. The population of Tripura has increased by 18 times from 1.73 lakh in 1901 to 31.91 lakh in 2001. The density and growth of population has serious implications for development and according to demographers the population growth of the North East India including Tripura is accelerating. Density of population in Tripura is very high i.e. 304 per square kilometre (2001) which was 263 in 1991 and in 2011 it rose 350 per sq. km. The sex ratio was improving from 945 in 1991 to 950 in 2001. The literacy rate of Tripura exceeded the all India average of literacy rate. It was 60.39 percent (Males: 70.8 percent and Female: 50.01 per cent) in 1991 which became 73.66 per cent (males: 81.47 per cent an females: 65.41 per cent) in 2001. In 2011 Literacy rate to 87.75 persons. The percentage of urban population is low i.e. 17.02 percent which is much lower than the national norm of 27.78 percent (2001). There was virtually no any urban centre except Udaipur, once the capital of the princely state–Tripura. But it was not defined as an urban centre till 1961. In 1871 a Municipality was instituted at Agartala and it was the only urban centre up to 1951. In this state the most conveniently placed villages eventually took the shape of urban centre either due to these were administrative centres or market places. Kailashar, Udaipur, Khowai, Belonia, Dharmanagar, Amarpur, Sonamura, Kamalpur, Sabroom, Kumarghat, Ranibazar, Teliamura became urban centres mainly because of administrative reason. In 1901 the total urban population of Tripura was only 6,415 and 2001 is after 100 years it became 543,094 urban persons. Agartala, the capital of Tripura is the only city of the state of over 2 lakh population. It is the principal administrative, educational and trade centre of the state. It is connected with Assam by the National Highway No. 44.

Agriculture : It may be mentioned that the area of planned economic development in Tripura started from the year 1951 after its integration with India. There was no pressure of population on land in the princely state of Tripura. At that time population was mainly tribal and practised jhuming on the hill slopes and the state was self-sufficient in food. The government and the people did not feel the need for industrial development. But the partition of India, caused waves of inflow of displaced persons from the neighbouring areas of erstwhile East Pakistan and now the composition of the population, with substantial majority being refugees. The rice production has also been increased. But inspite of it the state is not self sufficient in food products.

After independence agricultural programmes could not receive as much input as social service and transport sectors. However, the measures were taken to make agriculture more extensive as well as more intensive. Some schemes for agricultural development like reclamation of waste lands, construction of minor irrigation and extension of horiticulture have been introduced in Tripura during the First Plan Period. Greater emphasis was laid on intensive agriculture through the use modern agricultural techniques, high yielding seeds, chemical manures and in secticides. Various schemes implemented during the third and fourth plans were mostly on the expansion of agricultural output. Because of such efforts foodgrains production increased from 1.35 lakh tonnes in 1950-51 to 3.64 lakh tonnes in 1973-74. This increasing trend of foodgrain is continued. In 1993-94 the total cropped area was 2,60,800 hectares and foodgrain production was 45,54,000 tonnes. The yield per hectare was 1746 kg in the same year.

Rice is grown in the plains as well as in the hills and it is main foodgrain in Tripura. Popular high yielding varieties of rice are taichung, IR-8 monohar sali, jaya, padma, jamuna, etc. Cultivation of other crops like potato, sugarcane, pulses, jute, cotton, sesamum mesta etc. are also expanded considerably.

Like Assam ecological conditions are also favourable for

tea cultivation in Tripura. There are 58 tea gardens over 6,500 hectares of land in Tripura. About 9,000 persons were employed in tea plantations which produced 5.2 million kilogram annually. At present tea industry of the state suffers from transport and labour problem.

Animal husbandry is also carried on along with agriculture in Tripura, Livestock includes cattle, buffaloes, goats, ducks, pigs, fowls, pigeons etc. The quality of these animals is poor and so efforts have been made to develop hybrid varieties.

Natural water bodies for fishery are very few in number and as such development of pisciculture is restricted to tanks, ponds and swamps. Some fish breeding farms are being developed in Tripura.

Industry : Tripura has to face many hurdles for industrialisation. It is already mentioned this state integrated into India on October 15, 1949. At that time Tripura had Asiatic feudal economic structure like any other neighbouring state of the region. Basic infrastructures for the development of industries like power, important minerals, transport and communication were poor or absent. Even today the situation has not improved. Besides, the state suffers from acute locational disadvantage.

During the second and third plans industry and mining sector received only 5 percent of the total plan expenditure. It dwindled to less than 2 percent in the fourth plan period. Industrial institutes had been set up to provide training units. Promotion of industrial training facilities and growth and development of village industries during second and third plan period. The schemes implemented in the successive period were mostly of service nature like financial assistance, supply of industrial raw materials, marketing of products, subsidising cost of power etc. In fact little attempts have been made during the last two decades to add new dimensions to the small industrial sector Tripura.

Oil and natural gas are the potential discoveries in

Tripura and in future petro-chemical industries may be developed. The existing industries of Tripura include Tripura Jute Mill Ltd., 14 brick kilns, village pottery, leather, carpentry, bio-gas, handloom and handicrafts and sericulture industries.

Transport and Communication : Tripura is surrounded by Bangladesh on three sides and it shares 839 km long border with Bangladesh. Besides it is mostly a hilly state. For all these transport and communication system is poorly developed in Tripura. Ironically the state has only a token presence of railway tract of only 44.72 km. Dharmanagar is connected by a 30 km gauge route with Silchar and in 1990. The route is extended to Kumarghat. So the economic development of Tripura is inevitably dependent on road transport.

The national highway No.44 is regarded as Tripura's life line which connect Agartala with Shillong via Badarpur is neither reliable nor very effective. This road is subjected to inundation and land slides during the rainy season. Apart from national highways there are state PWD roads, district roads and Panchayat roads. The state PWD constructed about 4200 km of road by the end of the fifth plan period. The village roads and Panchayat roads are mostly unsurfaced. The Agartala-Udaipur-Sabnum is the state highway. The important district roads are Dharmangar-Kailashahar road, Kamalpur-Dalubari road, Khowai-Teliamura road, Teliamura-Ampi road, Harishnagar-Madhupur Bazar road, Agartala-Ananda Bazar road, Kalacherra-Khowai road, Ambassa-Bagafa road, Pearicherra-Churaibari road, Dharmanagar-Tilthai road, Kumarghat-Kanchanpur road and Amarpur-Udaipur road. Within the state, The eastern hilly part is very poorly developed in road system while the western part is relatively more developed in road communication system.

In 1995-96, The total road length of Tripura was 14726 km of which 4577 km were surface roads and 10,149 km unsurfaced roads. The percentage of surface road to total road length in the state was only 31.03 percent. The Tripura

Road Transport Corporation has been operating about 200 services in about 50 schedules covering a length of more than 10 thousand kilometres daily by passenger services since its establishment in the 1971. The number vehicles registered in the state is about 15,000 which include buses, cars, taxis, jeeps, trucks, two-wheelers, three wheelers and others.

Air links with Tripura in tenuous. After the nationalisation of commercial air transport in India. Indian Airlines Corporation took ever the services. A new airport was constructed at Agartala and a few small air-port were constructed (one each) at Kailashahar, Kamalpur and Khowai. The Indian Airlines Corporation operates daily air sevice to these airport of the state from Kolkata.

22

Sikkim

The North Eastern Council was created by an act (North-Eastern Council Act of 1971) of Parliament in 1971 to look after the common economic interests of the seven political units of North East India, namely Assam, Arunachal Pradesh, Meghalaya, Manipur, Mizoram, Nagaland and Tripura. Recently Sikkim, the 22nd state of the India became a member of this council. Now North East India Consists of 8 states including Sikkim. The NEC Act has been amended in December, 2002 which allowed Sikkim to be the Council's eighth member.

Sikkim is a small mountainous state in the eastern Himalayas. The state is strategically located between Bhutan in the east and Nepal in the west and between Tibetan part of China in the north and Darjeeling district of West Bengal in the south. The length of the state from north to south is 117 km and width from east to west is 88 km. It covers an area of 7,096 sq. km with a population of 5,40,493.

Sikkim was to all intents an Indian protectorate prior to April, 1975. The monarchical ruler of this kingdom was called Chogyal. The Sikkim Assembly on April 10, resolved that "the institution of the Chogyal is hereby abolished and Sikkim shall henceforth be a constituent unit of India, enjoying a democratic and fully responsible government". In this connection a special opinion poll conducted by the Government of Sikkim on April 14, 1975 resulted in a total of 59,637 votes in favour of and 1,496 votes against the resolution out of a total electorate of about 97,000. Following this, the 38th constitution (Amendment) Bill was passed by Lok Sabha on April 23, 1975 and then by the Rajya Sabha on April 26, 1975 for the fulfilment of the wishes of the people of Sikkim

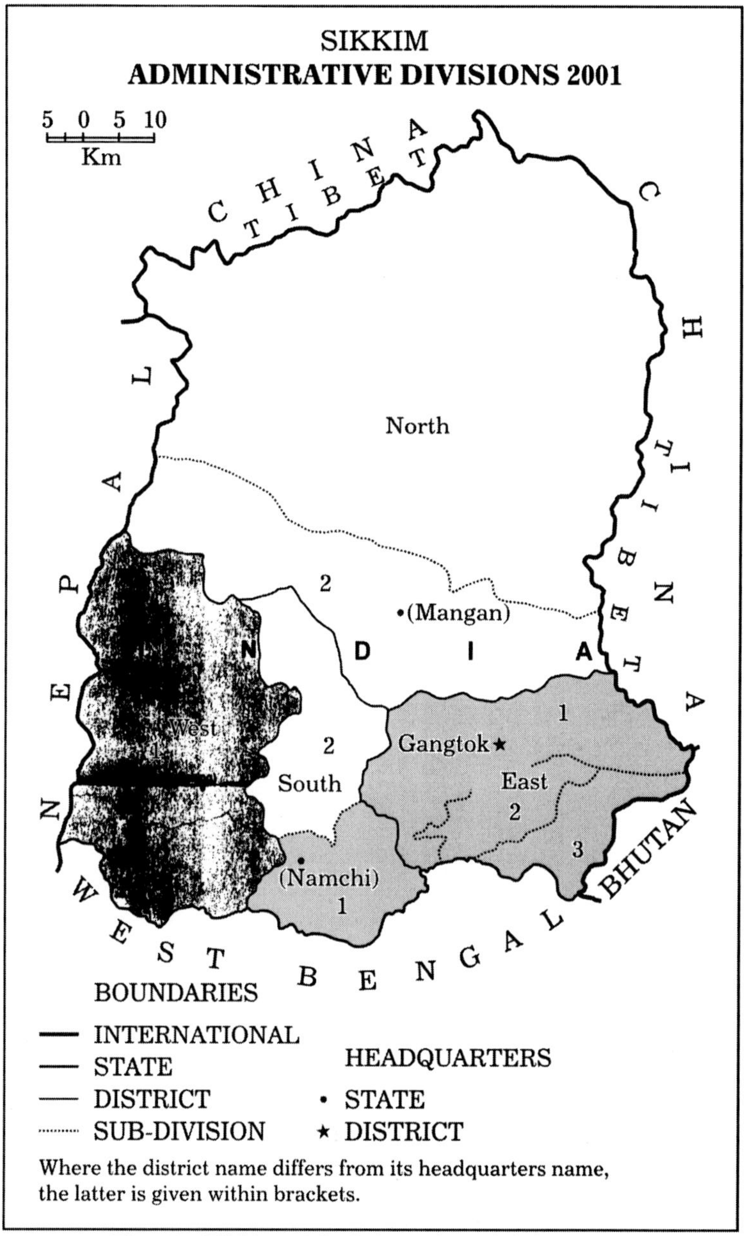

Fig. 19 : Sikkim : Administrative Divisions 2001

as expressed in the referendum held on April 14, 1975. The President of India signed the Bill which made Sikkim the 22nd state of India and abolished the monarchial rule of Choggal on May 16, 1975. At present there are four districts in the state. The name of these districts along with their population and headquarters are given below:

District	Area	Population sq. km.	Headquarters (2001)
East	954	2,44,790	Gangtok
North	4,226	41,023	Mangan
South	750	1,31,506	Namchi
West	1,166	1,23,174	Gyalshing

Physical Features : The state consists of a mass of deeply-dissected highland. There are large number of mountains above 7320 metres and more. Kanchenjunga (8598m), the world's third highest peak, rises from this part of Sikkim. The Singalila range forms the boundary between Nepal and Sikkim and the range rises to a height of 3685 metres, on which lies the Chiabhanjan a principal pass between Sikkim and Nepal. The Donkya range, separating Sikkim from Tibet lies on the east. This is a very high mountain range which act as watershed between the Chumbi valley and the upper courses of the Tista in the west. The famous Jelep La Pass (4386m) lies on this range. This pass is a traditional trade route between Tibet and India through Kalimpong and Lhasa. Nathu La is also an important Pass and a trade route connecting India and Tibet. The Chola range is situated in the centre of the state and it joins with the hills of the Darjeeling region of West Bengal.

Drainage : Sikkim is drained by the river Tista and its tributaries. These rivers originate from the Great Himalayas and flow mainly from the north to south direction. The rivers cut through the Darjeeling ridge (2170-2480m) in a narrow gorge, to spill on to the plains below. The erosional activities of these rivers are very intense and the head of the gorge at the tributary Ranjit confluece is only 232 metre. Most of these rivers are snow-fed and they carry huge amount of water all the year round. They are youthful in character. The principal tributary of the river Tista is the Ranjit and it meets with it at right angles near Melli. Another glacier fed river is the Ratong. All the rivers of Sikkim including Ranjit and Ratong are very turbulent and swift flowing. During the rainy season they cause menacing floods on the lower reaches of the rivers. The catchment area of the Tista river system receives average annual rainfall between 300 cm to 450 cm. So the rivers are very active and young and their erosional activities are more.

Climate : Sikkim enjoys a moderate climate with cold humid winters and cool summers. The mean temperatures vary between 27°C-31°C and diurnal range are very high. Temperature never comes to a freezing point in the southern part of Sikkim even during the winter. Thus sub-tropical climate prevails in this part of the state. But the northern part of the state is cold and summer is practically absent in this part. Snow fall occurs on the high mountains (above 2400 m) every year. The state receives rain from the monsoon winds. Generally it receives rains from early April and continues to receive high rain (over 300 cm) up to the end of October. On the south facing slopes rain is almost continuous from June to September. Only November and December are dry. During the Summer season the river valleys are hot and somewhat malarious.

Natural Vegetation : Sikkim is the smallest state of the region with an area of 7096 sq. km and of their area under forest is 3121 sq. km. or about 44.07 percent of the total area of the state is forested. There are broadly three categories of forests in Sikkim: tropical, temperate and alpine forests. The tropical forests are mostly found in the lower ranges and river valleys of the state and important forest species are sal, simul, toon and bamboos. Temperate forests are seen in northern Sikkim in the form of coniferous trees. The important trees are silver fir, the chirpine, junipers and deoder etc. The Alpine vegetation are found to grow at height between 2,900 and 3,800 metres. Several species of rhodondendrons, rhubars and other herbs are the important plants of the alpine forest. There are about 350-400 species of orchids in the forest of Sikkim.

Population : The population of Sikkim is composed of the Lepchas, the Bhutias and their allied clans and the Nepalis. The original inhabitants are the Mongolian Lepchas. They are amiable but not very effective. They are Buddhist by religion. Now the Hindu proportion of the population is increasing with the immigration of Nepalis from Nepal. It is believed that the Bhutias came from Tibet in the early part of the 14th century.

The Nepalis came into Sikkim during the 18th and 19th centuries and now they form the majority community in the state. The society is multiethnic. The existing official languages are Nepali, Lepcha, Bhutia and Limboo. Recently the government of Sikkim has accorded State languages status to Tamang, Gurung, Rai, Sherpa, Mangar, Newar and Sunwar.

As per 2001 census the total population of Sikkim was 5,40,493 of which 2,88,217 were males and 2,52,276 were females. The number of females per 1000 males was 875. The literacy rate was 69.68 percent of which 76.73 percent males and 61.46 percent females. The overall density of population in Sikkim was 76 per square kilometre. The infant mortality rate was 875. The decadal growth of population of the state had gone up to 32.98 percent in 1991-2001 from 28.47 percent in 1981-91. In 2011 total population increased to 6,07,688 with a density of population 86 per sq. km.

The distribution of population in Sikkim is very uneven and is governed by topography, climate, availability of water, accessibility to the areas and cultivable lands. The population of Sikkim is concentrated mostly in wet and warmer parts of the south and in and around the district headquarters, and trade centres like Lachung, Singhik, Rangpo, Rhenock and Namchi. The sparsely populated areas of Sikkim are the northern cold mountainous areas and the interior hilly areas of the state. Only 11.10 percent of the total population of the state live in small urban centres. These urban centres are developed mainly due to administrative functions and commercial functions. The main urban centres of Sikkim are Gangtok, Singtam, Rangpo, Jorethang, Nayabazar, Mangan, Gyalshing and Namchi.

Agriculture : The economy of Sikkim is mainly agrarian. The state has hilly terrain and as such the agricultural land is limited being about 15 percent of the total area of the state. There are three types of agriculture at practices are seen in Sikkim: shifting, terraced and plantation agriculture. Shifting or jhuming is the most common agricultural practice in the difficult terrain of the state. The important crops of the jhum fields are rice, maize, potatoes etc. Terraced cultivation is done on the hill slopes. Generally the hill slopes are carefully terraced and cultivated by means of contour irrigation. Rice, maize, millets, oranges, apples, bananas, apricots, potatoes and cardamom are grown on terraced fields. Good quality apples are raised at higher altitudes. Oranges and potatoes are grown on extensive areas and there two are the important items of the states economy. Rice and maize are also grown on a limited area in the wet and warmer parts of the south. Cardamom and tea are the major cash crops of the state.

These two crops are grown on shaded moutain sides. Cardamom and tea plantation are closely linked up with the economy of Sikkim. Sikkim is one of the largest producers of Cardamom in the world. Sikkim tea has been getting high price in market and it has earned a considerable foreign exchange for our nation. Tea cultivation has also contributed to soil conservation of the hill slopes of the state.

The northern part of Sikkim is not favourable for growing crops due to very cold climate and heavy snowfall. In this area sheep and yak are carefully reared. Yak is generally reared as a pack-animal and its milk and hair are also useful. Thus pastoral activities are well developed in Northern Sikkim.

Industry : Sikkim is poor in industrial raw materials. A very small quantity of low grade coal and silver deposits have been discovered at Dikchu. This area is located at a height of about 1000m and 20 km from Gangtok town. Except a very small quantity of low grade coal, Sikkim has no other power resources. But the state has a recognized capacity of generating 8000 mw of hydel power. Power is very much essential for agricultural and industrial prosperity. The state has a vast hydro-electric power potential if harnessed from its swift-flowing mountainous river. It is to be noted that the proposed III phase Tista Hydel Project of 1200 MW has been pending with the government of India. There will be employment generation, booming industrial in Sikkim if the above project is commissioned.

The traditional industrial projects of Sikkims are brass and metal work, handicrafts, handloom and fur products. A number of industries have been setup in Sikkim after its merger with India. A paper and pulp mill has been setup at Melli, which is situated at the confluence of the Tista and the Rangeet. The mill has a daily capacity of 25 tonnes of strong kraft paper including absorbant and abrasive paper.

There are some important tourist centres in Sikkim, namely Gangtok, a natural garden at Bakkhin, Yoksum, Dhubbi Monastery, Tashing Monastery, Rumtek Monastery, Khanchendzonga National Park etc. The central government already relaxed the innerline permit system for Sikkim and now the state has been getting a number of tourists. The state has vast potentiality for the development of tourism. Because the whole state is the land of abundance, beauty and adventure. Thus there is enough scope for tourism development by utilizing its tourist resources.

Transport : It is mentioned that the state is entirely mountainous and about a third of the landforms is covered with dense forest. It is the least populous state in India. For all these transport and comunication system is poorly developed. It is to be noted that the states does not have any railways, air links and navigable rivers. The only link with other part of India is the single line National Highway number 31A, This highway is also frequently disrupted especially during the rainy season. This road was constructed as a cartroad in the first decade of the 20th century. In 1960 it was declared as National Highway No. 31A with little improvement. This is a single lane road with sharp bends and poor visibility which should be widened to accommodate double lane traffic. At present it connects Gangtok with Kalimpong and passes through Darjeeling district of West Bengal where there is frequent break down of law and order leading to closure of this highway at an smallest pretext. Apart from National Highway 31A, there are several other metalled roads connecting Gangtok with several central place like Rangpo, Rhenock and Namchi. Besides Gangtok- Kalimpong road, Tista-Siliguri Bridle Road, there are several other circuitous connecting some interior places with trade centres. The North Sikkim highway is a good metalled road which runs towards north from Gangtok to Singhik and Lachung. Nathu La-Gangtok is also and important road.

Sikkim has no railhead of its own and the nearest heads are at Siliguri and Darjeeling which are located in West Bengal. Similarly Sikkim has no airport of its own and its nearest airport is at Bagdogra about 120 km away from Gangtok Air communication to Sikkim is absolutely necessary and the government of India should construct an airstrip at Gangtok at an early date.

Slowly and steadily the socio-economic changes have been taken place in Sikkim since 1980s. Some selected idicators of such aspects have been given below in tabular forms (**Source :** Statistical Hand Book, Assam, 2012).

Sikkim

1.	Population Nos	: 60766
2.	Decadal Growth rate 2001-11	: 12.36
3.	Density per sq. km	: 86
4.	Sex Ratio per 1000 male	: 889

5. Literacy rate : 82.20%
6. Household Nos : 128131
7. Percentage of Households having drinking wither within premises : 52.6%
8. Percentage of Household having electricity : 92.5%
9. Percentage of Household having Latrine Facilities : 75.0%
10. Poverty Head Count Ratio (%) (using Tendulkar Methodology) 2009-10
    a. Rural : 15.5
    b. Urban : 5.0
    c. Combined : 13.0
11. No. of Establishments (Agri + Non Agri) : 19362
12. No. of Workers : 68489

Bibliography

Abbi B.L., "North East Region: Problems and Prospects of Development", (Ed.), CRRID, Chandigarh, 1984.

Agarwal, A.K "Economic Problem and Planning in North East India", Sterling Publisher Private Limited, New Delhi, 1987.

Ahmad, Aijazuddin "Social Geography", Rawat Publication, Jaipur, 1999.

Bhattacharya, N.N. "The Contemporary Geopolitical Problems of North East India", *North-Eastern Geographer*, Vol. XXIII. No 1-2, 1991, Pp. 1-5.

________ "Some Problem of Forest Rsources in North East India" in *Forest Resources in North East India*, Datta Ray and Alam (Ed.), Omsons Publication, New Delhi, 2002.

________ "Planning Regions for Balanced of Development in North East India" in "*Regional Development in North-East India*", (Ed) Deb B.J., Reliace Publishing House, New Delhi,1995.

________ "Impact of Land Reforms in Assam", in *Impact of Land Reforms in North-East India*, Das Gupta, M. (Ed.) Omsons Publication, Guwahati, 1991.

________ "The Role of Small Towns in the Development Process of North-East

India" in *Urban Development in North-East India*, Datta Ray, Neog and Mazahar ed., Reliance Publishing House, New Delhi, 1998.

_______________ "Formation of Appropriate Development Paradigm of North-East India" in *Development Priorities in North-East India*, Deb, B.J. (Ed) Concept Publishing Company, New Delhi, 2002.

Bhattacharyya N.N. "Status of and Constraints to Industrial Development in North-East India", in Social Constraints to Industrial Development in North East India, (Ed) Datta Ray and Baishya, Concept Publishing Company, New Delhi, 1998.

_______________ "Growth and Changing Face of Guwahati since 1972" in *Guwahati the Gateway to the East*, (Eds) Alam, Das and Borah, Concept Publishing Company, New Delhi, 2001.

_______________ "Tribal Population of the Brahmaputra Valley under Changing Socio-Political Situation" in *Agenda for North East India*, (Ed) Datta Ray, Concept Publishing Company, New Delhi, 2002.

_______________ "Trend of Population Growth in North East India" in *Population, Poverty and Enviroment in North East India*, (Eds) Datta Ray, Mazhari Passah and Pandey, Concept Publishing Company, New Delhi, 2000.

_______________ "Rural Development in North East India: A Note" in *Dimensions of Rural Development in North-East India*, Datta Ray and Das (Eds) Akansha Publishing House, New Delhi, 2004.

_______________ "Literacy Scenario in North East India"

in *Education in North-East India*, (Eds) Lyndem and De, Concept Publishing Company, New Delhi, 2004.

________ "Spatial Growth of Shillong Since 1991" in Shillong: *A Tribal Town in Transition*, Sengupta and Dhar. (Eds), Reliance Publishing House, New Delhi, 2004.

________ "Environment, Land and People of Jaintia Hills" in *Jaintia Hills: A Meghalaya Tribe- Its Enviroment Land and People*, Reliance Publishing House, New Delhi, 2002.

________ "Settlement in North-East India: Some Perspective", *North-Eastern Geographer*, Vol. 18, No. 122, 1986.

Bhattacharyya, N.N. and Bora, A.K. "Floods of the Brahmaputra River in India", *Water International*, Vol. 22 No. 4 December 1997.

Bhakta, G.P., "Geography of North-East India", Akashi Book Depot, Shillong 1992.

Borpujari, H.K. "Problems of The Hills Tribes-North East Frontier-1873-1962", Spectrum Publication, Guwahati, 1981.

Bareh, H., "The History and Culture of the Khasi People", Spectrum Publication, Guwahati, 1985.

Banerjee, M., "Lack of Entrepreneurship and Industrial Development in Meghalaya" *in Sociological Constraints to Industrial Development in North East India,* (Eds) Datta Ray and Baishya, Concept Publishing Company, New Delhi, 1998.

Chaudhary, P.C., "The History of Civilization of the People of Assam", Department of Historical and Antiquarian Studies in Assam, Guwahati, 1959.

Das, M.M. and Datta L., "Regional Variation in Land use and Agriculture in North-East India" *North-Eastern Geographer*, Vol. 18 No. 1 & 2, 1986.

Devbarman, S.S., "Sociological Constraints of Tribals on Industrialsation in Tripura" in *Sociological Constraints to Industrial Development in North-East India*, (Eds) Datta Ray and Baishya, Concept Publishing Company, New Delhi, 1998.

Dutta, A.K. *The Brahmaputra*, National Book Trust, India, 2001.

Dutta, S.K. "Palaeogeography of Assam Plateau", in *21st International Geographical Conress-1968*, Dept of Geography, Gauhati University.

Goswami, P.C., "The Economic Development of Assam", Kalyani Publication, New Delhi, 1988.

Gopala Krishanan, R "The North East India, Land, Economy and People", Vikas Publication, New Delhi, 1991.

Kyndiah, P.R. "Pillars of Mizo Society", Cambridge Laser Print, Calcutta, 1999.

Mackenzie, A, "The North-East Frontier of India", Mittal Publication, Delhi, 1989.

Singh, B.M. "Sikkim's Economic Development" in *Regional Development of North-East India*, Deb. B.J. (Ed) Reliance Publishing House, New Delhi, 1995.

Sarin, V.I.K., "India's North-East in Flames", Vikas Publishing House, Sahibabad, 1982.

Spate and Learmonth India & Pakistan, Methuen & Co. Ltd. London, 1967.

Sukhwal, B.L. "Modern Political Geography of India", Sterling Publishers, New Delhi, 1985.

Thakur, S; Chutia, D., Talukadar P., and Chutia D.J. — "Transport Scenario of N.E. India-Problem and Prospects", Vasundhara, Vol. 1. No. 1 2004.

Taher, M., — "Physiographic Framework of North East India" North-Eastern Geographer, Vol-18 No. 182.

Taher, M., and Ahemed, P., Devi — "Geography of North-East India", Mani Manik Prakash, Guwahati, 2002.

Unpublished Ph.D. Thesis

Devi, T.R. — Handloom Industry in Manipur, Manipur University, 2000.

Hazarik, J., — Geopolitics of North East India, Gauhati University, 1994.

Singh. L.I., — Patterns of Rural Settlement in Manipur: A Morphological Study, Manipur University, 2002.

Singh, S.H., — Tea Plantation in Barak Valley: A Strategy for Future Development, Manipur University, 2002.

Journals :

IASSI Quarterly, Vol. 12, January-June 1994, Nos. 3 & 4.

North-Eastern Geographers (Some Volumes).

The North Eastern Hill University (Some Volumes).

Journal of North-East India Council for Social Science Research (Some Volumes).

Govt. Publications :

Statistical Hand Book, Assam, 1988, 2002.

Census of India, 1971, 1981, 1991, 2001.

Economic Survey, Assam, 2001-2002.

Basic Statistics of North Eastern Region, 1987, 1995.

Other Publication :

Manorama Year Book, 2003.

Index

B

C

D

E

F

G

T

U

V

W

Author Index